Meaningless Citizenship

Meaningless Citizenship

Iraqi Refugees and the Welfare State

Sally Wesley Bonet

University of Minnesota Press
Minneapolis
London

The University of Minnesota Press gratefully acknowledges the financial assistance provided for the publication of this book by a grant from the Colgate University Research Council.

Published by the University of Minnesota Press
111 Third Avenue South, Suite 290
Minneapolis, MN 55401-2520
http://www.upress.umn.edu

ISBN 978-1-5179-1111-9 (hc)
ISBN 978-1-5179-1112-6 (pb)

A Cataloging-in-Publication record for this book is available from the Library of Congress.

Printed in the United States of America on acid-free paper

The University of Minnesota is an equal-opportunity educator and employer.

UMP BmB 2022

For Mama and Teita

Contents

Introduction

The Mirage of Refuge

Fatima[1] sat on the couch, holding the greeting card that that she had asked me to interpret for her. Her head was bowed and out of my field of vision, but I could see her tears falling to the thin carpet under her feet. I sat quietly for some time, unsure of what to do or say. The card, which had come from the hospital, read "We are so sorry for your loss, but we wanted to let you know that we are planting a tree in the honor of your child." I began to wonder if I should take my leave, feeling increasingly uncomfortable that I had inadvertently come upon information that Fatima[2] had not meant to share with me. Over the past several months, we had discussed so much: what had driven her and her family out of Iraq, her growing concerns for the son she had left behind in the care of her father, her anxieties about her children's education in their public school, and her frustration with how little financial and navigational support her family received after they resettled here. We had also laughed together: when her daughter Layla unsuccessfully attempted to imitate my Egyptian accent; when Fatima told the story of how she had met her husband, who was smitten at first sight; when Fatima and Layla put on a fashion show for me after buying some clothes from a discount store, with Layla teetering on high heels and giggling as she attempted a catwalk. This moment, however, was meant to be a private one, but Fatima's inability to decipher the card in English had placed me in this position, a trespasser in her world and suffering. As I rose from my seat, telling Fatima that I would come back another time, she held my hand and said, "No *habibti,*[3] stay."

Fatima wiped her tears on her sleeves and told me the story. A few months before, she happily discovered that she was pregnant, which she never expected to be at her age. The mother of five children, the eldest being twenty-one years old, Fatima had assumed that her child-bearing years were behind her. She and her husband Mohammed had celebrated

1

the news, as they both felt that children are a blessing from Allah, and looked forward to the newest addition in her family. At the outset of her pregnancy, she had seen a doctor at a hospital near her home in Philadelphia, who told her that since hers was considered a "geriatric pregnancy," she was to "take it easy" and come back for regular visits and checkups—both things that she could not afford to do. Since her state-funded health insurance lapsed soon after her first visit to the doctor, she refused to seek out medical care, having heard from others in the Iraqi refugee community how expensive out-of-pocket visits could be. Even though Mohammed had begged her to leave her difficult and physically taxing job as a housekeeper in a local hotel, Fatima refused, knowing that her family desperately needed her income to survive. A few months into her pregnancy, she began to experience severe cramping while at work. By the time she arrived home, she knew that she was losing the baby. Mohammed took her to the local emergency room, where her fears were confirmed. Beyond their devastating loss, Fatima and Mohammed had to grapple with an enormous ER bill, since both of them were uninsured. A local nonprofit that served Philadelphia's Arabic-speaking immigrants was negotiating with the hospital on Fatima's behalf, but she had yet to receive word about the results. After retelling her story, Fatima said, "I didn't expect this. I had hoped for a different life here, but I guess it is just not to be." Like all the other Iraqis I spoke to, Fatima's dreams of a better life were nowhere to be found.

Through three years of ethnographically capturing the lives of Iraqi families, I gained a window into the complexities of refugee life. Many questions fueled my research. What did it mean for Iraqi refugees to be living in the United States, the very nation that had caused their displacement as well as the devastation of their home country? How did these refugees, who would eventually be eligible for legal citizenship, understand themselves in relation to the American nation-state? How did poverty and the subsequent need to depend on the various institutions of the welfare state texture their lives? How did they interpret their interactions with these institutions? And finally, how did these encounters inform their notions of citizenship? To answer these questions, I spent countless hours with refugee families, mostly in their homes, but also when I accompanied them to schools, welfare offices, hospital waiting rooms, and refugee resettlement agencies. I witnessed, firsthand, the resilience of those who had suffered losses that I could not begin to understand or imagine. I looked on as families ate and laughed together, supported each other fiercely, and sought after a better life as a collective. While my time with families had many moments of levity and joy, the immense struggles they faced often took priority in their lives and our conversations, and were quite simply undeniable. Adults struggled with brief and inadequate financial supports; unstable, low-wage jobs with no benefits or pensions; and deep concerns for their children's education. Many Iraqi youth—who came to the United States with hopes for a better future vis-à-vis education—struggled in underresourced public schools while others were excluded from education altogether. Making a new life in the United States, the country that caused their displacement, the proverbial "belly of the beast," was inherently a contested process.

In spite of all of this, the Iraqi refugees I have been privileged to know came to the United States with hope—dreaming of better lives for themselves and their children. However, what they found in the United States surprised them. Iraqi refugees not only experienced the devastation and fallout of American neoliberal imperialism in Iraq, but after their resettlement came face to face with a more insidious, pernicious, and invisible war that was occurring on U.S. soil—the systemic neoliberal destruction of the welfare state. Through their encounters with a hollow welfare state, Iraqis become intimately acquainted with the contradiction of American empire. They learned that the country that once claimed to bring Iraq "human rights" struggles to fulfill that obligation to its own citizens. Instead of a better, settled life, Iraqis encountered neglect, exclusion, and more suffering—robbed of the right to social inclusion and full citizenship. The veneer of American values—such as freedom, democracy, and human rights, exported to countries like Iraq—quickly cracked to uncover what really lay beneath: a nation-state that prioritized the needs of capitalism above the survival and well-being of its citizens, particularly those of the poor and marginalized.

Refugee Families and the Institutions That Shape Them

Scholarship that has centered the lives of refugees resettled to the United States has provided the inspiration and backdrop to this study. In her seminal book concerned with Cambodian refugees, Ong (2003) explores the meaning of citizenship for "disadvantaged newcomers," which is primarily "a matter of figuring out the rules for coping, navigating, and surviving

the streets and public spaces of the American city" (xiv). Like Ong, I too
sought out ways to understand what citizenship meant for refugees who
were struggling to eke out a living, and who were increasingly displaced
from the lives they had hoped to find in the United States with every passing day. Instead of refuge, they found a welfare state on its last legs, hollowed out by neoliberal policy. While the refugees whose stories are at
the heart of this book might share common struggles with those in Ong's
analysis, it must be noted that the lived experiences of Iraqis are textured by
several unique elements. First, as Muslim refugees arriving in the United
States in a post-9/11 era, they are framed as the ultimate "other"—a threat
to national cohesion and security. Iraqis faced immense Islamophobia in
the United States, shaped by Bush-era "War on Terror" rhetoric that tied
Saddam Hussein—and by proxy Iraqis in general—with Osama bin Laden
and the global "axis of evil." This ire was further exacerbated by the xenophobic attack on Muslim refugees promoted by Donald Trump, who
campaigned on promises of creating a Muslim registry and whose Muslim
travel bans and halting of the refugee program in the name of "heightened
security" barred refugees and immigrants from entering the country. This
book builds on the work of education scholars (Abu El-Haj 2015; Ali 2017;
Jaffe-Walter 2016; Maira 2009) whose work with transnational, Muslim,
and im/migrant[4] youth in the West highlights the ways that interactions
with teachers, schools, and society ultimately cast them as impossible subjects of the nation-state—putting into question Western exceptionalist notions such as democratic citizenship, humanitarianism, and acceptance of
cultural difference.

Rather than focusing solely on youth, however, this analysis widens
the ethnographic scope to better understand how refugee *families* are
being dispossessed of the rights they hoped to find in the United States.
Furthermore, this analysis takes into account refugee worlds that lie beyond schools and classrooms. Abu El-Haj adeptly contends that schools
are important sites of "everyday nationalism," and "centrally implicated in
the discursive and institutional processes through which belonging and
citizenship rights are created and negotiated" (2015, 9). Indeed, many eth-
nographies of migration concerned with refugee life in the United States
(Besteman 2016; Inhorn 2018; Tang 2015) have critically examined the limitations and inherent contradictions of many of the various institutions of
the state. However, in order to capture the complexity that defines the lives
of refugee youth and their families, we must examine other institutions

of the state as critical to the process of citizen making. Through a multi-sited, multilingual ethnography, this book illustrates the ways that *all* of the state institutions that refugees encounter, navigate, and are embedded within are inherently educative ones, teaching them about the limitations and even meaninglessness of citizenship, while shaping them into laboring subjects in service of capitalism.

This book also attends to the role that the United States played in the displacement of Iraqi refugees who can trace their forced migration directly to the American imperialistic military ventures in their country. Additionally, like many before me (Abu El-Haj 2015; Burde 2014; Nguyen 2012) I consider the ways that American imperialism and specifically the endless War on Terror have indelibly affected those who inadvertently find themselves directly in its path. For more than three decades, the Iraqi families I came to know had been subjected to brutal wars, inhumane sanctions, and finally full-scale occupation at the hands of the United States, forcing them to flee and leave all that they had known behind and to attempt to build new lives in the very country that caused their displacement. In U.S. history, Vietnamese refugees have held a similar place, coming to the "proverbial belly of the beast" (Nguyen 2012). However, Iraqis have lacked the broader support afforded to Vietnamese refugees, both in numbers allowed into the country and in more robust state programs—all bolstered by the American war on communism, where the massive influx of Indochinese refugees was framed as those who "voted with their feet" for democracy. As I will outline throughout the book, the devastation of their country and indeed their lives has inspired little political will to resettle and support Iraqis within the United States.

Iraqi Refugees

In recent years, a small but growing body of scholarship concerned with the lives of Iraqi refugees has emerged. Omar Dewachi's (2017) work provides a medical history of Iraq, problematizing the notion that the devastation of Iraq's healthcare system began with the American invasion of 2003. Dewachi brings forth the ways that imperial forms of government—first at the hands of the British Mandate and then through American interventions, sanctions, and wars—have been upheld, challenged, and collapsed through medicine in Iraq. Dewachi rails against orientalist presumptions that frame Iraq as inherently "ungovernable" or "unruly," arguing that decades of wars and sanctions hollowed out the medical system, and indeed the very project of state making. Inhorn's (2018) analysis follows the barriers to healthcare, and in particular to equitable reproductive health, experienced by Iraqi and Lebanese refugees to the United States. Like Dewachi, Inhorn critiques the effects of American wars and sanctions that have destroyed Iraqis' lives, and in particular their health. Inhorn's qualitative research with Arab refugees in Detroit highlights the ways that refugees, who cannot afford expensive fertility treatments, are forced into states of "reproductive exile." Chapter 5 of this book takes on the ways that paltry post-resettlement medical supports have exacerbated the precarity that textures the already diminished health and well-being of Iraqi refugees. In contrast, this analysis attends to refugee trauma, framing it not simply as a personal, psychological set of symptoms but as a collective debilitation foisted upon Iraqis at the hands of American empire. Furthermore, *Meaningless Citizenship* centers the ways that the exclusion from adequate medical care in the United States informs refugees' understandings and critiques of citizenship.

In her journalistic account of the lives of twenty-two im/migrant students who have recently arrived in the United States, including a few Iraqi refugees, Thorpe (2017) focuses on Mr. Williams, a Denver high school English language acquisition teacher, and his students. While Thorpe captures daily life in the classroom as well as some of the realities students and families face outside of the school, she does not pay adequate attention to the conditions that displaced refugees in the first place, nor to the various conditions beyond the school that continue to limit refugees. Like Thorpe, whose work centers im/migrants' sense of belonging, Crane's (2021) qualitative study examines the barriers that Iraqi refugees experience in achieving this in the United States, specifically in a post-9/11 environment. The first text to dedicate its full attention to Iraqi refugees in the United States, Crane's work brings into focus the various struggles that they face in their new context. Unlike Crane's account, which traces the challenges experienced by Iraqis as a result of Bush's War on Terror after 9/11, *Meaningless Citizenship* argues that in order to understand the liminality of the Iraqi refugee experience, both in Iraq and the United States, we must look back further than the 2003 American invasion of Iraq to the decades of political interference as well as the brutality of the First Gulf War and the subsequent sanctions, all while simultaneously paying attention to the dismantling of the American welfare state that poor refugees look to for support. I argue that we must move beyond psychological analyses of refugees' sense of belonging as well as outdated arguments about acculturation and assimilation, and look instead to the ways that the gutted welfare state in effect doubly displaces them from "the right to have rights" (Somers 2008) that allow them to become full citizens. Crane rightly tends to the ways that Iraqi refugees are racialized in a post-9/11 U.S. context, but problematically concentrates on the intergenerational tensions between young people and their stricter and oftentimes more religious parents about various issues, including the appropriateness of dating. This discourse of cultural difference has long been attached to Muslim im/migrant youth (Sarroub 2013; Zine 2001), problematically positioning young people as those who consistently struggle to negotiate between two allegedly irreconcilable cultures, risking the buttressing of the problematic notion of a fundamental clash between cultural systems (Abu El-Haj and Bonet 2011, 35; Jaffe-Walter 2016). In contrast, *Meaningless Citizenship* situates both refugee youth and parents as those entangled with and excluded from various arms of the state that shape them as particular types of citizens.

This book is an effort to share the lives of the refugee families whom I have had the privilege of knowing, for whom global neoliberalism, disaster capitalism, and American imperialism are intertwined social experiences. Their pre-migratory histories and encounters with and exclusions from various arms of the American welfare state reveal the hollowness of American exceptionalism. The experiences of refugees with these institutions—including public schools, resettlement agencies, welfare offices, and hospitals—uncover the broken nature of the American resettlement program, but more important are an indictment of the smokescreen of the democracy promised to them and their fellow Iraqis through the imperial project. The lives of Iraqi refugees provide a scathing critique of the lie that undergirds the "freedom" that America exports through imperialistic machinations of war and occupation, revealing that the only freedom pursued both in Iraq and the United States is that of markets and unfettered capitalism. Rather than access the right to a settled life and full citizenship, they, like those who came before them, became entangled in the project of being made into laboring subjects, those whose lives are created, limited, and evaluated by their ability to work. Below, I outline the changing face of American imperialism, and the role of global disaster capitalism in the devastation of Iraq, as well as the welfare state in the United States.

America's (Disavowed) Neoliberal Imperialism

Many Americans do not like to think of their nation-state as an empire, including former president George W. Bush—who declared in a West Point speech that "America has no empire to extend or utopia to establish" (Harvey 2003, 4) and who ran a campaign that opposed the use of U.S. soldiers for nation-building. But what else was Bush's war on terror and its resulting invasion of Iraq if not "an exercise of imperialism" (Ignatieff 2002)? There is no doubt that those facing the barrel of American guns in the name of peacekeeping, security, and freedom have long suffered the direct results of U.S. empire. The United States is the only nation that "polices the world" through more than forty military bases on six continents (Savell and 5W Infographics 2019), that "deploys carrier battle groups on watch in every ocean; guarantees the survival of countries from Israel to South Korea; drives the wheels of global trade and commerce; and fills the hearts and minds of an entire planet with its dreams and desires" (Ignatieff 2003). In order to qualify as an empire, the United States need not be the most powerful nor even the most hated, but rather the enforcer of a global order that aligns with American self-interest, decrees America's demands, and subjects other countries to laws and regulations from which it excuses itself, such as the Rome Statute of the International Crime Court (Ignatieff 2003).

U.S. imperialism departs from earlier versions of empire in striking ways. While older forms of imperialism were political projects based on the command of a territory and the ability to marshal its resources to meet economic, political, and military goals, the new American imperialism is a capitalist one—a scattered political-economic project in terms of both space and time, in which control and use of capital is the priority (Hardt and Negri 2020; Harvey 2003). The current face of American imperialism is dissimilar from the empires of the past, built not on colonies and the "white man's burden," but rather on a global hegemony imbued with promises of democracy and human rights, and most important, free markets (Ignatieff 2003). Even though American imperialism took on a bolder quality after 9/11 and the subsequent global War on Terror, the United States has had a long history of imperialistic ventures abroad, even if it refuses to recognize them as such. Since the United States emerged from World War II as the global superior power with only the Soviet Union as a serious opponent, it has claimed to be the foremost defender of freedom, which in reality is the freedom of markets and private property rights (Harvey 2003, 31). To stave off the prospect of growing international socialism and to safeguard European democracies post–World War II, the United States "magnanimously" helped rebuild war-torn economies such as Germany and Japan (Harvey 2003). The Cold War afforded the United States with the means to allegedly act in the world's general interest, fighting the "good fight" against communism, which threatened the endless accumulation of capital (Harvey 2003). In spite of the rhetoric pumped out by the United States of its role as the "defender of democracy," it has consistently prioritized order and stability that ensured the interests of capitalism over democracy. The United States supported countless military coups all over the world—including in Iran, Guatemala, Brazil, Chile, Indonesia, and the Dominican Republic—which overthrew democratically elected governments and caused innumerable deaths, large-scale poverty, and the destruction of states on a massive scale (Harvey 2003). Even before Bush's War on Terror, the United States placed itself at the helm of collective global security, using the United Nations and NATO as tools to combat the influence of anticapitalist governments such as Russia and later China (Harvey 2003, 53). Contradictory to its claims of ensuring peace, security, and stability, the United States has supported state-sanctioned terrorism in countries like Bolivia, Poland, Russia, and Afghanistan, to name a few—all to ensure the creation and continuation of governments that were aligned with American interests (Harvey 2003; Klein 2007). In other words, even as the new American empire "is continually bathed in blood" its "concept of Empire is always dedicated to peace—a perpetual and universal peace outside of history" (Hardt and Negri 2020, xv).

Another distinguishing aspect of current American imperialism is its grounding in neoliberalism. After decades of economic growth under Keynesian state-interventionist economic policies—which included the expansion of public expenditures, building the welfare state, promotion of "full employment" as well as social welfare policies in order to provide a safety net for the working class, and making active interventions in the economy (Harvey 2007)—neoliberal logic began to take hold in the United States in the 1980s. At first a small and obscure school of thought led by University of Chicago professor Milton Friedman, who argued that society functions at its best when individuals and markets are free from government intervention, neoliberalism has become the new hegemonic "common sense" (Forgacs 1988). According to neoliberal logic, corporate growth, achieved through corporate tax cuts and lowered wages, will eventually trickle down and benefit all citizens. Notions of public good and shared consequence began to erode as concepts of personal responsibility began to take their place. In this formulation, the role of the government was to "back off" from its former stance on regulations and to allow the markets the freedom they needed to fight stagflation and promote economic growth.

American Neoliberal Imperialism Devastates Iraq

These logics not only transformed the institutions in the United States that serve refugees, but also shaped the ways in which American imperialism manifested globally. An essential and often disregarded aspect of Friedman's neoliberal theory is what Klein (2007) calls "disaster capitalism," or the framing of major crises as opportunities for corporate aims, typically achieved by breaking down and selling off the state to private corporations while citizens are still in shock. According to this frightening logic, the only way to achieve the "natural health" of an economy was to subject it to "shock treatment"—Friedman's three-part formula of deregulation, privatization, and cutbacks—which consistently resulted in the (often further) impoverishment of citizens and the simultaneous accumulation of mass wealth for large, multinational corporations. This theory informed American imperialist actions globally, but in particular in the Middle East. With nearly 65 percent of the world's oil, the region offered untold riches to corporations. After 9/11, earlier conversations about invading an Arab country began to take root in the government. Knowing that the closed economics of the Middle East would not be penetrable through peaceful means, plans for war were put into place. While some (Klein 2007) argue that several countries were considered—including Egypt, Syria, Iraq, and Iran—others contend that many members of the Bush administration had long had Iraq in their sights, ever since the unsettled end of George Bush Senior's Gulf War (Harvey 2003; Saleh 2020). Iraq would be the first country that would be invaded in the Middle East and then transformed into a free-market democracy, and would act as the catalyst for the region (Klein 2007, 415). The attacks of 9/11 provided the Bush administration with the perfect opportunity, whose justification for the war in Iraq was threefold: the link between Saddam Hussein's regime and Osama bin Laden's terrorist network, Iraq's persistent possession and development of weapons of mass destruction (WMD), and Hussein's horrific human rights violations. This departed from the Bush administration's justification for the war in Afghanistan, which was centered on the decimation of al-Qaeda and punishing the Taliban government for providing haven to the terrorist group. Bush's justification for both wars served as a means of appealing to the authority of the United Nations, which bans preemptive wars. Of the three reasons put forth by Bush to wage war on Iraq, only the last was true, as Hussein had used chemical weapons on his local opponents during times of war—an endeavor made possible through U.S. military and intelligence support. There was no tie between Hussein and bin Laden; in fact, bin Laden openly referred to Hussein, a secular ruler, as an "infidel" (Marr and al-Marashi 2017). The WMD were also a fiction.[5] The Iraqi government attempted to stave off war through diplomatic means, offering that the United States send thousands of troops or intelligence agents to scour the country for the alleged WMD. This did not stop the Bush administration, since war was a necessary step on the way to corporate profits. Bush's promise of "spreading freedom in the region" was actually nothing more than the "freedom for Western multinationals to feed off freshly privatized states" (Klein 2007, 416).

The devastation in Iraq began with a "shock and awe" airstrike campaign that was meant to shock the senses of Iraqis (Klein 2007). First, their hearing was attacked. As U.S. soldiers approached Baghdad, they bombed the Ministry of Communication, several telephone exchanges, as well as television and radio transmitters, leaving terrified families hiding in their homes, unable to access news of what was happening outside of their doorsteps or to call their families and loved ones to check on their safety. Next, their sight was targeted: in an instant, the entire city of Baghdad, which housed five million people at the time, found itself in the dark after electric facilities were destroyed. Desperate, Iraqis began to loot destroyed infrastructure, businesses, and homes, including the National Museum and the national library, which held "nothing less than the records of the first human society" as well as the nation's most prized collections of cultural heritage (Klein 2007, 425). U.S. troops did not commit these crimes, but also did nothing to prevent them or stop them once they began. This all fit the Bush administration's design for Iraq: a shock and awe campaign, the deliberate devastation of its infrastructure, standing by as its history and culture were plundered, and then, when the people were still stunned, selling the state off piece by piece to the highest bidder.

Within a few months of the American invasion, Iraq was in a predictable humanitarian crisis. Unemployment had reached an astounding 70 percent and malnutrition was widespread, with the ability to purchase subsidized foods—a holdover of the Hussein regime—the only thing protecting Iraqis from outright starvation. It was against this backdrop that U.S. occupation forces enacted economic shock therapy, setting up of the Coalition Provisional Authority (CPA) that formed the Iraqi Governing Council (IGC), a limited government with little authority to change any edicts by the U.S. occupation forces or enact new laws. The IGC gave the U.S. military control of the armed forces, and turned over the finances of the country to American supervision. Given full authority over the Iraqi economy, the CPA issued four orders[6] that enacted the full privatization of public enterprises, full ownership rights by foreign firms of Iraqi business, full repatriation of foreign profits, the opening of Iraq's banks to foreign control, national treatment for foreign companies, and the elimination of nearly all trade barriers (Harvey 2010). The labor market was to be strictly regulated and a regressive flat tax was to be implemented. None of Iraq's two hundred public firms survived the capitalist disaster attack, fettered by constant blackouts and the occupying forces' lack of willingness to offer them contracts. Contracts for the reconstruction of the economy worth billions of dollars were handed out to multinational companies, who chose to import their own foreign workers rather than employ Iraqis. De-Ba'athification[7] efforts resulted in the laying off of 500,000 state employees, mostly soldiers but also teachers, doctors, nurses, and engineers. After handing out Iraq's billions to private contractors, the CPA dissolved, leaving no one responsible for the mess it left behind.

A global and local uproar arose in response to U.S. imperialist actions in Iraq. Rights activists argued that these orders were in violation of both the Geneva and Hague Conventions, as an occupying power is mandated to protect the assets of a country rather than sell them off. The legality issue was resolved by appointing a "sovereign" government in 2004, whose confirmation would make the CPA's economic policies lawful. Before handing over the reins, the CPA increased the numbers of laws that would specify free-market and free-trade rules, and spelled them out in minute detail, ensuring that they would be very difficult to reverse. As a result of corruption, mismanagement, and a lack of regulation, many of the projects that were handed out to contractors and subcontractors remain unfinished, some of them were never even started. Billions of dollars spent on basic services such as electricity worsened the situation rather than fixing it. Iraqi quality of life plummeted as access to clean water, electricity, safety, and security dwindled further. As public anger grew, sectarianism began to take root and violence became endemic. When the occupation failed to provide basic services, militias filled the growing vacuum (Klein 2007, 454). Iraqis watched their country's riches handed over to private companies that were not in fact more efficient than the state. Faced with unemployment, malnutrition, an alarming rise in child mortality mostly caused by preventable diseases such as diarrhea, Iraqis began to express desire for a theocratic government, and took up arms against the occupation. According to an Iraqi-American CPA aide, "the economy [was] the number one reason for the terrorism and lack of security" (Klein 2007, 450). While it might have been a massive failure in providing Iraqis with "freedom" and "a better life"—the rhetoric that the Bush administration used as justification—the invasion and occupation was actually "the purest incarnation of the ideology that gave it birth": disaster capitalism (Klein 2007, 455).

The (Unacknowledged) History of American Imperialism in Iraq

While Bush's actions have undoubtedly caused mass destruction, dispossession, and deprivation in Iraq, it is critical not to ignore the long history of American imperialism there. In order to understand Iraq, one must be familiar with its land and the diverse groups of people who live within its current borders. The state of Iraq, which has only existed since 1920 when the three provinces of Basra, Baghdad, and Mosul were combined under the British Mandate, encompasses 167,618 square miles and shares borders with Iran, Saudi Arabia, Syria, Turkey, Kuwait, and Jordan.[8] The long-term project of Iraqi national unity has proven to be difficult for various governments due to the diversity of its inhabitants and the divisions between them, which are mostly based on language and religion. The three groups[9] that constitute the majority of Iraq are the Arab Sunnis, the Arab Shi'a, and the Kurds.[10] The vast majority of the population is Muslim (97 percent), with Shi'a significantly outnumbering Sunnis.[11] Even though Sunnis are a numerical minority in Iraq, they have historically dominated the political arena in the country—a trend that was first set by the Ottomans and carried on by subsequent governments, including that of Saddam Hussein. Arab Sunnis in Iraq tend to be urban dwellers, residing mostly in cities like Mosul and Basra. Through the exclusion of Iraq's Shi'a from the most important posts in the administration and military, they became increasingly alienated and have acquired the characteristics of a persecuted minority. The Shi'a, who tend to live in the south of Iraq, have had their own independent schools and sources of funding, since *khums,* a tax of one-fifth of one's income, is required of followers. The Kurds, who mostly live in the mountains and foothills of the northeast, are for the most part devoted, orthodox Sunnis. Over time, Kurds have developed an ethnic and national identity based on language, tribal connections, customs, and a common history of struggle for independent nationhood. There are also several religious and ethnic minority groups in Iraq, including Muslim minorities such as the Turkmen[12] and Shi'a Farsi speakers,[13] and non-Muslim minorities that have historically included Jews,[14] Christians,[15] Yazidis,[16] and Mandeans.[17]

From Revolution to the Iran–Iraq War

American involvement in Iraq began in earnest after the overthrowing of the Hashemite monarchy by a military coup by the leader of the Ba'ath Party,[18] General Abd al-Karim Qasim, in 1958—a move that also expelled the British from Iraq. The departure of the British changed Iraq's relationship with imperial powers, putting the country in the direct orbit of the United States (Saleh 2020). The United States perceived the overthrow of the monarchy as an act of insubordination that threatened the geopolitical and economic stability of the region. With the backing of the CIA and members of the U.S. National Security Council, Qasim was eventually killed in a military coup by Ba'athists in 1963. Five years later, a bloodless coup was led by military officers including General Ahmed Hasan al-Bakr, who became president and prime minister. Saddam Hussein[19] first worked within al-Bakr's regime, as second in command, and then became the de facto leader of the country when al-Bakr retired from most of his political responsibilities in the mid-1970s. While Hussein was brutal to his enemies,[20] he was also adept at currying favor with the Iraqi population through various means, the most important being the support of a nascent middle class and the creation of a "modern nation-state with the best educated, healthiest, longest living population in the Arab world," through his social reforms (Marr and al-Marashi 2017, 124). By 1973, all foreign oil companies were in the hands of Iraqis, which caused a sudden flood of wealth into the country. Hussein's regime used this new flow of income to implement agricultural improvements, develop large-scale industries, invest in cultural sites, expand public services such as public education and universal healthcare, and establish a massive literacy campaign. This investment in public services rendered tangible, positive results. By the 1980s, per capita income increased tenfold, and Iraq belonged to the middle-income group of countries with a per capita gross national product of $2,800 (Popal 2000). During the 1970s and 1980s, Iraq also boasted a robust healthcare system that provided cutting-edge, universal healthcare to its population, which raised the life expectancy of Iraqis by a full decade. Similarly, by the 1980s, Iraq possessed one of the best public educational systems in the Arab world, a result of mandatory primary education backed by a robust economic commitment to K–16 education (De Santisteban 2005). By the end of the 1980s, over 90% of elementary-aged children were enrolled in public schooling, with approximately equal participation between girls and boys. There was also an increase in the enrollment of women in higher education, with 47 percent of graduates being female.[21]

The Islamic Revolution in Iran in 1978–1979 that overthrew the shah, a former close ally of the United States, and the subsequent American hostage crisis provoked the United States to search for new allies in the region. Meanwhile, Ayatollah Khomeini's open calls for Iraq's Shi'a population to revolt and even to kill Hussein enraged the Ba'ath Party. Feeling confident with a full treasury and new weapons, Hussein went to war with Iran, assuming that it would be an easy and short venture with what he believed to be a weak nation. It proved to be neither, but instead lasted nearly eight years. The documents indicating whether President Carter gave Iraq the green light to invade Iran remain classified (Saleh 2020). The United States, which was growing increasingly wary of an Iranian leadership that had the potential of destabilizing the oil-producing Gulf, provided Hussein with a plethora of supports during the war, including removing Iraq from its terrorist nation list and replacing it with Iran; convincing allies to stop selling weapons to Iran and sell arms to Iraq instead; providing intelligence, arms, money, and foodstuffs to Iraq; and actively engaging in military action to support Iraqi forces. The United States also facilitated the sale of the necessary materials for the production of chemical and biological weapons to Hussein, who used them against Iraqi Kurds—an action the United States would later decry and use as a rationale for regime change in

Iraq. After nearly eight long and bloody years, Iran realized that it was engaged in a war not only with Iraq but with Western powers, and accepted the United Nations Security Council's Resolution 598 that demanded a cease-fire linked to withdrawal to internationally recognized territories, the exchange of POWs, and an investigation of responsibility for the war. On the same day, Hussein accepted the resolution and presented his own peace program that included the resolution's terms. The war was over and neither side had won, with over 500,000 lives lost on both sides.

From the Gulf War to the Sanction Era

The human, economic, and social costs of the Iran–Iraq war were immense for Iraq. Approximately 125,000 Iraqis were killed and nearly 255,000 were wounded. The burgeoning middle class began to erode, and those employed by the state struggled to make ends meet. The war also undermined prior gains in women's rights and caused a massive brain drain on the country brought on by the exodus of more than one million professionals. Hussein's once full treasury was depleted by the war, which cost the country over US$1 billion a month, leaving him in debt to the West and Gulf states to the tune of US$30 to 40 billion. The Iraqi economy was worsened further by Hussein's decision to liberalize the economy, causing wealth to concentrate among entrepreneurs and contractors while most of the population struggled to put food on the table. Aware of the danger posed to rulers who do not provide their people with basic necessities, Hussein demanded that his debt to the Gulf States, including Kuwait, be forgiven. His request was summarily refused. This refusal, coupled with oil prices plummeting after Kuwait's flooding of the market, were perceived by Hussein as acts of war against Iraq. It was during this time that the United States began to turn on Hussein, citing his use of chemical weapons on his own people[22] as proof of his regime's brutality. Amid the uproar against Hussein, the fact that the United States had lent him support in his efforts to acquire biological and chemical weapons was conveniently ignored. After the war ended, a U.S. Senate bill that sought to impose sanctions on Hussein's regime was opposed by the Reagan administration since Iraq was one of America's largest agricultural export markets as well as one of the major suppliers of oil to the United States. Additionally, the United States continued to provide Iraq with dual-use technologies, those that can serve military as well as civilian purposes. As a result, Hussein was largely ignorant of the growing ire against him in the United States. In fact, Hussein attempted to test the waters about an American reaction to his invasion, hinting at his intentions in meetings with American officials who assured him that the United States would not retaliate if Iraq invaded Kuwait. A misinformed, desperate, angry, and greedy Hussein decided to invade Kuwait, which he framed as "the bank next door." On August 20, 1990, Iraqi forces crossed into Kuwait.

What Hussein had misjudged was that he had laid claim to two things that the United States would not tolerate, money and oil. As one member of Congress stated, "if Kuwait produced bananas instead of oil," then his actions in Kuwait might have been permitted (Polk 2005, 146). The international response to the invasion of Kuwait was swift and hostile. Only five days after the invasion, U.S. deployments were dispatched to the Gulf to protect its oil interests. International diplomatic attempts to avoid the war, which Hussein mostly agreed to, failed. The United States, now keen on regime change in Iraq, was determined on war. On January 17, 1991, the United States launched Operation Desert Storm with an air strike on Iraq, the likes of which the country had never before experienced. U.S. forces dropped 80,000 tons of bombs targeting not only military facilities but also those critical to civilian life, including water sanitation and sewage plants, power stations, oil refineries, roads, factories, bridges, and roads—damage that has been estimated at US$232 billion. Iraqis struggled to access electricity, clean drinking water, and healthcare. The colossal U.S. aerial attack had devastated Iraq before any ground troops became involved. When Iraq announced that they would withdraw from Kuwait, President George H. W. Bush admitted that "instead of feeling exhilarated, [his] heart sank" (Polk 2006, 150)—he wanted war. With no other recourse, Iraq capitulated on February 27, and Bush ordered a ceasefire the following day. Enraged, Hussein ordered his forces to set alight nearly six hundred of Kuwait's oil wells, which burned for over six months and created a massive environmental hazard. Within two months of the ceasefire, the United Nations Security Council passed two resolutions that required Iraq to return all looted property to Kuwait, pay reparations to Kuwait, and destroy all of its WMD. Iraq's financial assets abroad were frozen and the country was banned from exporting oil, the state's major source of income. These two resolutions put Iraq in a catch-22 situation: until reparations were paid, the sanctions remained in place, and with the sanctions in place, the state could not afford to pay the reparations.

Iraq suffered the longest and the most severe sanctions[23] ever to be imposed on a country (De Santisteban 2005). Armed with its UN veto power, the United States controlled all relevant decisions, including which materials were allowed into the country, including ambulances, chemotherapy medications, chlorinators for water sanitation, and even pencils. The sanctions, framed by some scholars and human rights activists as the "invisible war" (Dewachi 2017; Saleh 2020), theoretically targeted Hussein and his Ba'ath Party but instead strengthened the government while weakening and dividing the Iraqi people. The poor, elderly, women, and children were the most affected, while a small group, mostly made up of the Ba'ath Party, grew immensely wealthy through the selling of banned items on the black market. The Iraqi dinar became worthless[24] and per capita income dropped by approximately 70 percent. The sanctions also arrested the state's ability to rebuild infrastructure that had been devastated by U.S. military actions. This had an immense and disproportionate impact on the most vulnerable Iraqi civilians. Schools fell into disrepair and were abandoned. Hospitals ran out of everything from life-saving medicines to soap for linens. Infant mortality rates soared to unprecedented levels in the country's modern history. Families struggling to survive were forced to sell their belongings and parts of their homes such as windows and doors (Saleh 2020). Daily electricity outages and water shortages, the lack of public transportation, the lack of access to the once state-funded public kindergartens and schools made life for women particularly difficult. Essentially, the sanctions "reduced the country to a pre-industrial state" (Arnove 2000, 14). Nearly a decade after the sanctions were imposed, despite evidence from UN arms inspectors and other international agencies that Iraq had been successfully disarmed, sanctions remained in place. President Bill Clinton boldly stated that the sanctions would last "until the end of time" or until Saddam Hussein "was no longer president" (Arnove 2000). Between 1990 and 2003, nearly 500,000 children died of malnutrition and a lack of basic services (Saleh 2020). When asked by a journalist about the death of half a million children, Secretary of State Madeleine Albright replied that the "price was worth it" to disarm the Hussein regime (Saleh 2020).

From the War on Terror to Modern-Day Iraq

George W. Bush's plans for Iraq laid bare the realities of the new American imperialism (Ignatieff 2003). Until then, the face of American imperialism in Iraq had changed from supporting coups and regimes to waging wars and sanctions on Iraqi soil. However, Bush's imperial logic and tactics favored coercion over any semblance of cooperation, prioritized unilateralism, and relied on American military strength to ensure global dominance of oil resources (Harvey 2003, 75). On the first anniversary of the 9/11 attacks, President Bush declared his imperial intents in a *New York Times* op-ed, that the United States sought to build "a peaceful world of growing freedom serves American long-term interests, reflects enduring American ideals and unites America's allies . . . where repression, resentment and poverty are replaced with the hope of democracy, development, free markets and free trade" (Harvey 2003, 5). Bush's statements might not have been a formal declaration of empire, but they undoubtedly constituted imperial intent (Harvey 2003). Noteworthy is the fact that even amid flowery discourse laden with American exceptionalism, the freedom envisioned for Iraqis was one where neoliberal priorities took primacy. Ensconced in false promises of progress, peace, and security were the primary goals of neoliberal imperialism, which would be facilitated by the invasion and occupation of Iraq.

After declaring a War on Terror and invading Afghanistan a few weeks after the attacks of 9/11, Bush rationalized a war in Iraq by falsely claiming that Saddam Hussein's regime had WMD, that he was linked to Osama bin Laden's "axis of evil," and that Iraqis must be freed of his tyranny. On March 18, 2003, President Bush gave Saddam Hussein forty-eight hours to leave Iraq, indicating that war was sure to follow. Two days later, Coalition forces led by the United States illegally invaded Iraq under the name of Operation Iraqi Freedom. The campaign began with airstrikes that were meant to "shock and awe" Iraqis, this time targeting Iraqi command and control facilities as well as military installations. Thirteen thousand cluster munitions that exploded into two million cluster bombs were dropped on Iraq, leveling entire areas of the country.[25] Within three weeks, ten thousand Iraqi civilians and tens of thousands of Iraqi soldiers were killed. By the middle of April, the Iraqi Army ceased to exist, and Bush declared Iraq as liberated,[26] even though it would take another eight years for American troops to leave Iraq. The American invasion and occupation further exacerbated the untenable living conditions created by the sanctions. Perhaps the single most devastating aspect of the occupation was the annihilation of law and order in Iraq. The failure to provide enough troops to ensure security, coupled with the American dismantling of the Iraqi military and police force, plunged the country into perpetual chaos[27] (Dewachi 2017). Rather than "liberating Iraq" and providing its people with safety from the oppressive regime of Saddam Hussein, occupying U.S. troops looked on as life in occupied Iraq became textured with widespread looting[28] of state property, diminishing security, sectarian violence, terrorism, and overall instability. The lack of security encouraged the emergence of militias, while unprotected and permeable borders allowed for the entry of insurgents as well as smuggling and other criminal activities. Crime could no longer be prosecuted and eventually lost its definition. The United States ultimately tried to recreate an Iraqi army and police force, but this was a failed effort.

With the occupation came the additional blow to the Iraqi economy, further incapacitating critical institutions and systems. Power outages increased and water running from taps ran brown and was undrinkable (Ismael 2008). The lack of electricity impeded the capacity to rebuild or even sustain water purification plants, oil and gas refineries, hospitals, and industrial plants. Public infrastructure was sabotaged further by the CPA's fire sale of state institutions. Fuel and electrical shortages had a devastating effect on hospitals in particular, leaving them unable to provide their patients with critical care (Dewachi 2017). Whole cities were without essential workers including police, firefighters, sanitation workers, healthcare professionals, and teachers. The health, safety, and security of the Iraqi people plummeted to an all-time low, making life intolerable. The harm done to Iraqis was not limited to the indirect fallout from the American invasion and occupation but also involved direct, dangerous, and at times deadly encounters with its military machinery. In the absence of a functioning police force, security fell to U.S. forces, who used increasingly harsh, countercultural, and humiliating tactics against civilians. Undertrained young soldiers used excessive force, killing innocent civilians in the process. Finally, U.S. top-down attempts to create an ethnically and religiously balanced democratic government backfired—causing an unprecedented rise in sectarian tensions and violence that came to a head in 2006, with the al-Qaeda bombing of the al-Askari mosque in Samarra, one of the holiest sites in Shi'a Islam. In order to survive the violence, civilians had to either choose to align themselves with a militia for protection, or flee.

Since the American invasion in 2003, approximately 2.5 million Iraqis have fled their country, over 2 million Iraqis have been internally displaced, and nearly 7 million (nearly 20 percent of the population) are currently in need of humanitarian assistance (UNHCR 2019). The uprisings and resulting violence, the withdrawal of U.S. forces, and the growing Arab Sunni discontent with the government's pro-Shi'a policies all contributed to the rise of Sunni extremism in Iraq, which culminated in the rise of the Islamic State of Iraq and Syria (ISIS)[29] terrorist group. By 2014, ISIS had captured entire Iraqi cities, imprisoning and massacring Shi'a civilians and military personnel, and causing a migration crisis within the country. At its height, ISIS took hold of about 40 percent of Iraq, targeting not only Shi'a, Christians, and other minorities[30] but also systemically eradicating pre-Islamic cultural heritage and religious sites. By the end of 2017, Iraqi forces, aided by U.S. and Coalition forces' airstrikes, were able to take back 95 percent of territories once held by ISIS, but the damage caused by ISIS still textures the lives of Iraqis to this day.

The U.S. Response to the Iraqi Refugee Crisis

Millions of Iraqis have been displaced as a direct result of the human, infrastructural, economic, and cultural destruction inflicted by American imperialism. And yet, the response of the United States to the Iraqi refugee crisis can be described as paltry at best. In total, the United States has settled less than 125,000 Iraqi refugees since 2008, which averages to 10,000 Iraqis resettled each year. The resettlement of Iraqi refugees began in earnest after the signing of the Refugee Crisis in Iraq Act in 2008, which framed resettlement as a way to intervene before refugees "became a fertile recruiting ground for terrorists" and before the region became further destabilized. Resettlement in this case was primarily a diplomatic and strategic tool, rather than a response to humanitarian crisis created by the United States. The fact that the United States did not respond immediately to the refugee crisis is not surprising, since resettlement tends to be inversely related to American military action in a particular state (Berman 2011).[31] Low resettlement rates were exacerbated by the Bush administration's minimization of the humanitarian cost of its war in Iraq for several years after the invasion in order to avoid the perception that the American-led coalition had failed. The Bush administration was also keen to divert attention from the fiasco of the U.S.-created government that was unable to provide security within Iraq (Berman 2011). Humanitarian organizations have consistently criticized the United States for its response to the Iraqi refugee crisis, both as the country responsible for it and in comparison with other Western countries who have accepted more

Iraqi refugees per capita. At the time of this writing, similar critiques have emerged regarding the latest humanitarian crisis in Afghanistan caused by the U.S. withdrawal and the Taliban gaining control of the government. After twenty years of war, the United States is once again doing very little for the people whose lives have been destroyed by its military imperialism in their country, with a plan to resettle only 80,000 Afghanis in 2022, leaving vulnerable millions to fend for themselves in a state ruled by the Taliban and gutted by uncertainty, violence, and instability.

Undoubtedly, the United States should grant asylum to those whose lives have been devastated by the American imperial project. But as the testimonies of Iraqi refugees will demonstrate in this book, refugees' troubles do not end with resettlement. Refugees arrive to find diminished resettlement supports as well as hollowed-out state institutions. Upon arrival, refugees receive a standardized package of case-management services from their resettlement agency, as well as a one-time Reception and Placement Grant, which was approximately $1,000 per person during the years of my data collection—an amount typically used to fund rent and utilities for approximately 90 days after their arrival. Through the passing of the Refugee Act in 1980, refugees were brought into mainstream public assistance programs, making their access to much-needed support subject to state and local welfare policy. As such, refugees were only eligible for cash assistance and state-funded medical insurance for eight months. This brief period of support was intended to achieve the number one priority of the American refugee resettlement program: for refugees to achieve financial self-sufficiency as soon as possible by reducing their dependence on public assistance programs. Meanwhile, neoliberal "reforms" had long reshaped and in many ways gutted the very programs that refugees (and low-income Americans) depend on for survival. Once lauded as evidence of a robust state, the welfare state has since become faulted for being wasteful, ineffective, and even for creating the very conditions that it sought to cure by constructing a culture of dependency rather than self-sufficiency. Rather than the former goal of eradicating or even *attempting* to reduce poverty, supports are now given with the explicit goal of not only reducing welfare rolls but also governing the poor and transforming them into productive market actors (Somers 2008). The institutions that were once theoretically charged with supporting refugees in the United States were gutted, such as refugee resettlement agencies, schools, public assistance offices, as well as clinics and hospitals. In other words, Iraqi refugee life has been ravaged by American neoliberal imperialism in Iraq and then once again by the evisceration of the welfare state in the United States.

Key Terms

The Welfare State

While Americans typically understand welfare to be limited to public assistance programs offered to low-income families or the unemployed, I rely instead on Michael Katz's definition of the welfare state as "a collection of programs designed to assure economic security to all citizens by guaranteeing the fundamental necessities of life: food, shelter, medical care, protection in childhood, and support in old age" (2010, 6). The main principle undergirding the welfare system was the conception of a society as male-headed households where men earned an adequate wage to support their wives and children, while women shouldered the unpaid labor of caregiving (Fraser 1994). This assumption was the bedrock of many welfare states at the time, discounting the lives of countless families who never fit this patriarchal mold. Most welfare states in Western countries provide social insurance programs that protect people from the unpredictability of the labor market. These programs were designed to replace the breadwinner's wages in case of sickness, disability, unemployment or old age (Fraser 1994). In the United States, these welfare programs provided relief by "decommodifying" labor, which gave the poor respite from the pressures of the market (Soss, Fording, and Schram 2011, 7). Unlike the United States, many countries provide a second tier of support that provides direct support for women whose primary occupation is mothering, caregiving, and homemaking. In the United States a last tier, also known as the "residuum," provides inadequate and often-times stigmatized support for those who do not fit the family-wage frame and thus have no claim to honorable support (Fraser 1994). Below I provide a brief description of the various welfare institutions that refugees living in poverty in the United States rely on.

Public Assistance Programs

What most Americans understand as "welfare" is actually made up of two separate programs, the Temporary Assistance to Needy Families (TANF) program, which offers cash assistance, and Supplementary Nutrition Aid

Program (SNAP)—often referred to as *food stamps*—for assistance purchasing food. The current TANF program replaced Roosevelt's Aid to Families with Dependent Children (AFDC, 1935–1997) and serves as the primary support for women's childrearing as well as the main support for poverty relief (Fraser 1994). When neoliberal notions of "moral hazard"[32] began to take hold in the United States in the 1980s, welfare programs were repositioned from a social virtue to social vice. In 1996 Bill Clinton signed the Personal Responsibility and Work Opportunity Reconciliation Act, which effectively abolished welfare as an entitlement, eliminating AFDC and replacing it with TANF—a more limited and restrictive welfare program currently available to low-income families, including recently resettled refugees. The program moved away from providing cash assistance and is now mostly used to fund services, classes, and other programming that removes barriers to work for recipients. The modern SNAP program also finds its roots in the Great Depression era and was unsurprisingly transformed under the Reagan administration. Funding for SNAP was slashed and the very nature of the program changed, which caused hunger to resurge all over the country at alarming rates.[33] Clinton's welfare reforms exacerbated the limits of the program and negatively affected refugees' access to food stamps. In order to receive benefits, SNAP recipients must register for work, accept any work available, and participate in programs that prepare them for work (Soss, Fording, and Schram 2011).

Public Education

Public education has long been a central element of the public welfare state (Katz 2010). For over a century, public schools have provided critical social services to children, including nutrition and health, especially in America's poorest neighborhoods. Schools offer free and reduced hot meals to students from low-income families on a daily basis, as well as health screenings and other important services. From a financial standpoint, families who live in poverty and whose children experience what Jonathon Kozol (1988) has deemed the "savage inequalities" in their schools receive more from public education than they contribute in property taxes (Katz 2010). This is no accident, since the founders of public education recognized the redistributive nature of public schooling. To find adequate support, early school promoters had to persuade both the wealthy and those who did not have children that a universal, free education would be in their own interests. They argued that public education would reduce crime, lower the cost of relief for the poor, prepare the masses for labor by furthering their skills and improving their attitudes toward work, and assimilate immigrants—all efforts that would save taxpayers money in the long run. Early school promoters were successful, so successful in fact that the redistributive quality of public education vanished from public consciousness, even though the term *public education* was a stand-in for *schools for the poor* at the time. Nonetheless, this form of welfare was taken up by taxpayers as a crucial public good, until the attack on the welfare state began to take hold in the 1980s.

Healthcare

Unlike other Western countries, the majority of social insurance in the United States is actually provided by a "private welfare state." A wide range of benefits, such as pensions and health plans, are not basic entitlements given to all citizens but are paid by private companies as a part of market compensation (Fraser 1994). Approximately 60 percent of Americans receive their health insurance as well as their pensions through their employers. This design was facilitated by the enactment of the Employee Retirement Income Security Act of 1974, which allowed private employers to deduct the cost of healthcare and pensions from taxes. This fact that this process is supervised through the government via intense regulation proves that the provision of private benefits is in fact a part and parcel of the welfare state (Katz 2010).

Citizenship

While definitions of citizenship abound, I rely on Somers's (2008) and Mink's (1998) analyses of the term. Put simply, Somers defines citizenship as "the right to have rights," arguing that the primary rights of citizens are rooted in recognition, inclusion, and membership in both a political body and in civil society. This notion of rights rests on a structural model made up of a triadic relationship between the institutions of the state, market, and civil society. When disrupted, this relationship, inherently marked by a constant struggle for balance and power, can cause citizenship to be endangered. Somers maintains that the past several decades have been marked by such an imbalance caused by the domination of the market, rendering once rights-bearing citizens into those whose lives are marked by social exclusion and rightlessness. While other scholars have referred to this phenomenon as neoliberalism (Harvey 2007; Lipman 2013; McCluskey 2003; McNevin 2006), Somers argues that we are currently living in an era of "market fundamentalism," which she defines as "the drive to subject all of social life and the public sphere to market mechanisms" (2). This process has allowed for disproportionate market power to jeopardize citizenship by pitting the market and the state on one side and civil society on the other. As a result, "the risks and costs of managing human frailties under capitalism once shouldered by government and corporations get displaced onto individual workers and vulnerable families" (2). The spread of neoliberalism has resulted in a contractualization of citizenship, where the relationship between the state and its citizenry is transformed, framing social inclusion and moral worth as conditionally earned privileges, given only to those who are able to reciprocate with something of equal value.

Similarly, Mink (1998) frames citizenship as the web of relationships between an individual and the state that sustains rights and obligations. Mink centers her analysis on the complex relationship between citizenship and the U.S. welfare state. In the U.S. constitutional democracy, the basic rights given to citizens are political, such as the right to vote or jury duty. While the strongest obligations are enforced by law, such as military conscription during times of war, some are completely ethical, such as community or public service. Alternatively, U.S. citizens' political rights are explicitly identified in the Constitution as interpreted by the Supreme Court, such as the right to counsel, the right to vote, and the right to trial by a jury of one's peers. These political rights are *enjoyed* by citizens, but not *earned*. They are bestowed on citizens through the mere existence of the democratic political community. *Theoretically* these rights are universal, without the need to prove that citizens deserve them. These political rights are attached to individuals because they are members of the community. Also, since we all theoretically enjoy these rights, we are all equal. Needless to say, the history of citizenship within the United States has proven the fallacy of this claim. Indigenous peoples, African Americans, Mexican Americans, immigrants, and women were all barred from rights of American citizenship, proving that full citizenship has been far from universal but rather categorical, with citizenship dependent on racial, cultural, and gender status of individuals for most of U.S. history.

Mink argues that even if certain political rights are universalized and become available to everyone, this would not guarantee equality among citizens. To universalize rights, we must attend to the social inequalities that might act as a barrier to accessing political rights. For example, a person who struggles with housing insecurity cannot register to vote without a stable home address. In this case, housing insecurity threatens a citizen's political right to vote.

Most serious democracies, Mink argues, have recognized that moving from categorical to universal citizenship requires alleviating social inequalities, which includes policies that guarantee the economic security of their citizens. These policies and provisions are what Mink defines as social rights, or specifically, "primordial claims to those social supports that enable one to live and participate in . . . [their] . . . community" (1998, 12). Unlike other democratic industrialized countries, the United States has not offered generous social rights such as universal healthcare or robust labor market programs that protect workers' rights, but instead has provided a patchwork of minimal supports for different categories of needs. Social rights such as unemployment insurance are given in lieu of protections against an all-powerful market in several European countries, which include the prohibition of firing, generous parental leave, and several weeks of mandated paid vacation time. In the place of universal healthcare for all citizens, the United States provides access to Medicaid for its poorest citizens. Rather than providing a living wage, the United States provides limited and ever-decreasing TANF and SNAP support. While political rights are legally grounded, social rights, referred to as "entitlements," are derived from claims from the political majority that are won through the legislative majority, and as such shift with political change (Mink 1998). Theoretically, social rights enable equality by neutralizing inequalities among citizens. This includes providing welfare supports for poor Americans, including refugees.

Scholars argue that neoliberalism has further skewed the meaning of citizenship in the United States by making the fulfillment of obligations a *condition* of civic membership. Civic incorporation now centers market priorities, situating welfare recipients not as those who have "the right to have rights" (Somers 2008) or as political members of a community, but as those who need to be managed and disciplined through supervision, surveillance, and instruction. Citizenship, then, is understood through the lens of the market. As such, citizens are now mainly defined and evaluated by their self-discipline and as those who labor and consume. Those who fail to "manage their daily affairs," such as the poor, are deemed as morally lacking citizens (Soss, Fording, and Schram 2011, 23). As such the poor are excluded from civic participation, and are situated as civically inferior in comparison with their more financially stable counterparts. Neoliberal policies "prioritized social order [over] social justice, and civic compliance over civic engagement" (Soss, Fording, and Schram 2011, 48). Any attempts to include the poor as citizens and enable them to be active, full members in their communities have been replaced by neoliberal paternalist efforts to transform them into self-disciplining market actors.

Definitions of citizenship that critique the neoliberal project often disregard the ways that conditionality has long been encoded in the American citizenship-making process, one that rested on the exclusion of all but middle-class, white men. Saidiya Hartman's (1997) analysis of the experiences of freed slaves revealed the false promises that have undergirded the creation of "laboring subjects"—people whose identities are both created and limited by labor (Reddy 2017)—in the United States for over 150 years. Hartman contends that the freed slave "was nothing but burdened, responsible, and obligated" (125). In fact, a freed individual was essentially a project, a subject to be transformed into a "rational, docile, and working class" entity through pedagogical manuals, freedmen's school, and religious instruction taken up by teachers, missionaries, and plantation managers (Hartman 1997, 127). Texts, lessons, and sermons centered on all aspects of life, including labor, consumption, and even hygiene, all aimed to fashion a consuming and self-disciplined subject. The most valuable virtue imparted by the texts was "the willingness to endure hardships," which would alone guarantee "success, upward mobility, and the full privileges of citizenship" (Hartman 1997, 129). By framing freedom as a debt, purchased through the "precious blood" of their countrymen, the freed individual was and would remain a debtor, obligated to others. In this formulation, individual responsibility was the antidote to slavery, erasing its entire legacy and putting the burden on those who had suffered most under its brutality. In this way, the immense struggles that freed slaves faced, including a lack of land, the constant threat of starvation, and a lack of education—all created by slavery—were never addressed or considered. As such, the freed were subjected to a system of "indebted servitude," where debt ensured their submission.

One risks stating the obvious in observing that the histories, contexts, and lived experiences of those who survived the ravages of chattel slavery are vastly different from those of modern-day refugees. That said, Hartman's analysis allows us to understand that there are parallels in the promises made to those who must fulfill the needs of capitalism: you can gain access to freedom, social mobility, and indeed full citizenship only through your willingness to be a disciplined subject, and most important a dedicated "laboring subject." Also, Hartman's notion of debt can illuminate for us the expectations placed on Iraqi refugees, who have "magnanimously" been allowed entrance into the United States and taken away from the devastations of war and forced displacement—conditions that were engineered and manufactured by American imperialist ventures in Iraq (Nayeri 2019; Nguyen 2012). *That* is the debt that refugees must pay, by ensuring that they are not a financial burden to the country that has "freed them" from their formerly tumultuous and dangerous lives.

Organization of the Book

This book is a testament to the failure of the United States in providing Iraqi refugees with the social rights needed for full citizenship in their new communities. In spite of being subjected to the devastation of American military imperialism in their home country, they all came to the United States with hopes of accessing the allegedly universal citizenship available to them as future legal citizens. As those most closely acquainted with the transnational rhetoric of American exceptionalism[34] (Koh 2002; Lipset 1997; Madsen 1998; Tyrrell 1991), Iraqi refugees had hoped to find the promises embedded within that narrative. However, as refugees living in poverty, they quickly discovered that the social rights that they had assumed they would find—those that might level the playing field and give them the ability to realize the settled lives they dreamt of—were never actually promised but instead always out of reach. Effectively, Iraqis suffer not only devastation of their own country at the hands of American imperialism but also the neoliberal and disaster capitalist hollowing out of the very institutions that might have theoretically provided them with critical social rights in the United States. The lives of the Iraqi refugees at the heart of this book reveal how the shrinking of the welfare state and the American resettlement program shape the ability of refugees to access the rights of citizenship. Furthermore, *Meaningless Citizenship* traces how the various institutions of the welfare state contribute to the creation of poor refugees into laboring subjects, whose worth as citizens rests on their ability to be "industrious, responsible, thrifty and sober" (Reddy 2017, xvii) and most important not financially dependent on the state. Chapter 1 documents how the ravages of American imperialism shaped refugees' hopes for a better life. The destruction of Iraq and their subsequent forced displacement to neighboring countries where they had limited rights shaped their aspirations for a "settled life," one where they could finally find the safety and stability they needed. These hopes collided with the nature of post-resettlement (lack of) supports in the United States, forever shaped by neoliberal reforms to the welfare state. This chapter explores the ways that the emphasis on self-sufficiency, as defined by the Office of Refugee Resettlement and local refugee resettlement agencies as immediate employment, limits refugees' ability to become full citizens while also disciplining and shaping them into low-wage laboring subjects. Through their encounters with the refugee resettlement agency, refugees learned that social mobility is nothing but a false promise, accessible only to financially stable immigrants/refugees (Ong 1999). Chapter 2 underscores the ways that the punitive policies and practices of the welfare office—designed with the main goal of reducing welfare rolls rather than eliminating poverty—impede refugees from achieving the financial independence required of them. As a result of their disciplinary encounters with the welfare office, refugees question and reject the empty promises of citizenship. This chapter not only highlights the human cost of the hollowing out of the welfare state but also underscores the agency of refugees as they resist the abuse and neglect they experience at their local welfare offices. This chapter concludes with an analysis of refugees' pre-migratory expectations and the disparate realities they face upon arrival.

Shifting the focus from refugee adults to refugee youth, chapter 3 explores the ways in which the gutted public education system affects their dreams of "the good life" (Berlant 2011)—aspirations formed in contexts rife with loss, suffering, and liminality. This chapter investigates the ways that budget cuts as well as teacher and staff layoffs effectively incapacitated schools' ability to adequately meet the needs of refugee students, who came to their classrooms with a host of unique challenges including fragmented educational trajectories and trauma. Furthermore, these Muslim refugee youth who arrived in a post-9/11 era were forced to navigate entrenched Islamophobia in their schools. Chapter 4 homes in on the educational experiences of young adult refugees, whose age, pre-migratory histories, and post-resettlement responsibilities collided with a gutted adult education landscape that excluded them from accessing secondary and higher education. The chapter focuses on the discrepancy between the pre-migratory aspirations of young adult refugees and their lived realities in the United States that shaped them into laboring subjects.

Chapter 5 points to the physical and mental health needs of refugees. The chapter examines the ways that American resettlement policies limit refugees' ability to access, navigate, and maintain adequate and consistent healthcare for needs that can often be directly tied to American imperialism in Iraq. Soon after their arrival in the United States, refugees came to understand that healthcare was not in fact a right, but a privilege afforded to those fortunate enough to procure full, gainful employment. Shut out of an American healthcare system that prioritizes profit over health, refugees began to question their citizenship rights. The concluding chapter takes up the ways that current xenophobic, nationalist, and Islamophobic refugee policies continue to contribute to the precarity experienced by asylum seekers and refugees to the United States, focusing on the destructive policies of the Trump administration. The book concludes with policy recommendations inspired by the lives and testimonies of those whose stories are at the heart of this book.

1

Resettlement

The Creation of Self-Sufficient Subjects

I walked up the short flight of stairs to the first floor of the split-level home and was greeted by Nadia at the door. Since her husband was at work, and her daughters at school, it would be just the two of us. Nadia led me to my usual seat on the couch and went to the kitchen. As she prepared tea, we chatted. After a few minutes, Nadia brought me a cup of sweet cardamom tea, her specialty, and some *maamool* cookies, which she knew were my favorite and had baked earlier that morning. As she settled onto the couch next to me, we caught up on each other's news. After the conversation died down, I said, "Alright! Let's get down to business." She laughed and told me to finish my tea first before we got to the "bad news." That made us both laugh. As per our weekly tradition, Nadia retrieved a stack of mail and handed it to me. One by one, I opened each document: the travel loan payment, the electricity bill, the water bill, a credit card statement, and documents from the welfare office. I read each one, interpreted its contents, and handed it back to Nadia. With each bill, I noticed the concerned look growing on her face. I knew that her husband, Sayed's, hours at work had been reduced, and I wondered how they would make ends meet.

Nadia's experience highlights the heavy burden of survival that low-income refugee families experience on a daily basis. The ritual framed above—where I opened, read, and deciphered the documents that penetrated refugee households—was a common one across all of the families that I worked with. As one of the few English speakers that families were acquainted with, and the only one who visited their homes regularly, it fell to me to help them make sense of their "financial responsibilities"—a term they learned from their resettlement agents soon after their arrival to the United States. This ritual gave me a window into the human cost of the American resettlement program's emphasis on self-sufficiency, defined by the refugee resettlement agency as immediate employment. Subsequently, refugees were forced into low-wage jobs and scrambled to make ends meet. I spent countless hours at kitchen tables and living rooms, observing families as they tried, often in vain, to stretch their meager salaries far enough to meet their needs.

This was not the life that refugees had imagined for themselves. Refugees like Nadia came to the United States with hopes of a better, "settled life," or one that is free of violence, conflict, instability, and dispossession, so that *finally*, all might be well. Refugees came to their new contexts with the expectations of adequate supports that would facilitate their new lives. However, upon arrival, refugees quickly learn of the barriers that lie between them and the settled life they imagine, put in place by a refugee resettlement program that prioritizes economic self-sufficiency above all else. This chapter focuses on the ways that an emphasis on self-sufficiency, defined by immediate employment, limits the capacity of refugees to achieve the settled life for which they long. By focusing on the pre-migratory journey of Nadia and her family, I document how the ravages of war shape refugees' hopes for a settled life in their new contexts. Then, by tracing the post-resettlement life of Nadia's family and others, and in particular their experiences with their caseworkers, this chapter makes visible the ways that definitions of self-sufficiency as immediate employment hollows out refugees' aspirations and instead fashions them into laboring subjects.

A Family's Journey of Displacement

Nadia's Family

In early 2013, I received an email from a colleague who was in search of a fluent Arabic-speaking tutor for an Iraqi refugee student. Soon after, I began providing daily tutoring support for Zeina, a seventeen-year-old Iraqi refugee and ninth-grade student at Liberty High, a large urban neighborhood high school in Philadelphia. A few days after I met Zeina, she informed me that her mother, Nadia, would like to meet me, and had extended an invitation to me to their home. I readily accepted. My first visit was on a weekend, when everyone was home. Nadia, a forty-nine-year-old mother of two, was warm and chatty. Standing at 5 feet 2 inches, dressed in a purple track suit, with her brown hair tied in a neat ponytail, Nadia looked much younger than her age. I soon noticed that Nadia walked very slowly and at times winced when she walked up stairs—a result of her early-onset arthritis. In our first outing together, I found out that Nadia wore the hijab outdoors, but as was custom in many Muslim countries, she did not wear it in the house in female company. Sayed, her husband, was tall and lean, and had a much darker complexion than Nadia. He looked his age, fifty years old, with greying temples and worry lines etched on his forehead. He was quieter than Nadia but was also warm and welcoming. Zeina took after her mother: short, with pale skin and a ready smile. Dima, her younger sister, who was thirteen the first day I met her, was very quiet and shy. She looked most like her father, tall and olive-skinned, and seemed a little serious for her age.

During my first visit to Nadia's home, I took in the warm, cozy, and inviting feeling of the apartment. Every surface in the house displayed attention and care: The walls were a freshly painted white, with the accent wall closest to the kitchen painted a bright yellow. Behind me on the couch was a colorful hand-knitted blanket. On the coffee table sat a green vase filled with faux sunflowers that complimented the yellow accent wall. Framed pictures of the small family sat proudly on both side tables, of them at the mall in Iraq and the beach in Syria, which Nadia then explained was taken before the "bad times began." On the wall facing the couch hung a beautiful hand-stitched tapestry, embroidered with verses from the Quran—the one item in the room Nadia had brought from Iraq. In the kitchen, Nadia's self-proclaimed "kingdom," which was visible from the living room, everything was arranged in order. A hand-built shelf stood above the small counter, Sayed's handiwork, which gave her more counter space. On the shelf, all of Nadia's spices, teas, and staples were arranged in glass jars, and labeled in her beautiful Arabic handwriting. Tea towels that complimented the colors in the living room hung from the stove handle. The kitchen was spotless, as well as the rest of the house. As I would learn from later visits, it usually smelled either of the incense that Nadia loved or of one of the incredible meals she was cooking. A couple of visits later, when Nadia gave me a tour of the house, it became clear that she had done an equally masterful job of decorating her daughters' room. Since Zeina and Dima both loved Hello Kitty, the room was painted pink with large Hello Kitty stickers glued to the walls, and identical overstuffed Hello Kitty pillows on each of the girls' twin-sized beds. As it turns out, Nadia and Sayed did all the painting themselves, since the landlord refused to paint the "the once dingy walls" himself. She explained that the duvet covers and other Hello Kitty paraphernalia the girls had asked for were too costly, so this was all she could afford. Her own bedroom seemed sparse in comparison, a queen bed and a small accent rug, but it, like the rest of the apartment, was spotless. Nadia told me that she and Sayed had turned a terrible apartment into something livable, and a semblance of her old home in Baghdad.

During our first visit, Nadia, Sayed, and I chatted for over an hour. They asked me about my family, how I had come to find myself in Philadelphia, and other questions. This made sense to me; I was teaching their daughter every day, and they wanted to know more about this new person in Zeina's life. The visit was a success, I assume, as Nadia invited me to return. In fact, after this first visit, I began visiting Nadia at least once a week. Since Nadia was often alone at home while her daughters were at school and her husband was at work, I would visit with her during those hours. Eventually, when I asked Nadia's family if they would like to be a part of my study, they readily agreed. Nadia was especially eager to join, happy to, as she put it, "set the records straight about refugees." Early on in my visits to their home, Nadia and her husband Sayed told me how their family had come to be resettled to the United States. They told me that they wanted to tell the story "from the beginning," so that I had an idea of what life was like for them before the war.

Dreams of Happily Ever After

Nadia and Sayed had what they both referred to as a "true love story." One afternoon, on her way home from spending time with friends, Nadia's car broke down. Sayed, a mechanic at the time, stopped to help. They spent the three hours that it took him to fix the car—which Sayed later admitted that he had elongated purposefully as it would have normally only taken him an hour or so to repair the car—talking and laughing. They exchanged telephone numbers, and soon after, as is traditionally expected, Sayed asked Nadia's father for her hand in marriage. Smiling as they both recounted their "meet-cute," Sayed explained, "I was captivated at first sight." Nadia refused to marry right away, insisting on getting to know him well first. They had a long engagement, where she "tested his personality," but eventually they married. Sayed told me that he was ecstatic when she agreed to marry him. "She is a distant relative of Kathem Al Sahir," a famous Iraqi singer. "You know who my distant relative is? Muntadhar Al-Zaidi, the journalist who threw his shoes at President George Bush in Iraq. She comes from artists, and I come from rebels!" We all laughed.

Nadia spoke of the first years of her marriage as "the good years before the troubles began." Sayed established a car dealership, which became very successful. They lived in a beautiful neighborhood, close to Sayed's family. Nadia nostalgically spoke of how her four-bedroom apartment was furnished beautifully, and how the girls never wanted for anything. She would spend her days with family members, friends, and her family. Her family would vacation near the beach each summer. She even cultivated a small garden on the balcony attached to her room, where she and Sayed sat and drank their evening tea after he returned from work. A year after they were married, Nadia became pregnant with Zeina, and a few years later with Dima. Nadia described this as the happiest time of her life. "Life in Iraq before the war was good for us."

Dangers and Daughters

According to Nadia, the situation in Iraq became unlivable soon after the American occupation of Iraq in 2003. The violence intensified after the bombing of the Al-Askari mosque in 2006, one of the holiest sites for Shi'a Muslims. Nadia stated that after the bombing, "people were being killed simply because of their last name, because of their identity as Sunni or Shi'a." On one afternoon, when Nadia was hanging the laundry from the balcony facing the back of the building, she heard her neighbor screaming her name frantically. It turns out that a man in a car had tried to abduct Dima, who was only three years old at the time, only to be foiled by the neighbor who pulled Dima out of the car before he sped off. When Nadia heard this story, she was horrified. For months after this happened, Nadia had recurring nightmares of losing both of her daughters to masked men who could walk through walls. She began to wonder if she could keep her children safe in an increasingly violent city.

A few months later, at the end of her eldest daughter Zeina's school day, armed men began to shoot at the children as they were heading home. Nadia recalled the event, one she told me was "seared in her mind":

> We got there right after it happened, so we saw all the blood. We almost lost our minds, and thought Zeina was dead. We went to the hospital that the children were taken to. Honestly at that point, I thought my daughter was dead, she was gone. I died a million times in those few minutes. We were both crying, and I was

screaming her name, and looking for her everywhere. I had to look for her among the dead children. It was horrible. And then I saw her. Her leg was wrapped, she had been shot in the knee, and she was sitting at the edge of a cot, getting stitches and crying her eyes out. And I thanked Allah for saving her. They wanted to do X-rays and scans on her, but Zeina was so terrified, we took her home, promising the doctors we would bring her back.

Nadia took Zeina home, thinking she was out of harm's way. But that night, she realized that Zeina had also injured her head. As it turns out, the school guard had picked up Zeina and rushed her out of the school once the shooting began. As he ran holding her, he was pushed by everyone else running for their lives, and was accidently thrust into the school's metal gate, ramming Zeina's head against the gate in the process. Nadia wanted to take Zeina to the hospital immediately, but when Zeina heard of this, she began to shake and cry, begging her parents not to take her there. "It's because that was where she saw the dead children," Nadia explained. Not wanting to cause Zeina any more suffering, she agreed not to take her to the hospital—a decision she would later regret when she arrived in the United States and Zeina was diagnosed with a traumatic brain injury.

After the shooting at Zeina's school, Nadia's nightmares and anxiety increased. She worried about her children constantly, even when they were inside the house with her. She would insist that her daughters play only in the parts of the house where she could see them. She began asking Sayed to leave Iraq, but he refused. His large family, including his elderly father, were all still living in Iraq, and he felt that he could not leave them behind. Nadia's desire to leave Iraq became the source of much tension in their marriage. Her suffering was compounded further by an incident that put her husband's life in danger.

Close Encounters with Death

A few weeks after the school shooting, Sayed was stopped by a caravan of cars on his way back from work, which had blocked the highway he usually took home from work every day. Three armed men got out of a black car with tinted windows, and commanded Sayed to get out of his car (a fairly new BMW), with his hands raised above his head. As Sayed slowly exited the car, he took the car keys with him. With guns aimed directly at him, Sayed asked permission to speak to the leader of the group, which was granted. He said, "Listen brother, I would like to give you this car, as a small gift to thank you for keeping our roads and our families safe. If you will do me the great honor of accepting this gift, I would be eternally grateful." With his gun pointed at Sayed, the leader walked up to Sayed, pointed it at his head, stood there briefly, with a blank stare, and then took Sayed's keys and walked away. Saying nothing, he motioned to the others, who got into their car. The leader got into Sayed's car and the caravan, now led by Sayed's car, drove off. Sayed, finally able to take a deep breath, stood in the middle of the highway and watched them drive off until he couldn't see them anymore. Sure that no one was turning back for him, he began his long walk home.

Nadia recalls, "He appeared at the doorstep hours later, dirty, dehydrated, and honestly, he looked like he had aged ten years. They say that this is what happens when you face death, and now I believe it. He didn't look like the man who had left the house that morning." The incident shook Sayed to his core. While he had been calm, collected, and quick on his feet in interacting with the armed militia, it wasn't until he arrived home that he allowed himself to collapse. Nadia reported that he took to their bed for some time, overwhelmed with the thoughts of what might have been if they had taken the car *and* his life. Sayed is what Nadia describes as a "sensitive soul," and it hurt Nadia to watch him suffer. He didn't talk much, but eventually made his way back to work. "He was changed though," Nadia said. "They didn't just take the car from him. They took a part of him too." After that incident Sayed began driving used cars, ones that wouldn't attract attention. And, according to Nadia, he often seemed distant, nervous, and "not his old self."

The Last Straw

The family's experience was also deeply impacted by the daily violence on the streets of Baghdad textured by the deadly presence of the American military in Iraq:

> One day we were driving to do our weekly shopping from the market. We were almost at the end of the street, and were coming at the end of it. That's when we saw them: American soldiers. They stopped the tank sideways, turned it against us, and began

shooting at us, shot after shot. I began to scream, "My daughters!," and the girls began to scream and cry. They kept shooting us one shot after the other. Sayed yelled at us, "Duck, duck, down into the car you and the girls!" Poor guy, he was trying to reverse the car and back out of the street, but he was so frazzled that he kept going forward. People were screaming, yelling at us to get out of the car, out of harm's way. Finally, Sayed just stopped. So we ran out of the car finally. I immediately began to check the girls' bodies for bullets and blood. Sayed and I then did the same. Because sometimes, from the shock, you've been hit and at first you don't know it. It was a miracle, we were unscathed.

Nadia recalled standing on the sidewalk, in disbelief, as those who had witnessed the incident came to offer them water and to be sure that they were safe. It was then that she learned that "the Americans," as they were referred to in Iraq, had closed the road. Typically, American soldiers signaled the closing of a street by rolling a tank onto it, and that once they close a street, they did so on both ends. After this, only local foot traffic is allowed. Nadia was certain that the street was open when her family drove through, and that the American soldiers closed it after they had passed. She explained that if an Iraqi saw an American military vehicle on the road, they would immediately avoid it and choose another route. She emphatically insisted that had she or Sayed seen anything to suggest that the road was closed, they would have never driven down it. More important, she questioned, "Why are they shooting at us?! What is our crime that they shoot at us!? All we were doing was shopping for food!"

Eyewitness accounts by journalists and the soldiers themselves confirm that American attacks on civilians were not atypical, but in fact a daily reality in Iraq (Crawford 2013; Hedges and Al-Arian 2009; Gonzalez 2003). An interview with renowned journalist Robert Fisk, given from Baghdad soon after the U.S. invasion of Iraq, revealed that hundreds of Iraqi civilians were dying at the hands of American soldiers who often indiscriminately fired their weapons when Iraqis approached, and showed little care to their civilian status. Interviews with American veterans revealed that this type of behavior was an everyday practice (Hedges and Al-Arian 2009). Iraqi families were regularly shot at for coming too close to checkpoints. One particularly gruesome confession involved a soldier firing at a man and decapitating him with a machine gun in front of his small son (Hedges and Al-Arian 2009). According to firsthand accounts, at the outset of the violence that followed the American occupation of Iraq (Gonzalez 2003), approximately one thousand civilians were dying weekly, 40 percent of those at the hands of American soldiers.

The attack on her family at the hands of American soldiers was the last straw for Nadia. That night Nadia told Sayed, "I will not stay in this country one more minute." Dima had almost been kidnapped; Zeina could have been killed in the shooting at her school; Sayed had narrowly escaped death in his confrontation with armed militia men; and finally, they had all been almost gunned down by American soldiers. "It was enough," Nadia declared. Sayed argued that since Allah had miraculously saved her family from each of these life-threatening disasters, He would continue protecting them. Nadia agreed; she also viewed the safety of her family as a gift from Allah, but perceived it also as a warning sign—Allah was telling them that it was time to leave. She informed Sayed that she and the girls would leave Iraq with or without him. Not wanting to lose his family, Sayed finally acquiesced. Nearly four years after the American occupation of Iraq, Nadia's family left for Syria.

Life in Syria

While Nadia felt safer in Syria, it was certainly not all that she had hoped it would be. Leaving her parents and siblings behind was extremely difficult, and she worried about them every day. A year after their arrival, Nadia was informed that her youngest sibling was killed on his way to buy bread for his wife and children. He left for the market and never came back. Soon after his disappearance, Nadia's brother was found in a mound of trash, shot in the head. Nadia's mother died two years later of a heart attack. Nadia was unable to return to Iraq for her family members' funerals due to the increasing violence in Baghdad. If she left, she was unsure that she would make it back to her daughters and husband as Syria had closed their borders with Iraq. Her own immediate family struggled in Syria as well. When they had first arrived in Syria, Zeina had seemed well, but soon afterwards became withdrawn, refusing to speak to her family. Nadia and Sayed attempted to encourage Zeina to attend school, in hopes that it would give their daughter much-needed social interaction with other children. But each time they tried, Zeina would cry hysterically and shake for hours. Finally, Nadia decided not to force Zeina to attend school. As a result, for the entirety of the family's stay in Syria, which spanned five years, Zeina was excluded from education. The family was also struggling financially. Sayed invested heavily in two business ventures that failed. As an Iraqi refugee, Sayed had to take on Syrian business partners, and in both cases, he was swindled out of the money he had invested. Since he could not register the businesses in his name, he had no legal recourse. Nadia describes this time of her family's life as "their time in hell."

Thankfully, a few years later, the family's situation began to improve. Nadia learned of the Center of Love, a nonprofit organization for children with disabilities, and began taking Zeina to their meetings. Slowly, Zeina began to "act more like herself" and even began to speak with her family again. Through a connection with an old friend from Iraq who had also settled in Damascus, Sayed found work at a television station as a technician, enabling him to earn a steady wage. However, by early 2011, political protests began to break out in their neighborhood, every Friday after prayers. As the protests became more volatile, Nadia's fears and anxiety returned. "We had left one war behind, and somehow landed in another one." As the political instability escalated, Nadia felt increasingly unsafe. When she walked to the market with her daughters, she would hear young men say loudly, to ensure that she heard them, "When the regime falls, *that* house is the first that I am going to hit!" Nadia's nightmares returned. To make matters worse, Sayed lost his job as employment opportunities began to shrink. Nadia and her family began to get desperate. With the help of a lawyer who regularly volunteered at the Center of Love, Nadia and her family applied for asylum through the United Nations office in Damascus. Nadia and Sayed had hoped to be resettled in Germany or Sweden, where they had heard the supports for refugees were robust and long term, and where they had several friends who had already resettled. However, they were informed that they were to be resettled to the United States.

Ever the backbone of her family, through it all, Nadia would encourage her husband, even when she herself had little hope. She shared:

I would always say to Sayed when we would face hardships in Iraq and then in Syria, "It's OK. Allah will give us better days once we are resettled. We will have a different life, a good life. We will live in a lovely home. We can plant things in our backyard, flowers and other things. They will help us until we can stand up on our own two feet." We would dream.

These dreams for a settled life had gotten Nadia and Sayed through the worst of times. These hopes were directly linked to the realities that textured refugees' lives. Lives that were marred by the American imperialist project that devastated Iraq, hollowing out its once healthy infrastructure that had included free healthcare, free K–16 education, adequate access to clean water and food, and secure streets free of violence. Lives that were then again hollowed out by the experience of forced migration to a land where second-class citizenship was the best refugees could hope for. Lives in search of something as simple as a garden. These were the lives of Nadia and Sayed and countless others who lost homes, families, loved ones, and pieces of themselves on their way to a dream of a settled life. And even though the United States was not their first choice, Nadia and Sayed had hopes for beginning a new and settled life there—one that was not to be.

Post-Resettlement Life: Expectations of Self-Sufficiency

Arriving in America

In summer 2011, when the protests in Syria began to gain international attention, Nadia's family was resettled to Philadelphia. Nadia told me that the day her family arrived in Philadelphia would be indelibly etched in her mind. "It was an omen of what was to come," she explained. After traveling for what seemed like days, Nadia and Sayed were shocked to find that no one was waiting for them. Not knowing what to do, she and her family sat in the arrivals area, waiting. Approximately eight hours later, a non-Arabic-speaking employee of their resettlement agency came and found them. Since Nadia and Sayed spoke little English, all Nadia and Sayed could understand from her was the word "sorry." They could not communicate with the caseworker for the entirety of the hour-long trip to their new home. Thankfully, Khaled, an Iraqi resettlement caseworker, was waiting at their doorstep. Nadia recalls how relieved she and Sayed were to have a fellow Arabic speaker to communicate with. Khaled explained that the person tasked with picking them up had been waiting for them at the wrong airport.

After sending the American caseworker home, Khaled led the family into their new apartment, attempting to give them a tour of the place.

Bleary-eyed and exhausted, Sayed and the girls plopped down on the couch, the only piece of furniture in the living room. Nadia remembered feeling "tired to the bone," but out of respect, let Khaled give her the tour. In spite of the state that she was in, Nadia couldn't help but notice the state of her new dwelling. And at each turn, as she took it all in, she visualized the home that she had left behind in Iraq. In this unfamiliar living room, the sole piece of furniture was the used couch where her family sat, with a long tear in the back cushions. Gone was the comfortable living room in Baghdad, with couches, ottomans, coffee tables, and pillows. A living room big enough for her extended family to gather, drink their afternoon tea, watch television, and spend time together. In *these* bedrooms, there were only mattresses on the floor. One bedroom for both of her girls. No desk for each of them to do their homework. No wooden closet to store their clothes in. Even the walls seemed dirty somehow. Who could she hire here to paint her walls every year, she wondered? Seeing how tired they were, Khaled left, promising to return the next day. Nadia tried to coax her daughters to go to sleep, but as exhausted as they were, they refused to sleep on the linens provided by the refugee resettlement agency. Nadia opened one of her suitcases and gave each of the girls their blankets, which she had brought with her from Syria. After her children and her husband were finally asleep, Nadia finally went to the bathroom, where she encountered cockroaches scurrying around once she turned on the light. She recounted distinctly thinking at that moment, "*This* is it? *This* is what they brought us to?" It was during that first night in Philadelphia that she decided that she would find a new place to live. Unbeknownst to her, that was not an option.

The next morning, Khaled picked them up and took them on several errands to the various places they would need to become acquainted with: the grocery store, the welfare office, the local clinic, and finally the resettlement agency. Once they arrived at the refugee resettlement agency, Nadia and Sayed were ushered into a conference room with others where they attended the federally mandated "cultural orientation": a PowerPoint presentation with Arabic writing on the slides accompanied with Khaled's prerecorded voice that narrated each slide. The presentation covered all aspects of life in the United States including transportation, banking, and public schooling for their children. It was during their cultural orientation that Nadia and Sayed had first heard that they were expected to become "self-sufficient" as soon as possible.

Post-Resettlement Realities: An Emphasis on Immediate Employment

Soon afterward, in a private meeting with Nadia and Sayed, Khaled informed them about their rights and responsibilities. Their rights included access to him, their caseworker, for ninety days, as well as a one-time Reception and Placement Grant, which ranges between $925 and $1125 per person (Thomas 2011). This resettlement stipend, which is funded through the Bureau of Population, Refugees, and Migration, was typically used to offset expenses such as rent, food, and utilities for the first few months after arrival. Refugees were also eligible to apply for longer-term cash and medical assistance for up to eight months through the Office of Refugee Resettlement (ORR), a branch of the U.S. Department of Health and Human Services. Refugee adults were eligible for state-funded health insurance for eight months, while children were covered by state insurance until they turned twenty-one years old. Khaled emphasized that it was their responsibility to pay their rent and utilities once their brief support ended. Furthermore, after a six-month grace period, they would be responsible for beginning to make monthly payments on their travel loan—an interest-free loan made to refugees to pay for the cost of airfare to the United States. For Nadia and Sayed, their travel loan sum was over $7,000, and their monthly payment was over $200. As a result, Khaled urged Nadia and Sayed to begin to search for work *immediately* to ensure that they had a steady income before their supports disappeared and their various financial responsibilities began to pile up. If not, they risked home insecurity.

This news came as a shock to Nadia and Sayed. They had been informed by UNHCR personnel in Syria that they would be expected to work, but that they would be given some time. Nadia recounted the UNHCR employee telling her, "You will go and after a while they will find you work. If they offer you a job that you don't like, it's your right to refuse it." This was certainly not the case. During my year-long placement at the refugee resettlement agency, I observed firsthand how the messaging about employment there was centered on immediacy, rather than choice or fit. The commitment to assisting refugees achieve economic self-sufficiency was front and center. Classes dedicated to employment readiness were offered to recently resettled refugees, and agency volunteers and interns spent much of their time shuttling refugees to and from job interviews. In fact, services pertaining to employment were at the heart of much of the case management offered to recently resettled refugees. Nancy, the director of the resettlement agency, confirmed this in an interview:

> One of our top priorities is to find our clients work. A lot of the refugees who come here struggle because their work experience, their credentialing, and their language skills don't really translate to the American workplace. We are always trying to connect refugees with access to entry-level jobs . . . so they can break their way into the American job market, and to build a resume with American experience.

Nancy, a middle-aged white woman who herself was married to a refugee, had always seemed to me sympathetic to the plight of refugees. She understood that her clients came to this country with a wide array of skills, credentials, and expertise that were often rendered meaningless in the American job market. In spite of this recognition, the solution she puts forth is one that is steeped in a hegemonic "common sense" (Forgacs 1988) informed by the capitalistic priority that undergirds the American resettlement program: avoiding dependency at all costs. Rather than granting refugees time to retrain within their former fields, or give them adequate time to learn English—both options that might lead them to better employment and eventually give them better life chances as well as lead to a long-term self-sufficiency—immediate, entry-level work was prioritized, defining self-sufficiency as reducing dependency on the state.

This prioritization of immediate employment was also underscored by Mary, the director of employment services at the agency. At a meeting with recently resettled Iraqi refugees, she implored them to accept the first job they were offered, no matter how troubling they found the nature of that job. She urged refugees to accept "part-time jobs with no benefits"; those "in a cold environment working with food"; custodial work that might "include cleaning toilets, which of course no one wants to do"; or working "longer than normal work days." Time and time again, Mary highlighted the importance of "keeping an open mind." The premise to Mary's logic was that once they built some job experience in the United States, as well as language skills, they could move onto better jobs. "But you have to start somewhere."

Soon after their arrival, Nadia and Sayed were pressured into finding immediate employment. At their first meeting at the resettlement agency, their caseworker Khaled informed them in no uncertain terms that finding a job, *any* job, was their number-one task. During that meeting, Khaled urged Sayed and Nadia to search for work, but given Nadia's health problems including diabetes and early-onset arthritis, as well as the need to support her daughter Zeina, who was still struggling, they ultimately decided that Nadia would not work outside of the home. All too aware of the ticking clock of dwindling resettlement support, Sayed felt backed into a corner. He had always been resourceful, finding a way to make a living and take care of his family. In Iraq, he had left high school to assist his father in supporting their family. Sayed had always been good with his hands, and loved cars, so eventually found work as an automotive repair technician in Baghdad. A few years later, with the help of his father, he opened his own automobile repair shop, and eventually saved enough money to establish a small used car dealership. A few years later, he began to sell new cars, even a few luxury models. This became a flourishing car dealership. When he, Nadia, and his daughters fled to Syria, Sayed had tried to establish first a bakery and then an automotive repair shop in Damascus, but both businesses failed after his Syrian partners cheated him out of his share. Eventually, Sayed found work as a part-time set-designer at a television station just outside of Damascus. This required him to learn a new set of skills, but also drew on some his strengths as a former business owner, such as communicating with people and managing several projects at a time. After one year, he became a full-time member of the set-design team, which was a relatively lucrative position at the time, especially for a refugee in Syria. The most impressive aspect of Sayed's rich professional history was the fact that much of his work had been acquired through experience rather than formal credentialing.

Sayed shared this with Khaled, who only reiterated what Nancy had stated earlier: Sayed's work skills would not easily translate into the American workplace. Khaled urged Sayed to be pragmatic, and to prioritize the needs of his family above his pride or discomfort with the nature of the jobs that were available to him. Khaled encouraged Sayed, reasoning that as his English got better and his résumé became more attractive to American employers, Sayed would eventually be able to access better employment opportunities. In essence, the message being relayed by the resettlement agency was that refugees needed to focus on getting a job as soon as possible, as this was for their own good. After searching for work for nearly two months in Philadelphia, Sayed was hired as a shelf-stocker at the local branch of a national superstore, earning minimum wage and working thirty-five hours a week without benefits. His monthly gross income was just over $1,200 a month, not nearly enough for four people to subsist on.

Self-Sufficiency: The Back Story

The messaging that refugees receive about employment does not come as a surprise to those familiar with the American resettlement program, since achieving economic self-sufficiency and avoiding dependence has long been the number-one priority. In fact, from the outset of large-scale involvement with refugee resettlement in the United States, refugees needed to prove that they would not be an economic burden. After World War II, there was a pool of approximately one million displaced persons (DPs) who could not safely return to their homelands. Harry Truman, the American president at the time, recognized the need to resettle some of these DPs to the United States both for humanitarian purposes and to demonstrate America's central role in the postwar order (Haines 2022). To convince Congress, Truman framed refugees as being worthy of assistance, and that they would eventually, in the long term, make contributions to American society. Congress was not swayed. As a result, advocates leveraged several arguments for the admittance of refugees, centering an economic one: refugees "could immediately fill needed slots in the U.S. economy," providing an "immediate economic advantage" rather than a burden (Haines 2022, 7).

In 1948, Truman signed the Displaced Persons Act, following the admission of over 250,000 European refugees. This legislation facilitated the admission of 400,000 more Europeans displaced by World War II. Even for these early waves of refugees admitted into the country, the Truman administration and Congress expected that they would provide for themselves by working the worst of jobs. They were required to do so for at least a year under a labor contract, and then were free to choose their own path. Theoretically, after this first year was over, refugees could go about enjoying their new life in the United States. Over the years, this system has changed. Now, there is no official labor contract for refugees upon arrival, but instead, refugees are pushed into accepting any kind of employment, as long as it is immediate. In this sense, they are fulfilling their obligation by taking jobs that no one else would want, like cleaning toilets. More important, by accepting these jobs, they are not a drain on the system. "The task of that first year (or so) is thus about learning to make money and simultaneously learning how to not cost anybody any money" (Haines 2022, 5).

After the fall of Vietnam in 1975, the United States was faced with the challenge of resettling hundreds of thousands of Indochinese refugees with temporary funding and a fragmented task force for refugee admissions. During this time, policy makers, advocates and activists were dedicated to assisting refugees to reach their full potential. Programs that allowed refugee professionals to access retraining in their former fields were developed to facilitate access to gainful employment (Haines 2010; Thomas 2011). Cash assistance and other supports given to refugees were framed as a means to facilitate long-term self-sufficiency, for instance by giving refugees a multiyear opportunity to learn English and to remedy any interruptions in their education (Hein 1993; Nezer 2013; Thomas 2011). With the help of religious institutions, financial supports for refugees lasted up to three years, rather than the current ninety days. However, once the Refugee Act was signed into legislation in 1980, the goal of long-term self-sufficiency dissolved and the notion of appropriate employment became synonymous with immediate employment (Bean, Van Hook, and Glick 1997; Haines 1988).

As a result of this understanding of self-sufficiency, most of the programming and services that resettlement agencies provide are expressly designed to encourage refugees to become employed and "get off" of public assistance (Haines 1988; Masterson 2010). Accordingly, resettlement agencies are now expected to place a higher priority on "hard services" such as employment training and access, leaving behind the "softer" services, such as long-term access to bilingual caseworkers, mental health services, and general language classes that do not center employment, in order to keep refugees from becoming dependent on the welfare system (Haines 2010; Nezer 2013; Takeda 2000; Thomas 2011). This reduction in services has a deleterious effect on all refugees, but especially those who have significant postarrival adjustment problems due to their pre-resettlement histories, which are often rife with challenges such as exposure to violent conflict, decimation of social infrastructures in their native country, loss of family and loved ones, and repeat migration. For several years, Iraqis were among the largest groups of refugees resettled by Nancy's agency, and by her own account, they struggled post-resettlement due to trauma and "what happened to them before they came." In spite of this acknowledgement, Nancy and her employees were directed by the ORR to center the priority of ensuring that refugees were economically self-reliant by attaining employment as soon as possible.

Promises for Self-Betterment through Low-Wage Work versus Language Learning

While learning English is one of the top priorities of the American refugee program, it is clearly second to the project of creating self-sufficient subjects. This is perhaps best illustrated through a conversation between Lian, a case manager, and Tamer, a twenty-eight-year-old, recently resettled, male Iraqi refugee. Tamer spoke little English and was resettled to the United States five months prior to this meeting. Tamer was desperate to find a job but was experiencing difficulty doing so. His resettlement cash assistance had run out two months prior, but he was able to survive by living with his older brother and his cousin, who were both employed at the time of his interview with Lian. Lian, herself an immigrant from China, described herself as "very dedicated to the refugee cause." She had immigrated to the United States for college and eventually found work with nonprofits that assisted immigrants like herself. Now in her mid-thirties, she remembered what it felt like to be "new in this country," and chose to work with newly resettled refugees as a way to help them make a home for themselves in the United States. She welcomed my presence at the agency, preferring to use me as an Arabic interpreter, rather than LanguageLine, a phone service that provided simultaneous interpretation for refugees. She asked me to interpret during her conversation with Tamer. Earlier that week, Tamer had been accompanied by an agency volunteer on an on-site job interview at a meatpacking facility. He was offered a job there, but had turned it down.

TAMER: You know that I have been looking for work for several months now. I have also been attending English classes five times a week, even though the classes are so far from my house. I am willing to work anywhere really. But this place is just too cold. I have circulation problems and asthma, and if I worked there my condition would get worse.

LIAN: Tamer, I think it is important for you to be realistic about the jobs out there. While it is great that you are taking all of these

English classes, right now, your English is very limited and there are very few jobs out there for people with such limited English. Honestly, you cannot be picky. You simply cannot.

Lian's response to Tamer's concerns about the job site confirms the agency's stance regarding refugee employment: appropriate work is *any* work, as long as it is immediate. Lian exhorts Tamer not to be too fussy, and to accept any offer, especially given the fact that he did not speak English. Their exchange, and in particular, Lian's emphasis on his English proficiency, illustrates how language learning—the second pillar of the American resettlement program, and a presumed pathway to better employment—is used by case workers as a tool to push refugees into low-wage labor.

Tamer's commitment to improving his language skills, which was costly in both time and resources, was an optimistic investment in his future— one mostly shaped by the discourse of agency employees. During my yearlong residency at the resettlement agency, I observed how caseworkers, ESL teachers, and volunteers consistently communicated to refugees that with better language skills came better opportunities. Eager to access the settled life that they had hoped to find here, refugees optimistically bought into this promise. In hopes of bettering his chances of acquiring gainful employment, Tamer attended language classes at the resettlement center every day that they were offered there, only to learn a harsh lesson: his dedication to language learning was encouraged and applauded as long as it was in service of attaining immediate employment. If refugees dared prioritize language learning over the search for or acceptance of immediate employment, they were harshly disciplined by resettlement agents. For then, dependency was at stake.

The prioritization of self-sufficiency over language learning is actually one that is federally mandated and not particular to a resettlement agency's internal policy. The Refugee Act of 1980 states that the main goal of resettlement agencies is to provide refugees with enough English language proficiency "*in order for them to become financially self-sufficient*" (Halpern 2008, emphasis added). In other words, learning English upon arrival is not framed as a method of integrating refugees into their new social contexts, a stated goal of the Office of Refugee Resettlement, but rather primarily as a way for them to avoid dependency on the state. Agents like Lian, Nancy, and Mary enacted federal mandates by ensuring that refugees were putting forth the necessary efforts to find immediate employment rather than spending unwarranted time in language classes. This was accomplished by ensuring that language classes were filled with refugees who were actively searching for employment, arguably to make them more "employable."

Koyama's (2013) ethnographic research with twenty-five refugee resettlement agencies and organizations found that refugees' employability may in fact be *inversely* related to their English proficiency level. Iraqi refugees who had arrived in the United States with special visas after assisting the American military as interpreters during the war were considered "unready to work" by their resettlement agencies (Koyama 2013, 961). As former lawyers and engineers, members of the middle class in their native Iraq, and fluent in English, they were resistant to accepting menial work and subsequently deemed "noncompliant" by their resettlement agents. Furthermore, even though they came with high levels of education, they were deemed as "uneducable" since they refused to learn how to become employable in the United States by accepting the first job that they were offered. In other words, these Iraqi refugees were *too* educated and *too* fluent in English to be employable. Koyama's research suggests that "employable" refugees are those who unquestionably accepted entry-level work.

This point was corroborated by Susan, the director of case management at the resettlement agency. A white woman in her early sixties and a year away from retiring her current position, which she had held for the past ten years, Susan was described by her coworkers as having a "harder edge." Personally, I experienced Susan as an extremely honest, no-nonsense sort of person who spoke her mind with ease. When asked about the greatest challenges facing Iraqi refugees, she shared:

> I think the most difficult thing we have to do [at the agency] is help our clients come to term with the fact that we are resettling them into poverty. No one wants to see them there, and no one wants to accept that, but the reality is that they are going to become a part of the American poor, and really there is no escaping that. That is a difficult message to give and an even more difficult one to accept, but it is the reality for these people. And there is no escaping it. I mean maybe there will be some hope for the second generation, depending on their circumstances. But for those who have resettled here, that is their reality. Even for those who have jobs, which are so hard to come by, they are going to be stuck in poverty.

A [minimum-wage] salary, even when it is supplemented with welfare checks and food stamps, is a salary that will keep people in poverty. . . . There is really no way out of it. This is especially a problem for Iraqi families because they have big families.

Unlike her colleagues who communicated their optimistic messages of better futures to refugees, Susan laid bare the brutal reality of the American resettlement project. Refugees were being resettled into poverty, and there was simply no escape from that. Susan's testimony clearly dispels the notion that immediate employment can act as a bridge to a better life, and in fact admits that it does nothing but trap refugees into poverty. Susan reluctantly suggested that life might be better for their children, a question I will explore in upcoming chapters, but makes plain that the fate of refugee adults was sealed. This troubling admission, rare among resettlement agency employees, reveals the fallacious nature of the promise of better future employment and life chances vis-à-vis work experience and language learning.

Broken Promises of Full Citizenship through Self-Disciplined Labor

Hartman's (1997) analysis of the experience of freed slaves suggests that in order to achieve full citizenship, subjects must prove their worth as good and willing laborers. Accordingly, Iraqi refugees must pay their debt to the country that gave them "refuge." In this formulation, the very pre-resettlement conditions that were directly caused by American imperialism—loss, dispossession, trauma, lack of access to education and other key services due to the crumbling of state institutions in their home country—are all collapsed and ignored. Rather than addressing these circumstances by providing refugees with adequate support, services, and training to allow Iraqi refugees to regain some of what they lost, the responsibility of obtaining the ever-elusive settled life is placed on their vulnerable shoulders, emphasizing low-wage labor as the way to achieve it. In other words, promises of a good life—as defined by success, upward mobility, and the full promise of citizenship—is all within reach, as long as refugees labor (in low-wage jobs) for it.

Beneath this false promise lie three undeniable facts. First, that a "reserve army" of labor will always be necessary to fulfill the needs of a capitalist society like that of the United States (Bowles and Gintis 1976).

As such, since the inception of the refugee program in the United States, refugees have been expected to fill needed slots in the American economy and, more specifically, accept low-wage labor that provided little income and security. Only then would they prove that they were worthy and that they provided an immediate economic advantage rather than placing a financial burden on American taxpayers. Second, in order to prevent dependency, refugee adults *must* accept any kind of work, as long as it is immediate. This explains why refugees like Tamer were framed as troublesome. By refusing immediate employment, refugees break the unspoken social contract: you were admitted to this country, but you must not come with a cost.

Finally, to encourage refugees to accept unattractive jobs, resettlement agency personnel promise them better employment opportunities once refugees have furthered their language skills and/or their work experience. The central problem with this practice is that once refugees are limited to low-wage employment upon arrival, they are effectively stuck in the low-wage labor market and permanently excluded from economic advancement in the future (Haines 2022). For how will experience in custodial work or employment at a meat-processing plant necessarily prepare them for better work opportunities? Also, where will refugees improve their language skills when their time is taken up by low-wage work? The reality of low-wage labor is that one needs to work as many hours as possible in order to survive, so when might someone like Sayed find the time to attend language classes? The assumption here is that refugees might learn language "on the job" or become more fluent over time. While it is true that working alongside native English speakers might further refugees' *spoken* English, this does not further their reading or writing skills, a key component to *actual* employment advancement. Nearly all of my refugee participants spoke very limited English and would certainly not be able to further their language skills since they worked full-time, low-wage jobs. In order to gain actual literacy skills, refugees would need to attend language classes. However, the only consistent language classes were held at the refugee resettlement agency, on the other side of the city from where most Iraqis were resettled, during working hours. There, classes dedicated to employment readiness were offered to refugees for the first ninety days, and other English classes were offered by a rotating body of volunteers. Furthermore, as Tamer's experience highlighted, refugees were only encouraged to attend language classes *if* it served the purpose of accessing employment. In sum, the notion of refugees bettering their language skills was simply not possible: the pressures to get and keep a low-wage job would not allow it. Realistically, these promises of economic advancement and social mobility were nothing but an instrument of capitalism, transforming recently arrived refugees into the newest members of America's working poor.

· · ·

Refugees come to their new contexts with dreams of a settled life. Having experienced the loss, trauma, and privation that accompany forced migration, Nadia had hoped for "better days," where the new country that had offered her refuge would provide her family adequate support until they could stand on their own feet. In other words, Nadia had hoped to finally find a safe harbor after all that her family had experienced in Iraq and then again in Syria. This vision of America, as a haven for those searching for a better life, does not fall far from the historic stance of the U.S. government with regard to refugees—one that has been used as further evidence of its moral supremacy and dedication to human rights (Haines 2010). However, the history of the American refugee program gives us insight into the lasting confusion about its *actual* purpose. While the program certainly provides safety for those who come from violent and unstable contexts, it has also *always* required that refugees become good im/migrants, provide for themselves, and contribute to the economy of the United States (Haines 2022). Furthermore, the refugee program has acted and continues to act in the service of capitalism, fashioning refugees into laboring citizens. By emphasizing a definition of self-sufficiency as immediate work, refugees become locked into low-wage labor and join the American poor.

It's important to note that this analysis is not a critique of refugee employment altogether. It is the *conditions* and the *terms* of work that I am critiquing here. As Soss, Fording, and Schram contend, welfare agencies "function as workforce intermediaries" (2011, 15). They are designed to serve both welfare recipients and employers, and to facilitate the employment relationship between the two. Rather than marshalling the needs of workers and employers in reciprocal ways, however, welfare agencies are "designed to service the 'low road' of capitalism by offering up labor on whatever terms the market will bear" (15). Welfare agencies offer employers subsidies for hiring welfare program recipients and leavers, using taxpayer dollars while asking nothing in return (46). Agencies offer recipients meager and inadequate supports, designed to ensure that public assistance is not seen as a workable alternative to even the worst jobs available (45). Finally, agencies use state power to force welfare recipients into low-paying jobs that both disregard their needs and make advancement impossible (15). In other words, the experiences of refugees like Sayed and Tamer underscore the realities created by the modern welfare state. As Soss, Fording, and Schram argue,

> Welfare programs today demand "work first," while giving little serious attention to the disabilities, life problems, family needs, and resource deficits found among the poor. In the process, they actively diminish opportunities to acquire education and other forms of human capital that people need to get better jobs. Under the banner of "valuing work," we have constructed an aggressive work-enforcement system that rides roughshod over all countervailing values and willfully ignores the conditions of labor markets and poor people. (16)

As such, the findings of this chapter beg the question: what might the alternative be if another definition of self-sufficiency is put forth and normalized within the refugee program? What is possible if we rely on an alternative understanding of self-sufficiency that includes the factors necessary for long-term stability including safety and security, such as long-term subsidized healthcare, childcare, and, most relevant to this analysis, extended financial support? (Haines 2010). Unlike immigrants who might come to the United States with educational, linguistic, and professional backgrounds that prepare them for the transition into American life, refugees often lack these important building blocks to ensure their success in their new contexts (Masterson 2010; Thomas 2011). As a result, refugees need additional supports, such as increased financial assistance, which would allow refugees to learn English in adult language classes—rather than the expectation that they would learn it "by osmosis" or "on the job"—for a longer period of time. Long-term financial support would also allow refugees to retrain in their former fields, allowing them to build on their existing skills, careers, and bodies of knowledge, rather than being pushed into low-wage employment. One can only imagine how different

Sayed's life would be if he had the opportunity to retrain in his former field. Allowing refugees to achieve the settled life they had come to the United States in search of requires reimagining and rethinking the priorities of the refugee program. This includes the other ways that we define self-sufficiency as reducing dependence on public assistance, which is the topic of the next chapter.

2

Welfare

The Fashioning of (Non-)Citizens

I wish I hadn't come here as a refugee. Then we could have rented any house we wanted to, and then our life would have been good. Then we could have cut any ties we have to the welfare office, the resettlement agency, and anyone else who is "helping" [she says sarcastically] them. But as a refugee, you can't cut those ties with them. They are after you. The welfare agent is after you. She is after you to cut down your food stamps. She is after you to penalize you for every little penny you get. That is how it goes for us.

—Nadia

In her testimony above, Nadia critiques the institutions that are allegedly in place to support refugees. She frames agents of the welfare office as part of a policing, punishing force that is in constant pursuit of refugees. In the same breath, Nadia raises questions about the meaning and the utility of the "refugee" label. Nadia's expressed desire to rid herself of this label reflects the frustration, disappointment, and anger refugees experience when the rights they imagined are owed to refugees are in fact nowhere to be found in their new contexts. Instead, refugees find themselves tethered to a welfare office that offers them inadequate and decreasing supports and one that punishes them if they dare to break ties with it.

This chapter underscores the ways that the welfare office—which is theoretically tasked with providing refugees with supports that are critical to their survival—limits refugees' ability to realize the settled life that they hoped for. Through their punitive encounters with the welfare office, refugees question and reject the empty promises of citizenship and learn to survive within the contradictions and crosshairs of American imperialism. By centering the ways that the gutted welfare state has functioned in the lives of refugees, I highlight the human cost of public assistance programs that have been indelibly marked by neoliberal paternalism (Soss, Fording, and Schram 2011). Rather than frame refugees as victims of a rigid and at times punitive welfare office, the chapter also highlights the various agentic ways that refugees resist its neglect and willful distrust of refugees and other dependents. The chapter concludes with a discussion of refugee rights, pointing to the dissonance between the expectations of refugees and the historic relationship between im/migrants, welfare, and citizenship in the United States.

Encounters with a Rigid and Punitive Welfare Office

Soon after they arrive in the United States, refugees learn about their rights and responsibilities. As outlined in the last chapter, in their first meeting with their caseworker Khaled, Nadia and Sayed were briefed on the supports that they could expect to receive. Along with the one-time stipend, which the resettlement agency used to cover their rent and utilities for their first ninety days in the United States, Nadia and Sayed were eligible to receive cash assistance from Temporary Assistance for Needy Families (TANF) and Supplemental Nutritional Assistance Program (SNAP, more commonly known as food stamps) benefits from the welfare office. Khaled explained that the amount of cash assistance would be determined by the number of people in their family.

Nadia and Sayed spoke to me about their expectations of support before they met with their welfare agent. They had anticipated that they would be provided with adequate supports that would supplement Sayed's meager income. They understood that the cash assistance and food stamps that they received might be reduced, but they had expected that this would only happen if there were a significant increase in their income. Unbeknownst to Nadia and Sayed, the ultimate goal that underlies the American resettlement program is self-sufficiency. While the definition of self-sufficiency at the refugee resettlement agency emphasized immediate employment, that provided by the welfare office was to remove refugees off its rolls as soon as possible. As such, refugees' supports are systemically reduced until they are eventually removed altogether.

Among my adult refugee participants, welfare reductions were one of the most anxiety-producing aspects of everyday life in their newly resettled contexts. During any given week, I would have several conversations with refugee families about how these reductions affected their day-today lives. The following excerpt of fieldnotes captures the essence of these discussions. As the opening excerpt of the last chapter outlined, helping refugees make sense of the bills and documents that penetrated their home was a ritual during my visits to their homes. The documents that I came to dread the most were ones from the welfare office, as I quickly learned that they rarely contained good news. During this particular visit, Sayed handed me a bill from his welfare agent and asked me to translate its contents. As he had feared, the document stated that the family's monthly allotment of food stamps was being reduced once again. Upon hearing this, Nadia and Sayed shared their frustrations with me:

> NADIA: But this is not right! Sally, we are barely making ends meet right now, with the food stamps being what they are. If they remove some more, what are we going to do?!
>
> SAYED: You know Sally, when we first got here we had almost $700 in food stamps. . . . OK, I understand [an] initial decrease, because I got a job and have an income now. But since then, every six months, the welfare agent cuts our food stamps even though there is no increase in our income at all! . . . It doesn't make any sense. And when we go to her office to try to reason with her, she won't budge. Isn't the whole point of food stamps to help us because we can't make ends meet on our own?!

After his employment, the support Sayed's family received was cut by 27 percent, a steep cut that he was willing to accept because he had been prewarned by Khaled, his case manager, that employment signaled to the state that he was no longer eligible for full support. However, what remained unclear to both Sayed and Nadia were the consistent biannual cuts to their family's food stamps. In one year, their food stamps were cut by nearly half, which was incommensurate with Sayed's 90 cents per hour income increase during that same time period. This left the family in an extremely precarious financial position. They resorted to using a credit card to make ends meet, and in spite of their best efforts to pay it off, they continually accrued more debt with high interest. Within six months, they had maxed out one credit card and were applying for another.

Like many other Americans living in poverty, they were forced to bury themselves in debt in order to survive. Unfortunately, this strategy only worked for a few months, as things took a turn for the worse. The branch of the superstore where Sayed was working began laying people off. Thankfully Sayed was kept on, but his weekly hours were significantly reduced. As a result, his take-home income barely covered the cost of rent. Desperate, Sayed and Nadia made an appointment to see their welfare agent, hoping to plead with her for additional food stamps and cash assistance. Below is Nadia's account of that appointment:

> We went to see her, and we told her everything. This wasn't news to her. She already knew what was happening. They require us to send a report to them every six months [which includes] information about our income and we send paystubs along too. . . . The welfare agent saw the decrease in our income, but still, she didn't increase our food stamps. We asked her why, and she said, "This is not how this works." She said something about the fact that the decrease in Sayed's income has to last six months before we can get assistance. But how does that make sense?! What will we do in the meantime? Starve?! Why won't she give us some of those food stamps back? All they know to do is take away, not give?!

As it turns out, Sayed's wage reduction would last for approximately seven months, which did not warrant a change in their welfare support status and caused the family's financial situation to reach a breaking point. Sayed was forced to borrow money from friends, a practice he abhorred, since his attempts at acquiring more credit cards were rejected. Buried in debt to credit card companies and friends, Nadia and Sayed became despondent. Luckily, through conversations with their daughter Zeina's psychologist, Nadia and Sayed learned that Zeina might be eligible for Supplementary Security Income (SSI), commonly known as disability income. As a young person with a developmental disability brought on by the traumatic brain injury that she suffered as a child, Zeina was eligible for support. The process took nearly a year, but with the help of the psychologist who helped coordinate other necessary paperwork, Zeina was eventually awarded SSI.

This brought much-needed income and relief to the family for less than a month before their SNAP benefits were once again slashed in half. During a meeting with their welfare agent to understand the rationale behind this cut, Nadia and Sayed learned that the extra SSI income signaled to the state that their household no longer needed as much SNAP support. Their welfare agent explained that in order for them to regain their benefits,

Zeina would need to move out of their home. Both Nadia and Sayed tried to reason with the agent, explaining that the nature of Zeina's disability necessitated that she live with caregivers who could support her daily needs, including ensuring she got to school safely; purchasing her food, clothes, and hygiene products; cooking her meals; and conducting all other caregiving work on her behalf. The welfare agent did not budge, explaining that this was the policy and that nothing could be done. Nadia and Sayed left the welfare office unsure how they would make ends meet. This left their family in the same precarious position they had been in before Zeina received her SSI income. They were left to wonder again how to survive.

The Effects of Institutional Surveillance

One of the most common complaints lodged by refugees about the welfare office is the feeling of being under severe and constant scrutiny. Refugees are expected to send in regular reports to their welfare agents, which are always accompanied by pay stubs and bank statements. If the refugees' welfare agent detects an increase in income, they inevitably suffer a decrease in benefits. Nadia spoke to me about the effects of this surveillance.

> The welfare agent has us so scared that we don't even put our money in the bank. It is your right to deposit money, your *own* money in the bank, whether it's money you earned or money you came into the country with. But due to our fear of being punished for having money, we don't put our money in the bank. Why should we have to live in this kind of fear? We are always scared that somehow she will find out about the money in the bank and cut our food stamps even more. And now we are scared that someone will break into our home and find this money. It is like our last days in Iraq, when we had our money at home. Look what has become of us. We have no peace of mind.

The hawkish gaze of the welfare agent and the resulting cuts to their benefits caused Nadia and Sayed to revert to saving their money at home, a long-time war survival practice that they were forced into when the banks had all but collapsed in Iraq, and then again when they lived in Syria. Here they were, in a country with a functioning banking system, and yet they had to hide their money in their home yet again. As a result, Nadia relived the same kind of fear that she experienced during wartime, knowing that her family's chance of survival was only a break-in away. Since Nadia spent most of her days alone in a city that was foreign to her, this fear fell mostly on her shoulders.

Welfare surveillance also affects refugees by stymieing their hopes to improve their financial situations for fear of losing their welfare benefits. Sayed approached me in early 2013 with a business proposal. He and an Iraqi coworker had reached out to several car dealers in New Jersey who were selling vehicles that were on the lot that had been damaged by Hurricane Sandy. These "salvaged" cars were being sold for a fraction of their worth, and Sayed would purchase them and export them to Iraq. He explained that the cars' engines were actually in excellent condition, and that most of the damage was limited to the bodies—nothing that a good auto-body technician could not fix. He informed me that Iraqis loved American cars and that his business proposal was to export the damaged cars to Baghdad, where some of his former employees would repair them and then his relatives would sell them. He had already spoken with an acquaintance who had agreed to invest the money in the project to pay for startup costs. Sayed's business plan seemed viable. He was in fact a former car dealer as well as a skilled mechanic. He had spoken to me before this meeting of the best mechanics in Baghdad who could "turn a heap of junk into a piece of art." Sayed indeed had the experience and the connections to make this business venture possible. It soon became clear why Sayed had come to me with this idea rather than simply execute it:

> Well, you know how the welfare agent is with us. If we have any extra income at all, they will cut down our food stamps. You know how our financial situation [is]. Even with the food stamps, we can barely make ends meet. What would happen if this business fails? Yes, it is a good idea, and it has the potential to be very profitable, but what if it isn't? So we would want you to have the business in your name. You would have all the money and accounts in your name, and we would do all the work. That way the welfare agent would not be able to know that I was in business, and that wouldn't affect our food stamps.

Sayed's desire to move forward with his business venture was hampered by his awareness and fear of the surveillance of the welfare office. He wanted to better his family's situation but was afraid of what would happen if it failed. Without his SNAP benefits, his family would become food insecure. He and Nadia had learned the hard way that once benefits were removed, they were rarely returned. For ethical reasons, I refused Sayed's offer of entering into business with him. I apologetically explained to him that I was merely a graduate student and that I could not get involved in things I did not understand. I did not explain the true ethical reasons that held me back, such as becoming entangled in business dealings with my research participants—which might seem callous and overly stringent to him. Sayed responded to my refusal with kindness and understanding. He only had this to say:

> Right [he paused]. And I wouldn't want you to be uncomfortable or get involved in something you didn't want to either. It's just that if the welfare lady sees that we have made any money, she might take away our food stamps. I just really want to try to make our life better. This thing, I mean all of this, what I do every day feels like a waste, like I am throwing it away. I work so hard at an awful job where I will never get paid enough to meet my family's needs, and after all of this work, I throw all my money away in rent. I am worked to the bone, and I am getting older and soon this type of work won't be an option anymore. I want to have something for my girls, something for them so that in the end, they will have something to show for their father's hard work. But as long as we are being watched and everything that we earn or buy is being held against us, then that won't happen.

Exhausted by a life textured by low-wage, backbreaking work, Sayed had hoped to make a new life for his family and capitalize on his skills, knowledge, and connections in Iraq. However, his awareness and fear of the punitive measures taken by his welfare agent, coupled with his fear for his family's ability to survive if his business plan did not go as planned, stopped him from moving forward. This placed Sayed in an inescapable cycle where he was left with no alternatives for public assistance since any attempt to be freed from it would result in the removal of the very supports that his family needed to survive. As a result, Sayed and his family were shackled to these meager supports. In other words, the surveilling nature of public assistance is precisely what keeps refugees entangled with the system. From afar, for those who do not know the struggles, dreams, and attempts of refugees to better the lives of their families, their "continued dependence" might confirm public notions of those who depend on public assistance as those who are happy to "milk the system dry" or are "uninterested in becoming self-sufficient." Unbeknownst to them, refugees' own dreams of becoming financially independent and leaving welfare assistance behind are arrested by the very design of neoliberal welfare supports. Whether or not Sayed's business plans were feasible is beside the point. In fact, scholars have long pointed to the complex relationship between entrepreneurship and welfare. Scholars have rightfully critiqued the neoliberal notion that strong welfare states actually stymie entrepreneurship, which would have supposedly negative effects on society (Galbraith 2006; Henrekson 2005). Social entrepreneurship—which proposes the reconstruction of welfare by building social partnerships between the public, social, and business sectors—has received much criticism as it would break away from the commitment of the government to its neediest and instead prioritize funding for entrepreneurs using welfare funds (Cook, Dodds, and Mitchell 2003; Kibler et al. 2018). Sayed's experiences bring to the fore the limitations of a welfare system that tethers refugees to a welfare state that is designed to provide minimal and dwindling supports and that threatens their survival if they dare to break ties with it. Rather than find the settled life that they had hoped to find, refugees find their dreams are held hostage to a system that punishes them for imagining another world.

Resisting the Welfare State

Confronting the Oppressor

Increasingly burdened by a policing welfare state that seemed ever-impervious to their needs, many refugees begin to express a desire to be heard and to be able to speak back to the injustices that they experience at the hands of their welfare agents. Nadia grew weary of the endless hours she and Sayed spent attempting to stretch his salary, Zeina's SSI income, and their SNAP benefits as far as possible, which was becoming a nearly impossible task. Concerned with the fate of their survival, Nadia's frustrations grew, especially after her meeting with the welfare agent who refused to budge about the cuts to her family's support as a result of Zeina's SSI income. Upon realizing that the thick packet of documents that she received from the welfare office included information to make an appointment with a judge to make her case, Nadia was resolute:

I decided to make a complaint at the welfare office. I mean they can't just keep cutting our benefits like this with no explanation! I [will] ask [the judge], "Why are you doing this to us? Aren't you supposed to help us? Isn't this our right as a refugee?" But Sayed begged me not to go, and said, "Please don't get us into unnecessary trouble with these people." He was scared that if I go and complain, they would take away our food stamps and Zeina's stipend, and then we would be in a worse spot than we are now.

Ultimately, Sayed convinced Nadia not to request the appointment with the judge. When I asked her why she was swayed, she shared that Sayed's fears were not unsubstantiated. Sayed had reminded her of a story of an Iraqi refugee man, a father of six whose food stamp allowance had been reduced to $600 a month, which as Nadia shared, "was not very much when you have a big family." Frustrated, the man had made an appointment to see a judge. Once in the presence of the judge, the man complained that even though his income had not changed, his monthly allotment of food stamps was decreasing at an alarming rate. Nadia relayed the remainder of the story:

Do you know what the judge did? He said, "Oh you don't like that you have $600? Well then how about your family will only get $150 a month in food stamps from now on?" The man, he is an elderly gentleman, he just stood there, humiliated, knowing that if he said another word, the judge might take it all away. This is what they do if you complain. Sayed heard this story from the man himself. They work together. So he was worried that would happen to us. He convinced me that we can't afford to lose any more food stamps.

Employing Scott's (1990) concept of power relations and political life can help us understand the complex dynamics at play here. Scott's work on resistance contends that social intercourse between dominants and subordinates in a given context is the *public transcript,* or the open interactions between the two groups, such as modern social pleasantries that occur every day between the worker and the boss. Even if anger, resentment, suspicion, or fear might lurk underneath, the public transcript is the performance by both the dominant and subordinate groups of what is expected of them, such as civility and deference by the subordinates and strength by the dominant. The hidden transcript, on the other hand, is the "speeches, gestures, and practices that occur offstage" that often contradict what is visible in the public transcript. Scott argues that the discrepancy between the hidden and public transcripts can inform us about the impact of domination on public discourse. More important, Scott argues, all that lies in the realm of the hidden transcript—including rumor, gossip, disguises, linguistic tricks, metaphors, folktales, and ritual gestures—is, at its heart, resistance. Scott defines the infrapolitics of subordinate groups, then, as "a wide variety of low-profile forms of resistance that dare not speak in their own name" (19). These forms of resistance are by design invisible, to protect the political actors who understand, on an intimate level, that the balance of power is tilted in favor of the dominant. The concept of infrapolitics brings attention to the invisible resistance that undergirds more visible patterns of political action.

Applying Scott's notion of the hidden transcript to Nadia's situation, we understand her desire to speak to the judge as a longing to finally break from the confines of the hidden transcript and share her seemingly well-rehearsed speech in public. Standing before him, she would question him, finally demanding her rights, and ask the judge why these injustices were befalling her family. Alas, she was disciplined by the experience of a member of the refugee community who came before her. According to Scott, it is rare that subordinates make the hidden transcript public, except in cases when a person has reached the end of their rope and is emboldened to "speak truth to power." Sayed's coworker, who dared stand before the judge to ask for more public assistance for his family, had done just that: he "ruptured the political cordon sanitaire" between the hidden and the public transcript (1990, 19). And, as Scott predicted, this provoked a "swift stroke of repression" because, left unaddressed, this might lead others to "exploit the breach" of the stringent limits set by a dominant group and system (196). These decisive acts are meant to discourage others from venturing into limit-testing territory once again. "They are intended as a kind of preemptive strike to nip any further challenges to the existing frontier" (197). These acts of repression serve to discourage refugees from speaking up or seeking justice, effectively putting them in their place and silencing all those who might have any inkling of attempting to resist. The judge's strategy worked. Once she learned of this encounter, Nadia once again swallowed her frustration and resentment in order to ensure the survival of her family. Therein lies the effectiveness of these punitive measures: all that is needed is one terrible incident, one damaged life at the hands of an authority figure. The rest takes care of itself. The desire to break through the barrier between the public and hidden transcripts is subdued, and all is at it should be—or at least it appears to be so from the surface.

Trickster Tales

Scott (1990) argues that for underprivileged minorities, as well as the marginalized poor, open political action does not capture the bulk of their political life. For these subordinate groups, the use of disguise, deception, and indirection is often the crux of their resistance, all the while maintaining an outward appearance of civility, subservience, and/or deference. Through my weekly visits to the various families in my study, it became clear that much of the discourse about their assigned welfare officials was textured with anger, frustration, and growing resentment. This hidden transcript was shared with me in my conversations with families around kitchen tables as I opened letters from the welfare agent, or when they asked me to help them apply for yet another credit card. Given the tale of the man who lost nearly all his public assistance upon facing the judge, another form of resistance began to spring up in the community: feigning mental illness in order to garner more financial support from the system.

Fatima, an Iraqi refugee mother of six in her late forties, had fled with her family to Jordan before being resettled to Philadelphia. Her family also struggled with decreasing SNAP benefits. She and several of her family members were employed, but with ever-decreasing public assistance support, Fatima was always anxious about their ability to survive. During one of our conversations about her decreasing welfare assistance, Fatima excitedly shared a story of an elderly Iraqi refugee man that she had once met. When Fatima and her husband had met this man at the resettlement agency, she described him as looking "like everyone else." A few months later, while sitting in the waiting room of the welfare office, she encountered the man again. This time, Fatima described him as looking "scary." The man who was once clean-shaven had a bushy, long, and unkempt beard. His hair, once cut short, was long and matted, and looked to Fatima like it hadn't been brushed or combed in months. He was wearing stained, dirty, and ripped clothes. The most unusual thing that Fatima noticed was a full-body movement that rocked the man's body every few seconds. "It was like his whole body went through a convulsion, like this": she got up and demonstrated repetitive movement that began in the upper arm area and then shook her torso.

Fatima, who swore that she had never seen the man do this when she met him before, was sure that this was all a part of a performance. The man, Fatima explained, wanted to appear unwell, and his appearance as well as this new involuntary body movement were all a part of the plan. Incredulous, she exclaimed, "They believed him! And he ended up receiving a disability check, every month, something like $800!" With a wry smile Fatima recalled how she and her husband came upon the man in the grocery store in the neighborhood a few days later, only to find him restored to how he appeared when they first met. He was clean-shaven, his hair had been cut short, and he was wearing a crisp, clean suit. "And of course," Fatima stated, "there was no tic." Fatima shared that the man appeared two decades younger than he had a mere few days earlier in the welfare office. Smiling and shaking her head, Fatima proclaimed, "So you see, it was all a *huge* lie, a way to get more money out of the welfare people! And they fell for it!"

Looking at Fatima as she said this, I couldn't tell if she was resentful of the man or in awe of him for getting away with it. It was clear to me as Fatima recounted the tale that she had mixed feelings about the man's actions. She seemed incredulous that this man's simple performance of a neglect of personal hygiene and a repetitive body movement could so easily fool those in charge. How ridiculous! But as she enthusiastically retold the story, framing the welfare agents as those who could be so easily duped by the simple antics of a refugee, I could tell that she also took pleasure in all of it. For in this story, a refugee who basically stopped bathing, brushing his hair, and laundering his clothes had managed to trick the almighty welfare agents—the ones who remove supports from refugee families every month, leaving them increasingly vulnerable.

Nadia recounted a similar tale, one she heard firsthand by the protagonist herself:

> Sayed and I met this woman once and she told us how she tricked the people at the welfare office. She had a husband and only one

child, so they did not get a lot of food stamps. There is a doctor who gives you some tests when you apply for disability income. So she walks into this doctor's office with her husband, and they are sitting in front of the doctor and then all of a sudden, she begins screaming and hitting her husband. She takes off her shoe and hits him, over and over and chasing him in the doctor's office. She trashed the doctor's office! At first the doctor was trying to get between them, but then she began attacking the doctor too, so he backed away and walked out of the office. He had to call security and they held her down and took her away! All the while, she was screaming at the top of her lungs, hitting her husband. And her husband was just quiet and not responding. Well, at her next appointment, she did the same thing. So the doctor said that she was not well and that she needed help, so that woman ended up getting a lot of money. And you know what she said to me? She said, "I am an incredible actress. I should get an award really." She was proud of herself!

By the time Nadia met this woman and heard this story, Nadia had lived in the United States for nearly two years and was familiar with the possible legal repercussions of this woman's behavior. "She was playing with fire," Nadia stated. Nadia understood that if this woman continued to act violently in the presence of the doctor or the welfare agent in an effort to convince them of her instability, she could be deemed an unfit parent. Nadia told me later that the doctor could decide that "if she was hitting her husband" during these fits, "then she might be hitting her son, and she can't do that." The doctor or the welfare agent could report her to the authorities, and the woman could lose custody of her son. In her conversation with the woman, Nadia found that the woman was actually aware of this risk but had felt that there was simply no other way to procure the financial support that her family desperately needed. "This is what people do," Nadia bemoaned. "This is how they get the money they need from the welfare office."

As it turns out, these stories, which Scott (1990) calls "trickster tales," were persistent within the Iraqi refugee community. Trickster tales, often used by enslaved peoples, were usually fictional and even at times based on nonhuman characters, such as cunning smaller animals outwitting larger, more powerful ones. Scott argues that tricksters successfully make their way through treacherous terrain, not by strength, but through wit and cunning. Knowing that a direct confrontation with their antagonist is impossible, the trickster deceives them and takes advantage of their traits, such as gullibility. The tales in this study were of *actual* refugees who had managed to get the better of the welfare state. Both of the protagonists in Fatima and Nadia's stories fit the mold of these brave tricksters. Knowing the consequences of direct confrontations with welfare judges, they opted to resist by relying on the gullibility of their American state agents and playing into the perceptions of refugee performances: an elderly Iraqi refugee who, having lost kin and country, lost the will to care for himself; a refugee mother who simply snapped, as maybe her trauma was so severe that she simply could not contain her rage at all the loss she had experienced. These are conjectures, but for whatever reason, the tricksters found acceptable ways to resist. What is important is that these tales, which hailed the refugees who managed to play the system—the cruel, punitive, unforgiving welfare system—as those who secured what they needed by any means necessary, were told and retold.

It is important to note that political action in this case is reserved not only for the protagonists in the tale but also for those who retold the story, in this case Fatima and Nadia. Scott (1990) rails against the notion that offstage discourse is simply a substitute for real resistance, but rather that discourses and practices of resistance are mutually sustaining. The hidden transcript, in this case the retelling of trickster tales, is enacted among a host of under-the-radar strategies that fight domination and is no less important than other forms of resistance. Scott argues that these tales "are the infrapolitical equivalent of open gestures of contempt and desecration: both are aimed at resisting the denial of dignity to subordinate groups" (199). Among those who told and heard them, trickster tales were instructive—they celebrated and shared the weakness of the antagonist, who managed to outwit and ridicule his enemy. Trickster tales also instructed other members of the subordinate group of the limits and dangers of going too far. Hearing this tale must have been a difficult pill to swallow for Nadia, as a devoted mother. While the woman had succeeded in getting the support she needed, she also put her family in danger of being separated—a threat that is all too real for so many refugee families who face that threat repeatedly throughout the migration process. In fact, almost all of the refugees that I worked with had left someone behind and longed to be reunited with those family members. So while the protagonists had succeeded in tricking the enemy, the lesson of which lines should not be crossed were also made clear.

Using Scott's analysis to understand what is happening within the refugee community as political action and resistance is an important counter-
argument to the simplistic reading of the refugee protagonists' actions as
"welfare fraud." Furthermore, this framework allows us to understand
how both the enacting *and* the retelling of the trickster tales were equally
important acts of resistance in the face of the punitive and all-powerful
welfare state. Since public complaints to those in charge put their economic
survival in danger, refugees engaged in other practices and discourse as a
form of political action.

Refugees like Nadia had mixed feelings about the trickster tale she was
retelling, going so far as to find it morally reprehensible. She shared:

> We have never lied or tried to trick the welfare people. As devout
> Muslims, we don't believe in lying, or anything like this. But as you
> can see, people who lie and cheat so they can get more from the
> welfare office, they get what they need! And us, we have never lied,
> and is this our punishment? This is not right. But no one is listen-
> ing. They do not care. We go to the welfare agent, and we ask, we
> tell them about our troubles and how much we suffer, and they say
> to us, "This is how it is. We can't do anything for you." No wonder
> those people do what they do.

It was clear that while Nadia did not condone the actions of those who
bent the truth to access more supports, she understood them. Faced with a
strict, unmovable, and cruel welfare office, refugees felt punished for living
according to their ethical and religious beliefs. Nadia, who self-identifies
as a devout Muslim, is at once calling out the mother who put her family in
danger while also empathizing with her, and, even further, acknowledging
that this might indeed be the only way to deal with the welfare office. A life
of being constantly surveilled by a state that provided ever-decreasing supports robs people not only of their dignity, but also of their sense of self.
Arguably, the welfare state removes so much more than financial and navigational supports: it takes away pieces of the people that are on its rolls.

Welfare and Refugee Rights

The inflexible, punitive, and policing nature of the welfare institutions
and their interlocutors/agents takes up a great deal of space in the lives of

refugee families. Most of our conversations during my family visits with refugees were textured with discourses of injustice, confusion, and rage over the welfare agents' actions, as well as the devising of financial survival strategies. Importantly, Nadia and Sayed's frustration with the inflexibility of their welfare agent points to the dissonance that they and other refugees experience when dealing with systems and institutions that allegedly exist to help newly resettled refugees who are attempting to create a settled life for themselves and their families. For refugees, this form of support was put in place as a form of assistance, a helping hand from a state that understands the needs of refugee families. They imagine that this is a right given to refugees by a state that acknowledges the challenges that they face in transitioning to life in a new context. However, refugees are not aware that they will be thrust into a U.S. context that has been indelibly marked by neoliberalism, where the state institutions that they look to for help have in fact become in service of disciplining the worker into a low-wage existence. Understandably, then, when the supports that they relied on were removed without what refugees deem as due cause, they become frustrated and angry, not to mention confused.

A few months after she decided not to file a complaint with the welfare agent, Nadia shared her frustrations with me:

> I wanted to go ask that judge, "What are my rights? And where are my rights as a refugee?" But you know what I have learned? There are no rights. A refugee would look around and say, "What is the difference between me and any other immigrant, or anyone else for that matter? There is no difference." The help they give you for a few months, and then you have nothing? What kind of help is this?! Where are my rights?!

Nadia's testimony revealed her new understanding of the state of refugee rights in the United States. Analyzing her experience with the welfare state, Nadia questioned how she, a refugee, differed from anyone else. The brevity of the resettlement period, after which refugees are expected to become self-sufficient, flattens their pre-migratory experiences and throws their lot among all those whose survival depends on public assistance. She had once believed that financial supports were *owed* to them as refugees—rights that should differentiate them from other immigrants and certainly other citizens. As an Iraqi refugee who had been displaced as a direct result of American imperialism, Nadia believed it was the moral obligation of the United States to care for refugees and to support them until they could *actually* become self-reliant. It was, according to Nadia, their right. However, after nearly two years of humiliating and frustrating encounters with the welfare state, Nadia concluded that refugees had no rights.

An interview with Susan, the director of case management at the refugee resettlement, shed further light on Nadia's conclusion:

SALLY: How do you think entitlements that refugees get now compare to public assistance that the average low-income American gets?

SUSAN: It's the same.

SALLY: So there's no difference in terms of having the refugee label or category?

SUSAN: No, I mean the resettlement funds is like a little cushion to begin with, so that maybe you can get settled with the housing, that's basically it. That money is used by the agency to cover their rent for about three to four months.

SALLY: And then after that it's the same for both groups?

SUSAN: It is the same. There's no difference. They are just like any other American who is on welfare.

Neoliberal paternalism has irrevocably transformed not only the shape of welfare programs but also the framing of those who rely on them. The Refugee Act of 1980 placed refugee funding under the umbrella of mainstream public assistance programs. As for other welfare recipients, the goal was to get refugees off the welfare rolls as soon as possible. Susan's testimony confirms that refugees have no "special" entitlements or rights but are in the same position as other welfare recipients: framed as morally lacking subjects who are unable to govern themselves while simultaneously receiving inadequate and brief supports meant to "incentivize work." Contrary to their hopes and expectations, low-income refugees in the United States do not receive support that is dedicated to meet their needs or that takes into account their difficult pre-migratory histories. In the current neoliberal welfare system, all of the aspects of recipients' lives, "mental illness, physical disabilities, educational deprivations, obligations to care for children or parents—are collapsed into the economic register, recast as 'barriers' to work that must be 'overcome'" (Soss, Fording, and Schram

2011, 49). The very facets of welfare recipients' lives that cause them to seek out support from the state, such as the harrowing experiences that Nadia's family experienced before arriving to the United States, are not taken into account as "needs" that must be tended to via support. Instead, refugees *and* low-income Americans are framed only as potential market actors and their needs as obstacles to achieving that goal. In other words, Nadia was correct: refugees do not have special financial rights, as their pre-migratory lives and the refugee label carry no entitlement.

Nadia, Sayed, and others in this chapter questioned the actions of their welfare agents that seemed to be in direct contrast to the inherent and unalienable rights refugees had hoped to find in the United States. Refugees bemoaned their lack of access to social rights but through encounters with the welfare state were learning that those were never a given. As Mink (1998) points out, the social rights or entitlements that Nadia evokes have always been inherently fragile and hostage to political winds, and as such never guaranteed. Additionally, as Susan's testimony reveals, in reality, refugees have no "special" rights, even though their very admission to the United States is often cited as evidence of America's exceptionalism and in particular a dedication to humanitarian ideals.

Nadia's notions of rights, nestled in ideas of what refugees are owed, are at the nexus of historical and current formulations of citizenship, neither of which promised full membership or rights to its subjects. While Nadia believed she deserved special rights, in reality, her struggles were not dissimilar from others living in poverty in America—those who have been made rightless by the vagaries of neoliberal paternalism and whose only worth was as potential market actors (Somers 2008). Nadia's questioning of citizenship also confirms the fact that welfare programs are sites of great consequence to democracy, citizenship, and power in the United States (Soss, Fording, and Schram 2011). Understanding this, Nadia rejected American citizenship, calling it a "farce." For what is citizenship without rights?

The experiences of refugees with the welfare office call into question the conflation of the reduction of dependence on public assistance, and the concurrent emphasis of "self-sufficiency" as the only measure of low-income refugees' "success." Rather than addressing the needs of refugees to allow them to actually become self-reliant, the definition of self-sufficiency has been reduced to whether or not refugees are receiving public assistance (Haines 2010). The social rights that refugees hoped for were for them simple enough: adequate, steady financial supports that lasted long enough in order for refugees to actually become financially self-reliant; a welfare agent who supported them rather than surveilled and punished them by cutting their supports for added income or other earned program supports; and the freedom to live as one wished without fear. However, as Nadia expressed at the outset of the chapter, for a low-income refugee who relies on the welfare office for support, that sort of freedom was simply not possible. Poverty places them in a toxic, cyclical, and inescapable relationship with the welfare office. Trapped, with no way out, refugees resist in creative, agentic, and most important, political ways (Scott 1990). However, this does little to change a welfare system that has been gutted by neoliberal paternalism.

In a neoliberal paternalist framing, welfare has been transformed from a system that was built to be of service to low-income (white) citizens to one designed to serve market logics. In this myopic view, the unique needs of refugees are absorbed into an economic equation, one that views their struggles simply as barriers to employment. Subsequently, like others living in poverty, refugees are expected to prove their worth in a welfare system where "the competent and self-reliant market actor—working, investing, choosing, and assessing returns—is made synonymous with a good citizen" (Soss, Fording, and Schram 2011, 22). For welfare recipients, citizenship is reduced to meeting the needs of the market, rather than being rights bearers or participants in a democratic community. Through their encounters with the neoliberal paternalist welfare state, refugees, like other low-income subjects, were meant to become self-governing market actors. Refugees question and even reject this definition of citizenship. Seeing through the "farce" of American citizenship, refugees like Nadia dare the nation-state to "keep the [green] card," or the pathway to legal citizenship, and instead provide them with the social rights they once thought citizenship might espouse. As we will see in the next chapter, refugee youth also came with dreams, hopes, and expectations of what they might find in their new contexts, looking to schools for support as a pathway to the settled lives they hoped for so desperately.

3

Public Education

Locked Out of the Right to Have Rights

My name is Ghada Musa. I am seventeen years old. I live with my sister,
my brother, and my mother. We came to America last year. I like it here.
I left Iraq when I was young because of war. My father died in the war.
We lived in Yemen before we came to America. I didn't like living in
Yemen. I had to work and go to school. That was hard. The school was
all Yemeni girls. The headmaster was Iraqi. He screamed a lot. The girls
in the school were very mean. They treated me differently because I am
Iraqi. They always told me "You are Iraqi!" They said this every day.
I always dreamt of coming to America! I want to go to college. I work
very hard in English class so I can learn English. I am happy that I am in
America. Here I can follow my dreams. Here I am not an outsider. I can be
an American, just like everybody else.

—Ghada Musa

On a warm October afternoon, I sat with Ghada Musa in the room she
shared with her older sister. It was a Tuesday, which meant that we would
work on her homework assignment for the next two hours. I had first met
Ghada at Liberty High, her urban public high school, through my part-
time work as the education programming director at a nonprofit teaching
Arab culture and language through the arts. Ghada, a seventeen-year-old
tenth grader at the time, signed up to join one of the afterschool workshops that we offered. When I met her, I was struck by Ghada's outgoing
and bubbly personality, her ready smile, and infectious laugh. A lover of
Egyptian soap operas, miniseries, and plays, Ghada shared the latest jokes
and "epic lines" from her favorite shows with me, making it her personal
challenge to make me laugh every time we met. Over the fall semester of
2012, I developed friendly relationships with the Arab youth who attended
the workshop, including Ghada. A few months after she began attending

the workshop, I asked Ghada to participate in my study, and she readily agreed. Eventually, I was invited to Ghada's home, and met her mother, Baheera; her elder sister, Samah; and her younger brother, Adam. Over time, I became a regular visitor to the Musa household and developed an especially close relationship with Baheera. During my weekly visits, I helped Ghada with her studies, visited with Baheera, and later on, helped Samah study for the GED exam—which I detail in the next chapter. Like all of the women in her family, Ghada wore a hijab in public, including at school, but at home she typically wore her long, chestnut-colored hair in a high bun. On this particular evening, Ghada asked me to help her complete an "All About Me" project that her teacher had asked everyone in her class to complete. Ghada dictated the opening paragraph to this chapter to me in Arabic, and I translated it to English. Ghada demanded with a smile, "Be sure to capture everything, including my excitement!" I assured her that there would be exclamation points to emphasize what she wanted to say. The next day, Ghada typed and printed the paragraph at the computer lab at school, and included a hard copy of it on a large poster board that she decorated with pictures of both the Iraqi and U.S. flags. The following week she informed me that her teacher hung her poster in the English as a Second Language (ESL) classroom, which made Ghada very proud.

It is not a coincidence that Ghada included Iraqi and U.S. flags in a project that was meant to capture both who she was and who she hoped to be, as these are powerful symbols of her dual aspirations as a refugee student: educational attainment and full citizenship. As evident from the excerpt above, Ghada's hopes for citizenship went beyond de jure citizenship, or the legal definitions of the term. She desired a form of citizenship that would ensure her both a sense of belonging as well as access to the rights she had been denied in Yemen, where her family had fled after the violence in Iraq had become unbearable. The financial strain on her family in Yemen had forced Ghada to work while attending school, but she held aspirations for "the good life" (Berlant 2011) in the United States where she could follow her dreams. She believed her hard work in ESL classes would lead to access to higher education, which she could leverage to a high-paying career. However, as this chapter will reveal, Ghada's schooling did not afford her the rights that she presumed she would find in the United States.

In spite of the many challenges that refugee youth face in their countries of origin and/or in their first countries of resettlement, they express aspirations for education, with the hope to make up for lost time (Bonet 2018; McWilliams and Bonet 2016; Shakya et al. 2010; Stevenson and Willott 2007). All of the refugee youth in this study rated education as their top priority in the United States, perceiving it as a bridge to upward social mobility that would allow them to pull themselves and their families out of poverty. Unfortunately, these youth were thrust into underperforming and increasingly underfunded urban high schools in Philadelphia. The students whose stories are at the heart of this chapter attended Liberty High, one of the largest public secondary schools in Philadelphia. Housing approximately 3,000 students at the time of data collection for this research, the school employed approximately 200 teachers, 6 counselors, 3 nurses, and 1 psychologist. These numbers were not atypical since the School District of Philadelphia has recently been the site of unprecedented neoliberal budget cuts at the state and local level, which contributed to the closure of over 30 neighborhood schools across the city, a result of the fiscal crisis caused by the expansion of the charter school movement (McWilliams 2019). The cuts, which were first implemented in 2012, precipitated in the layoffs of over 4,000 teachers and staff (Gabriel 2013), resulting in ballooning class sizes, overworked teachers, and gaps in essential services.

Refugee students arriving in this context were being educated in schools with diminishing supports and resources while they were simultaneously navigating the residual effects of their flight: trauma, fragmented schooling, and scarce time to compensate for the gaps in their educational foundations or subject matter. Often, these are framed by school personnel in the United States as "deficiencies in preparation" and quickly become barriers to accessibility. In other words, refugee youth's educational challenges will necessarily be read through a U.S. educational lens of ability and disability. Furthermore, refugee youth come to encounter gatekeeping in schools, which is often based on student identity, i.e., the degree to which students embody white and middle-class signifiers of academic performance. This chapter explores the difficulties in realizing the rights of American citizenship via public education through the experiences of three focal refugee students: Zeina, Layla, and Ghada. While adults often find themselves coming up against the limitations of the welfare and resettlement systems, refugee youth become "twice displaced" by their pre-migratory educational histories as well as the empty promises of a gutted public educational system that is not equipped to realize their "right to have rights" (Somers 2008).

Lack of Preparation for Disabled Refugee Students: Zeina's Story

Life before Resettlement

Zeina Jaafary, Nadia and Sayed's eldest daughter, experienced a six-year educational interruption before she was resettled to the United States. When I met Zeina, she was a ninth grader at Liberty High, and seventeen years old. I had been introduced to Zeina and her family through a special education lawyer who was searching for an Arabic speaker with a teaching background to tutor Zeina part-time. I was eventually hired as a tutor for Zeina for a few periods during her school day. Zeina immediately struck me as a chatty, warm, and bright young person. She usually wore her thick black hair in a ponytail and loved makeup, trying out new combinations of matching eyeshadow and lipstick every day. Zeina loved chatting with me about her favorite singer, Adele, as well as the books she had checked out from the library. At first, she was only comfortable speaking to me in Arabic, but over time, our chats grew to be mostly in English.

As detailed in chapter 2, Zeina's elementary school in Baghdad was attacked by armed gunmen when Zeina was only nine years old. She was shot in the knee and suffered a severe blow to the head when a school employee, who was trying to carry her to safety, accidentally rammed her head against the metal gates of the school. This resulted in a traumatic brain injury (TBI). During the shooting, Zeina witnessed the murder of her dearest friend, several of her classmates, and her teacher—events that took a great toll on her. According to her mother, Nadia, immediately after the attack on her school, Zeina began to have regular night terrors, waking up screaming and drenched in sweat. Zeina also developed a fear of unfamiliar adults, particularly of those in uniform including police, firefighters, security personnel, and all other armed authority figures. Zeina became increasingly anxious about leaving the house and even became reluctant to leave her room.

A few months after the shooting at Zeina's school, her family fled to Syria. It was then that Nadia began to notice how withdrawn Zeina had become: "Zeina refused to go to school. She would lock herself up in her room, refused to eat and drink. She even refused to talk to us! She would sit in a corner of the room all alone and talk to herself quietly." Nadia attributed Zeina's behavior to the trauma she had encountered, particularly that of watching her best friend, whom she had known and loved since they attended the same preschool together, die before her very eyes. Zeina, who broke into hysterics and shook uncontrollably for hours when her parents tried to encourage her to return to school, spent the entirety of her family's stay in Syria excluded from education.

Thankfully, Zeina began to improve once Nadia was introduced to the Center for Love, a nonprofit organization that served children with disabilities. Social workers came to visit the family at the house regularly, paying special attention to Zeina. More important, Nadia learned of field trips organized by the nonprofit, which encouraged Zeina to finally leave her corner of the room and to join other children in playing at the center. Slowly, Zeina began to act more like herself and even began to communicate with her family rather than keeping entirely to herself. Nadia had hoped that Zeina would express some interest in going back to school, but she continued to struggle with leaving the house, telling her mother that she was afraid to see "bad people with guns on the street." Social workers at the Center for Love suggested that Zeina attend workshops on their campus until she felt comfortable with daily school attendance again. Zeina, who had always loved art, began to attend weekly drawing and music workshops. Nadia later recounted that had it not been for the outbreak of the conflict in Syria, Zeina might have eventually begun to attend school in Damascus. Nadia expressed a great deal of gratitude for the nonprofit, not only for their work with Zeina. It was with the help of a lawyer who regularly volunteered at the Center for Love that Nadia's family ultimately made a successful application for asylum.[1]

Life and Schooling in the United States

Upon arrival in the United States, Nadia immediately sought out physical and mental healthcare for Zeina, to ensure that she continued to have the supports she needed. At the family's first healthcare screening, which was arranged by the refugee resettlement agency, Nadia requested that Zeina be seen by "someone who can help her like the people at the Center for Love [had]" as soon as possible. Fortunately, a new pilot program had just been launched in Philadelphia, offering free mental health care for refugee youth, and Zeina was eligible to participate. Within a month of her resettlement, Zeina began to see a psychologist once a week and continued to be under his care for several years. Additionally, as a minor, Zeina was eligible for state-funded health insurance until she was twenty-one years old, which ensured that she had access to much-needed medical care. With this health insurance, Zeina was finally getting medical attention for her injured knee, a heart murmur, and poor visibility in her right eye—all problems that surfaced after the shooting at her school.

With these mechanisms of care in place, Zeina had begun to slowly "return to her old self," according to Nadia. She began speaking with her younger sister Dima and even expressed some excitement about going back to school. Soon after their arrival, Nadia and her husband registered Zeina in her local neighborhood school. Within weeks of her registration, Zeina was evaluated by the school psychologist, who identified a TBI, significant developmental delays, trouble with communication, as well as trouble with memory, retention, and information processing. As a result, the psychologist's recommendation was for Zeina to be placed in the "resource room,"—a classroom for students with intellectual and physical disabilities—full time.

Zeina found her placement in this class demoralizing. In the first few weeks of her placement, Zeina would complain to her mother about her experiences in her classroom, which were mostly negative. Zeina felt neglected in the classroom, a fact she attributed to the more urgent needs of the other students. Zeina told her mother that she spent her time drawing and coloring, evidenced by the reams of artwork that Zeina brought home that littered the bedroom she shared with her sister. Nadia was angry. She felt that Zeina's teachers had exploited her daughter's love of art to fill her time and keep her busy while they helped other students. Furthermore, according to Nadia, Zeina felt shame about being in this class, because the other students were "different from her." Zeina later spoke to me about her experiences in the resource room:

> The thing is Miss Sally, I didn't belong there with them. The other kids, they were in very bad shape. One boy, he was in a wheelchair, and he couldn't move his arms or his legs, nothing from his neck down. And he was always drooling. Then there was this girl, she would pee herself all the time, so it smelled so bad in there. And

there was a boy, sometimes, for no reason he would jump out of his chair and start to scream and the teacher and the other grown-ups, they had to hold his arms because he would try to hit them. Why was I there? What did I do to be with those kids?

Zeina expressed shame at being placed among other students whose disabilities seemed to her more severe than her own, a sentiment that has been captured in the narratives of students who feel they have been unfairly placed in special education classes (Connor 2008). Like them, Zeina questioned her placement and wondered what she had done to deserve such a fate.

A few weeks after she was placed in the resource room, Zeina began to resist going to school. Nadia recounted:

She would fight with me every morning, asking me why she had to go when she wasn't learning anything. I would tell her that she had to go to school, that it would get better, but in my heart, I felt the same thing: she wasn't learning anything, and she didn't belong there. I would see the other children on the bus. Those poor children, many of them in wheelchairs, many of them couldn't speak and looked, just, well they broke your heart. It's no wonder that they didn't have time for Zeina. It was clear that she didn't belong there. But I didn't know what to do.

Zeina's resistance to schooling was not only rooted in her feelings of shame, but also in her awareness that she was unable to meet her academic goals in the resource room. To her family's delight, Zeina had expressed an interest in returning to school when she arrived in the United States, a desire that was now disappearing due to her negative experiences in the class. What I found interesting were the ways that Nadia's reservations about the resource room mirrored Zeina's feelings about her placement; she agreed that Zeina did not belong in the resource room, all the while expressing pity for the other students whose condition "broke your heart"—an affective register that has long been levied against persons with disabilities (Linton 1998; Shapiro 1994; Ware 2002). Nadia also expressed complex feelings about Zeina's teachers, who she felt both exploited Zeina's love of art to give her busy work to occupy her time, while also admitting that other students' "severe needs" understandably demanded more of their time. Ultimately, she felt unable to help Zeina, who was becoming increasingly resistant to going to school.

A few months after she began attending school in the United States, Zeina began to withdraw at home once again, keeping to herself, until she eventually stopped speaking to her family altogether. She would simply "go through the motions," Nadia explained: go to school, come home, go to her room, sit in bed, refuse to eat, and not speak to anyone. "I was terrified," Nadia recalled. "We were back to square one. I was losing her again!" Nadia attributed this to Zeina's classroom placement and to the way that Zeina felt about being in that room day in and day out. She had long stopped making art in the classroom, and her teachers wrote in her report card that she would sit in her chair and stare at the carpet all day. This seemed to Nadia as a sign of Zeina's "giving up," or that the other students were somehow "rubbing off on" Zeina. In other words, it was dangerous to leave Zeina in the company of these other students, whose embodied disabilities would bring Zeina down to their level.

Critical disability scholars have explored how these "troubling behaviors" that Zeina and her classmates were displaying, such as sitting in chairs, staring at carpets all day, or even drooling, can be seen from a different perspective. Taylor (2020) contends that special education contexts such as resource rooms, which completely exclude students with disabilities from their peers, assimilate disabled students to norms of incompetence and teach them to manifest the expectations placed on them. These expectations, some have argued, are exemplified in the very severe symptoms that Nadia rejected. Taylor raises questions about how behaviors that mark students as "severely" disabled can actually be a form of resistance to special education itself. In this case, both Zeina and her classmates can be read as engaging in acts of embodied dissent, rejecting the entire system that attempts to cocreate identities for them as "resource room" students.

Zeina's behaviors, both at school and at home, continued to be of major concern to Nadia. Zeina had also begun to restrict food and water, and Nadia was at a loss of where to go for help. When she had tried to speak with Zeina's teacher, through an interpreter, it was to no avail. The teacher felt that Zeina was displaying "symptoms of her trauma," reinforcing a medical model view of disability. In this model, the disability was positioned as living *within* Zeina, rather than in the surroundings or context, and was framed as a deficit (Stiker 2019). Nadia tried to explain that Zeina seemed to be regressing to her former state in Syria, and that her placement might be responsible for this, but the teacher did not seem to take this seriously.

Righting the Wrongs of Separate Schooling

The situation remained unchanged until Zeina's psychologist connected her family with a special education lawyer who eventually took on her case pro bono. The lawyer created a case against the school district, arguing that Zeina's needs were not being met at her school, and fought to secure placement for Zeina at an elite private school for students with special needs that would be paid for by the district. However, the district settled with the family out of court, agreeing to pay up to 1,300 hours of extra services for Zeina if she continued to attend her neighborhood public school. The school district also agreed to the lawyer's request, which stemmed from Nadia's advocacy, that Zeina no longer receive any instruction in the resource room. Instead, Zeina would work for a few periods a day with an Arabic-speaking tutor who could design a curriculum based on her needs and spend the remainder of the day in ESL classes and other electives such as music and art with her peers. I was hired for the position and began to work with Zeina on a daily basis.

Over the next two years, Zeina's academic progress was slow but steady. In addition to a custom-designed curriculum that focused on reading and writing, Zeina's one-on-one tutoring allowed her to receive additional support that supplemented what she was learning in her ESL class. She was introduced to the vocabulary words that her classmates would learn a week in advance, worked on homework assignments with me, and prepared projects ahead of time. In this learning environment, Zeina received instruction in an accelerated manner in a one-on-one setting within the school day, allowing her to spend most of the day with her peers. By the time she graduated, Zeina was reading and writing in English at a second-grade level, and was able to easily communicate with her teachers and classmates in English. This was especially impressive, given the fact that students who lack literacy in their own language can take up to eight times longer to reach a basic level in second-language reading (United Nations Educational, Scientific and Cultural Organization 2019).

The settlement with the district extended into various postsecondary programs where she could train in fields such as culinary arts, cosmetology, and other options that would accommodate for her needs and give her continued academic training. Zeina seemed to improve emotionally as well, although not without some setbacks. Over time, she began to demonstrate interest in interacting with her peers at school, and according to her mother, she began to "act more like herself" at home, too. Nadia attributed this to the fact that she was happy with her new placement, rather than being in the resource room. Unfortunately, this was not a linear process. Zeina continued to struggle with her former feelings of anxiety, withdrawal, and sadness, but for the most part she was what her mother deemed as "on the road to health."

The Making of Disabled Students

It is impossible to think about the ways that urban public schools fail to meet the unique and complex needs of refugee students without thinking about how ability and disability play out in the experiences of these young people. While it is beyond the scope of this text to provide a comprehensive analysis of this scholarship, disability scholars and activists have long argued that disability has historically been framed in psychological and medical models (Stiker 2019). This scholarship puts forth a social model that interrogates ableism, defined by Storey as "the belief that it is better or superior not to have a disability than to have one and that it is better to do things in the way that nondisabled people do" (2007, 56). Put another way, this literature questions the notion that disabled bodies are unnatural, highlighting the arbitrariness of able-bodiedness. Disability scholars have argued that schools have historically framed disability as a pathological and individual problem where disabled students are held to ableist norms without examining the problematic policies and practices of the school (Baglieri and Knopf 2004; Hehir 2002; Taylor 2012). Disabled students are assigned fictional institutional identities based on pseudoscientific "facts" into which children (and their families) have little input (Mehan, Hertweck, and Meihls 1986). Undoubtedly, these types of discourses were used to place not only Zeina but also her classmates in the resource room full-time.

Ferri and Connor (2006) point to the ways that schools teach explicit and implicit lessons about normalcy. Every time a child is given a designation of having a "special" need and is removed from their classroom, they deviate further from normalcy by the very act of their separation from their classmates. In this way, all children are learning critical lessons about belonging through their own positioning in and out of classrooms.

"Thus, classroom walls and more subtle divisions within the classroom act as literal and symbolic borders, assigning students to designated spaces that correspond to their perceived value in society" (128). It is particularly important to think about how these borders in Zeina's school—echoed as they were by her experience with harsh and unyielding borders in both Iraq and then Syria—reinforced notions of normalcy and belonging. Zeina and her classmates learned essential lessons about citizenship through their separation from their peers and classrooms.

The school evaluation conducted by the school psychologist stated Zeina's TBI significantly affected her academic functioning skills. Specifically, Zeina demonstrated some developmental delays. The TBI also affected her memory and concentration, making schoolwork difficult for her. This was especially true of tasks that involved recalling information, which left her reading and writing at a preschool level. Furthermore, she struggled with communication—not surprising since she was not an English speaker (Connor 2008). What was not taken into account was her complex and yet in some ways predictable pre-migratory history (Bonet 2018): the significant interruption in her formal education; her exposure to violence, conflict, and war (Meekosha 2011); and the lack of supports available to disabled refugees in their home countries (Mirza 2010). Alas, the school psychologist's assessment assigned Zeina an "institutional identity" (Ware 2002) as an intellectually disabled student, which segregated Zeina from her peers, all based on pseudoscientific pathologization (Mehan 2000). While I do not by any means discount the effects of the trauma that Zeina suffered due to the extreme violence that she encountered, I simply wish to question the arbitrary construction of labels that subject her to separate, and inherently unequal, classrooms.

Equally troubling, however, is the exclusion of Zeina's classmates, who were problematically described by both Zeina and Nadia as having "severe needs"—a sentiment that might be mirrored by school personnel to justify their exclusion from "mainstream" classes in order to meet their "special needs." These exclusionary practices remain in place in spite of the framework for children with disabilities in public education, which includes the Disabilities Act (IDEA, 1987/1997), in combination with Section 504 of the Rehabilitation Act of 1973 and Title II of the Americans with Disabilities Act of 1990. IDEA does not mandate "inclusion," but it does mandate that children be placed in the "Least Restrictive Environment" and that they be educated to the maximum extent appropriate with students who do not have disabilities (Baglieri and Knopf 2004). However, schools continue to interpret "inclusion" in a variety of ways. Some schools document the calculus of hours disabled students spend in general education classrooms to meet legal requirements, while others imagine inclusion as a technical problem where schools must find the correct mix of supports to facilitate the placement of students (Ware 2002). In other words, these practices hold up disabled students to ideals of normalcy while leaving unexamined the failures of schools to actually meet their needs (Ferri and Connor 2006; Taylor 2012). Rather than Zeina and her classmates being integrated into mainstream classrooms with their peers, they were segregated. In these spaces, they were separated from their peers according to ableist notions of students' capacities to learn and participate.

These deeply held beliefs were also reflected in Zeina and Nadia's feelings of pity for those students who "just break your heart"—a historical framing of disabled bodies, seen as "childlike, dependent, and in need of charity and pity" (Shapiro 1994, 14). These problematic attitudes stem from the internalized ableism endemic to the ways that schools themselves reinforce structural inequalities across lines of ability. Nadia and Zeina are not simply bad people with prejudices against the disabled, nor should they be written off as such. Rather, their attitudes point to the readily available ways of making sense of disability that are prevalent in the United States. These limited, deficit-driven narratives are leveraged explicitly against Zeina by her school, even as they trigger and frame her own and her mother's bias against her classmates. These biases ultimately work from within to undermine Zeina's experiences in school through internalized ableism. Schooling practices targeting young people with learning differences reinforce all of these harms.

The placement and educational experiences of Zeina and her classmates were also shaped by the bone-deep budget cuts that afflicted the School District of Philadelphia. Approximately 4,000 employees lost their jobs as a result of the cuts, which included special education teachers. Budget cuts frequently affect special education programs more severely than other programs (Pappas 2013). The cuts also resulted in the laying off of 1,200 classroom aides district-wide, including those who provided "therapeutic support services" (TSS). These aides, hired and supervised by special education departments, are typically assigned to work one-on-one with students who needed wraparound services in order to facilitate their learning in a mainstream classroom. Beyond their primary responsibilities, TSS aides often provide their students with social and emotional support beyond the bounds of the classroom, ensure student safety during transitional and break times, and assist teachers with other students who might need additional support. Using "their knowledge of the students and the community to navigate interactions with . . . cultural competence," aides are a critical support not only to their students but to the school as a whole (Deeney 2013). These cuts inevitably had a deleterious effect on the quality of schooling for students like Zeina at Liberty High. Coteaching opportunities between special education and mainstream teachers—which would ensure that students like Zeina were educated in mainstream classrooms—were dramatically reduced. Ratios of students with Individualized Education Programs to teachers increased dramatically. Finally, without aides to assist students within mainstream classrooms, many students like Zeina began spending much of their school day in the resource room. In other words, the financial realities that affected the school further constrained its ability to tend to her needs.

Moving Up While Slipping through the Cracks: Layla's Story

Layla's Family History

Layla Hassan was resettled to Philadelphia from Jordan with her three brothers, her mother, and her father. She was fourteen years old at the time. Prior to coming to the United States, she had been educated in Jordan after her family fled there to escape the growing violence in Iraq. By the time Layla arrived in the United States, she had completed the ninth grade. Unlike many of the youth in this study, she had the exceptional fortune of having no educational interruptions in her schooling. When Fatima, Layla's mother, took her children to Liberty High to register them, Layla was placed in the ninth grade because she had come to the United States without any transcripts, a process that will be taken up in more detail in the following chapter. Layla described herself as an "average student," adding that she was not "the smartest student in her class, but worked very hard." It had always been her dream to become a pharmacist one day. She was a little frustrated that she had to repeat the ninth grade, which she had already completed in Jordan, but later surmised that "it wasn't the end of the world." She was determined to do well, get her diploma, and enroll in a local college.

By the time I met Layla, she was beginning her senior year in Liberty High and was eighteen years old. Like Ghada, Layla was a member of the after-school workshops that I ran at the school, and agreed to participate in my study. This was not surprising since Ghada and Layla were self-reported "BFFs" (best friends forever) and did everything together. Unlike boisterous Ghada, Layla was shy and quiet, seeming tentative to speak even in front of her peers. She also wore a hijab at school, but her scarves were typically solid, earth-toned colors rather than the bold, patterned, and/or pastel scarves that Ghada wore daily. Rather than the shiny gloss or bright lipstick that Ghada preferred, Layla stuck with lip balm. Over time, Layla grew accustomed to my presence and was chattier, a fact I ascribe to Ghada dragging her to come talk to me after the workshop was over. Soon after handing her my consent form, Layla informed me that her mother, Fatima, wished to meet me. Similar to the other focal families in my study, over time I developed a friendly relationship with Fatima and was invited to come back to their home.

What became clear soon after I began to visit was the interdependence that marked the family structure. Like all her siblings, Layla was expected to help support their family of six. While her older brothers pitched in financially by working part-time jobs after school, she and her younger brother Ayman helped her mother by doing chores around the house. She helped her mother by being her mother's proclaimed "sous-chef." Sometimes Fatima even had Layla cook a dish on her own, which Layla proudly presented to me before our tutoring sessions, awaiting my sometimes-exaggerated "yummy" noises that made them both giggle. It didn't take long to see how close Layla and Fatima were, often breaking out into belly laughs together. They seemed at times more like friends than mother and daughter. As *waHda min il'ayla,* or an honorary member of the family, I too did my own part to help. During my visits to the Hassan household, I would assist Fatima by reading and deciphering mail as well as providing tutoring help for Layla and her siblings.

Obstacles to Graduation and Higher Education

Soon after meeting Layla, I learned that she had little exposure to English in Jordan. In my first interview with her, she told me, "When I first got here, school was really hard. I mean I was shocked." She explained that she went from not speaking, reading, or writing any English to learning all of her subjects in this new language. As such, her assignments were often well beyond her reach. During one of my visits to her house, Layla asked me to help her with an especially challenging assignment: her senior projects. In order to graduate, twelfth-grade ESL students at Liberty High were required to complete two projects. The first was a college poster, which needed to include facts, statistics, and useful information about a college or university that the student might be interested in attending. The second involved arguing one side of a controversial topic and deliberating its consequences. Students were expected to present this project in two formats: a five-page research paper, which included references to at least five sources that must include at least three academic papers, and a PowerPoint presentation before their entire ESL class.

In a private conversation, Fatima shared her concerns with me about Layla's ability to graduate, since she was having an extremely difficult time tackling these projects alone. Layla's parents were not proficient in English, and since she was academically ahead of her siblings, there was no one at home to help her. Knowing this, Layla asked her teacher for help, but she was informed that this was an independent project that she must complete at home. Frustrated with the lack of help available to her daughter, Fatima reached out to the director of the ESL department through an interpreter, who confirmed that the teacher could not help Layla with this project. Fatima's frustration was compounded by the fact that Mrs. Ivanov, the bilingual counselor, had been laid off in the latest round of cuts. In speaking with other refugee mothers, Fatima learned that Mrs. Ivanov had held after-school sessions to help immigrant and refugee students with their homework as well as other assignments—an essential resource for those who had no one to turn to at home for help. These mothers also informed Fatima that Mrs. Ivanov was also instrumental in helping their children navigate the college application process and gave them essential information including financial aid opportunities. Unfortunately, Mrs. Ivanov's position was eliminated as a result of the budget cuts that hit the district that year. Since she was not considered "critical staff," hers was one of the first positions on the chopping block.

To help Layla prepare for her graduation projects, I began to meet her at home once a week. Layla was eager to learn and was attentive during our tutoring sessions. She had prepared for the first project by selecting Temple University as well as writing down some facts about the university that she could find online and read independently, such as the address. The only information Layla had about the project was a handout, which included the question, "What university do you hope to attend? And why?"

In class, Layla had written, "I want go to Tambel because I be farmse there" [I want to go to Temple because I want to be a pharmacist there.] As we read through the rest of the questions, Layla struggled with decoding unfamiliar words such as "undergraduate," "majors," and "financial aid." After attempting to read a few sentences, she became embarrassed and frustrated.

My initial session with Layla revealed that she had some significant difficulties with reading and writing. Despite her ability to communicate in English, though, it was clear that she continued to struggle with sentence structure, grammar, and spelling, a difference long documented by language acquisition theorists (Cummins et al. 2005; Spada and Lightbown 2009). After a few sessions with Layla, I estimated that she was reading and writing at a first-grade level. Fortunately, Layla was literate in her own language, which made our work together easier (Cummins et al. 2005). After she successfully read a word, she could make a note of the definition in Arabic and then work on committing it to memory. That said, the task of reading just one screen full of informational text was slow, tedious work, with Layla slowly sounding out each unfamiliar word. Besides the few sight words that Layla was familiar with, most of the words were out of her reach. Soon after we began, she became frustrated and discouraged. Layla experienced similar difficulties in tackling her second graduation project. The more I worked with Layla, the clearer it became that she was woefully underprepared for these tasks.

None of this was surprising, for Layla had come to the United States with little to no instruction in English and had been in ESL classes for only three years. What I did find strange were the expectations placed on students like Layla, regardless of their academic abilities. Layla was required to complete this project to graduate, even though it demanded a high level of skills, including the ability to read several pages from college websites and synthesize and summarize information about these institutions, all the while dealing with unfamiliar, high-level vocabulary. This assignment was designed to help students to research local colleges and universities before graduation, as a means of encouraging students' interest in higher education. The irony should be noted that Layla was asked to prepare posters about colleges and universities that she would probably never attend. Even if Layla completed her required assignments, she would graduate while still reading and writing at an elementary level, which would place her in non-credit-earning college courses after her placement exams. It might be several years before she could receive credit for college-level courses. In spite of all this, Layla had progressed seamlessly from ninth to twelfth grade and was slotted to graduate with the rest of her class at the end of that academic year.

Layla's aspirations for higher education were also affected by the deep cuts to teacher and staff positions. These layoffs have had a particularly negative effect on refugee students since the cuts have eliminated the positions of staff that are critical to refugee youth's transitions within and beyond the school, such as school psychologists, reading specialists, bilingual counselors, and nurses. In Layla's case, the loss of Mrs. Ivanov harmed her academic attainment as well as her ability to navigate the unfamiliar world of college applications—a task that left Layla with no one else to turn to since none of her family members had attended college and none had the linguistic or logistical knowledge needed to navigate this unknown world. When refugee students at Liberty High had the option of meeting with the school's guidance counselors to inquire about college applications, many of them reported feeling overwhelmed. In a school of over 3,000 students, it seemed none of the counselors had the time to slow down long enough to accommodate the linguistic needs of refugee students during their appointments. The precarity exacerbated by these cuts collided with the unique needs of refugee students, creating a new set of challenges for refugee youth rather than being a site of promise that refugee students had imagined it to be.

Behavior as the Primary Determinant for Student "Success"

My work with Layla left me troubled, not only by the fact that she was required to complete two complex and difficult senior projects—an endeavor that she was *clearly* unequipped for—in order to graduate, but also that her seamless move from ninth to twelfth grade left her unprepared to achieve her dream of accessing higher education. The question that plagued me was, Why had Layla been promoted from one grade to the next only to be set up for failure in this particular way? Through my conversations with Fatima, it became clear that one possibility was that Layla was being promoted, not for her *academic* prowess, but instead for *social* perceptions about her as a student. According Fatima, Layla consistently brought home glowing progress and report cards, which framed her as "an ideal student"—a verbatim quote from one of her teachers. Additionally, in all the meetings that Fatima had with Layla's teachers, mediated by an Arabic-speaking teacher, she was told that Layla was well liked by her teachers and that she was doing very well in school. They reported that Layla was well behaved, followed the rules, and that she was a joy to have in class. In fact, Layla's ESL teacher told Fatima that "they wished all of their students were like Layla." In a family focus group, where all the family members spoke to their experiences with Liberty High, Layla and her youngest brother Ayman discussed the emphasis placed by teachers on behavior:

AYMAN: Most of the Arab kids got an F in math last year. A couple of us went to the teacher after we got our grade; we wanted to know why we got an F. We knew we weren't doing well, but we didn't think we were going to fail. When we asked him, he told us, "It's all about your behavior."

LAYLA: And that's why I don't say anything in class. I think that's what the teachers want. Even when I need the teacher to clarify or explain something, I don't ask because I am worried she will get mad. The teachers, especially the ESL teacher is very harsh. When other students have tried to ask her for help or for her to explain the problems again, she yelled, "Shut up! When I am talking, you don't talk!" So I haven't said anything in that class yet.

SALLY: What do you mean?

LAYLA: I mean that I haven't said one word in that class this year yet.

SALLY: But it's November.

LAYLA: I know. But it seems that anyone who asks for help or says anything gets into trouble, so I am not saying anything there. I am completely lost, but that doesn't seem to matter. As long as I am quiet, then the teacher thinks I am OK and they will leave me alone.

As Ayman and Layla's commentary suggested, a large emphasis is placed on students' behavior by their teachers. Layla, who was framed as a model student, was in fact struggling with reading, writing, and mathematics in much the same way that her brother Ayman was in his own classes. In her own words, she felt "completely lost" in her ESL class. However, Layla's strategy of keeping quiet, even if that meant that she remained unclear about her assignments and her lessons, seemed to be working. She had been promoted from one grade to the next with ease and brought home glowing report cards. Ayman, who was more vocal, tended to insist on asking for help, and complained when the teacher seemed to be acting with excessive harshness, brought home lower grades and at times failing ones. It is telling, not to mention troubling, that upon questioning of Ayman's grade, his teacher highlighted the centrality of students' behavior: the teacher's expectations of students' behavior and comportment in class can result in their failure in school. Like Zeina, Layla and Ayman were experiencing the ways that students' affective behaviors have consequences for their placement.

Layla came to her ESL classroom having had little to no instruction in English and was placed in classrooms where all of her instruction was in English, and where the use of her native language was discouraged. Upon arrival at Liberty High, Layla was placed in an intensive ESL track: her roster included four ESL classes, one math class, and one elective. However, by her senior year, her schedule looked quite different: she had only one ESL class, one math class, one history class, one science class, one music class, and a gym class. In other words, besides the one ESL class, the remainder of her roster read like that of a native English speaker. It was painfully clear from our sessions together that she was not receiving enough support as an English language learner, only receiving language support in one of her classes. Despite this, she was not only expected to complete senior projects but had also been subjected to state-mandated, high-stakes testing within one year of her arrival. In speaking with Layla, it became clear that her access to ESL support had been systemically reduced every year and that she was being pushed into mainstream schooling, arguably too soon. Had she spent enough time in her ESL classroom, perhaps Layla's reading and writing ability would have better matched the expectations placed on her. Furthermore, Layla and her Arabic-speaking classmates reported being punished when they attempted to help each other in their ESL classrooms. Teachers became angry when students spoke anything other than English. Rather than building on the literacies and competencies of students, teachers insisted on an English-only environment.

Discrimination and Islamophobia: A Post-9/11 Reality for Muslim Iraqi Youth

Resettlement as a Pathway to Citizenship

I began working with refugee youth and families as the tide was turning, both within and outside of the United States, against refugees. The Syrian crisis was unfolding, and soon the number of displaced peoples grew to the largest in recorded history. As masses of refugees made perilous journeys in rickety boats to escape the horror in their home countries, rhetoric that framed Muslim refugees as a menace to national security and identity gained traction in both Europe and the United States. Ghada Musa, the young woman whose testimony we read at the beginning of this chapter, had attended school in her native city of Baghdad for a few years until it became too dangerous for her to continue doing so, a reality for many children in Iraq. Ghada, her mother, her older sister Samah, and her younger brother Adam fled to Syria and then to Yemen, where they lived for several years before being resettled to the United States. Ghada enrolled in Liberty High soon after arriving in Philadelphia and was placed in the ninth grade, even though she was seventeen years old at the time and had completed the eleventh grade in Yemen. Since she was unable to procure transcripts proving her academic attainment, she was placed in the ninth grade. Life in Philadelphia proved to be a challenge for the entire Musa family. Baheera, her mother, suffered from several chronic illnesses and could not work, so both Ghada and her older sister had to work to support the family. After school, Ghada offered eyebrow threading—an age-old practice in the Arab world that recently became a trend in the United States—from the family home in Philadelphia to Arab women who lived in the neighborhood. Ghada was also responsible for assisting her mother with caring for their home and giving Baheera several insulin shots a day to manage her diabetes. Ghada was a hard worker and deeply committed to her family.

In my first interview with Ghada, I asked her about her dreams and hopes for the future. She informed me that she was determined to work hard in her English classes, graduate high school, and matriculate into college so she could become a journalist. "I like learning about people's stories," she explained. Ghada was grateful to have left Yemen behind, where she was reminded daily of her refugee status by her classmates. Unlike her Yemeni counterparts who wore a niqab, a Muslim covering that covered the face except the eyes, which is worn with loose-fitting clothing as well as gloves, Ghada, her sister, and her mother all wore hijabs, a head covering that only covered their hair, leaving the face exposed. This marked the women of Ghada's family as "different" and possibly less modest. Ghada and her sister had felt the social pressure to take on this more religious garb, but their mother insisted that they had already followed the rules of modesty by wearing a hijab. To cover up to fit in, rather than to follow their own religious/moral code, seemed unethical to Baheera. Unfortunately, in Yemen, this marked them as refugee *and* religious outsiders. Ghada and her family would always be refugees for legal reasons as well. Yemen, like most Arab countries, does not provide a route to legal citizenship for refugees, excluding them from particular employment opportunities, the ability to own property, and other basic rights enjoyed by citizens. Coming to the United States gave Ghada hope; it was here that she would no longer be an "other" but instead would "be an American, just like everybody else."

Islamophobia at Liberty High

In spite of Ghada's aspirations for inclusion, she admitted that she faced several challenges at Liberty High, including threats and violence at the hands of her fellow students:

GHADA: Like in gym, all the American kids in my gym always say awful stuff to me; they say to me "fuckin" and "bitch" and that kind of stuff. And it really bothers me. And I tell them, "STOP! Don't talk to me." And I even try to yell at them, but they don't listen, they just keep saying that stuff. Or sometimes some kids are playing with rocks, and then I am walking by and they throw a rock at me. One kid said, "Go back to your country. We don't want you here." He threw a rock at my head, but I ducked so it didn't hit me. And I was just trying to walk by, you know?

SALLY: Why do you think they do this?

GHADA: Because I am Muslim. [Pause] But you know when they do stuff like that, with rocks, I don't even respond.

SALLY: Why not?

GHADA: Because I am scared of what they will do if they get mad. They are already throwing rocks at me. What else will they do?

SALLY: So what do you do?

GHADA: I just try to avoid them.

In gym class, when students were free from the more stringent dynamics of a classroom and given more unsupervised time and freedom to interact with one another, Ghada was verbally abused by her peers. In this setting, with some adult supervision, Ghada felt emboldened to fight back, yelling at them to cease their insults. However, during instances when students were playing with rocks, presumably with no adult supervision, Ghada felt most vulnerable; students figured that they could throw rocks at her with no recourse. Here, with no adult in sight, no one that might act as an ally, Ghada had no recourse but to duck and avoid those students. Afraid of the consequences of responding to this abuse lest she incur further and perhaps more severe violence, Ghada was effectively silenced. In essence, her response to becoming a victim was to attempt to become invisible. Unfortunately, the visual marker of her Muslim identity, the hijab, would make this an impossible task. Interestingly, Ghada's hijab, which was the reason she was marked as a refugee in Yemen, was the same marker for otherness here, but in a very different way. At Liberty High, it marked her as Muslim, and hence a target. While Ghada could avoid specific students, she could not predict who might throw the next rock or levy the next insult, leaving her perpetually vulnerable.

Ghada's testimony also demonstrates the fragility of her hopes for citizenship, true inclusion, and refuge. It was clear from the discourse that surrounded the violence that she endured that she was not, as she had hoped to be, part of the imagined community of America (Anderson 2006). The cries for her to return to "her" country, as she was unwanted and unwelcomed "here," in "their" school and ultimately in "their" country, were accusations lobbed against many who find themselves outside the boundaries of the national imaginary, regardless of their citizenship status or even the fact that they served in the U.S. government. In 2019, President Trump tweeted that four congresswomen of color who critiqued the governments' immigration policies should "go back" to the "totally broken and crime infested places from which they came" rather than "loudly and viciously telling the people of the United States" how to run the government (Rogers and Fandos 2019). All but one of the congresswomen were born in the United States, all were U.S. citizens, and yet they were framed as un-American regardless of their public service to their country. In Ghada's case, her identity as refugee and Muslim in a post-9/11 context marked her as "un-American." These sentiments have been levied at Muslim youth who are traversing schooling in the post-9/11 environment, both in the United States (Abu El-Haj 2015; Bonet 2011; Ghaffar-Kucher 2009) and globally (Abu El-Haj, Ríos-Rojas, and Jaffe-Walter 2017). However, Ghada's identity as an Iraqi refugee in the land that displaced her has a specific and unique sting. The calls for Ghada to return to her country were unique in that hers was a homeland *at war with the United States*. In this framing, Ghada is perceived as a part of the enemy state, and perhaps linking her to the attacks of 9/11. Her body and presence in the United States is a reminder of those attacks and elicits vitriol that is not only verbal but also physical in nature. The students targeting her threw rocks aimed at her head, the very area covered by her hijab and marking her as Muslim.

Iraqis as the Ultimate "Other"

Ghada's experience was not an isolated incident. In fact, the harassment of Iraqi refugee youth in their schools was of major concern to Rasha, the director of a nonprofit organization dedicated to serving Arabic-speaking immigrants and refugees in Philadelphia. Rasha's organization, which has been serving the community since the 1990s, had fielded many similar complaints:

> RASHA: So the Iraqi refugee community, especially those who have arrived most recently, suffer from discrimination, especially in schools. We're hearing a lot of incidents of bullying, and kind of like being discriminated against because of their religion.
>
> SALLY: Can you give me an example of that?
>
> RASHA: Sure, so we had one client, Mohamed, he was an Iraqi refugee, and he was at a middle school that was practically 100 percent African American. On a daily basis he was called all types of names, because he was Arab and Muslim. He was called things like "Osama Bin Laden" and asked "What are you doing here?" and told "Go back to where you came from." We worked with the Human Relations Commission to actually pull him out of that school. It was *that* bad. And this is just one of the incidents that have been happening over the years. There were many more. Parents have complained to us in the past. Unfortunately the parents are scared to officially report things because they don't trust law enforcement, especially, well, because we come from the Middle East and so law enforcement is

viewed as not the protector but the aggressor. It's really tough for parents though. It's a really big issue.

Rasha's account demonstrated that Ghada was not alone in her experience at her school. Noteworthy is the fact that Rasha's organization served the entirety of the Arabic-speaking community in Philadelphia, which included groups that had been resettled prior to the Iraqis, such as Palestinians, Egyptians, and Moroccans, to name a few. However, Rasha points to the Iraqi refugee community as a group that particularly suffered from discrimination, and schools as being particularly volatile spaces for their children and a deep concern for parents. Like Ghada, Mohamed was being taunted by his U.S.-born peers as the only Muslim refugee student in a school that was nearly 100 percent African American. In this context, the student was presumably even more a target due to his phenotypical difference from the rest of his peers. Notably, in this instance, Mohamed was being called "Osama Bin Laden," the ultimate enemy of the United States and the enduring reason for U.S. military involvement in Iraq and Afghanistan at the time. As an Iraqi refugee, Mohamed represented the ultimate "other" and the country's ongoing War on Terror.

Refugee parents were wary of officially reporting incidents of threat and abuse, a fact Rasha attributed to their lack of trust in law enforcement. Coming from war-torn contexts where law enforcement officials were often embroiled in corruption and even outright violence against citizens, parents were reluctant to report these incidents in an official manner. Mohamed's case was a notable exception: the family had reported the incident to Rasha and asked her to assist them in communicating with school officials. Even though this young boy was being bullied daily, the school was slow to respond to the parents' complaints. Later in the interview, Rasha explained that change came for Mohamed only after the involvement of a task force with the Human Relations Commission, the Department of Justice, and the U.S. attorney's office in Philadelphia. Only then was Mohamed removed from his school and placed in another school, which was a feeder school to Liberty High School that boasted a great deal of ethnic and religious diversity. However, as Ghada's experience at Liberty High illustrates, a diverse student body does not guarantee inclusion or social cohesion (Tinke 2009)—a fact that has long been corroborated in the research of other educational anthropologists (Abu El-Haj 2015; Jaffee-Walter 2016; Olsen 1997).

Competition for Resources between Disenfranchised Students

We cannot take Rasha's statement that Mohammed's school was 100 percent African American acritically. African American students have and continue to face institutional and structural racism in their schooling, such as adultification, criminalization, and disproportionate special education referrals and disciplinary actions, as well as a historical education debt that is mistakenly framed as an achievement gap (Editors of *Black Issues in Higher Education,* Anderson, and Byrne 2004; Blanchett 2006; Ladson-Billings 2006; Love 2014; McLoyd 2014). Furthermore, African American students attend schools with the most deplorable conditions, usually completely segregated from their white counterparts, and yet ironically their schools are considered "diverse" and often boast the names of civil rights leaders and activists such as Dr. Martin Luther King (Kozol 1988, 2005). In these conditions, where young people find themselves in a pressure cooker and profoundly disadvantaged by institutional racism, incidents of "circular discrimination" tend to occur (Rosenbloom and Way 2004). An essential way that schooling environments harm students is by steeping them in problematic roles and narratives that do the work of forcing them and their peers into competition for scarce resources—including scarce emotional and psychosocial resources to create healthy identities as both citizens within the school and the nation. Hence, students who are effectively unable to ever be "good enough" to succeed turn their unresolvable trauma against others.

Philadelphia schools have been proven to be fertile ground for hostile relationships between student groups. Philadelphia was recently ranked as the fourth most segregated big city in the country, topped only by Chicago, Atlanta, and Milwaukee (Otterbein 2015). While African Americans make up approximately 43 percent of the student population in Philadelphia, they are concentrated in the west and southwestern region of the city, where they make up 80–100 percent of the student population (Statistical Atlas 2019). However, 96 percent of Pennsylvania's teaching staff are white (Research for Action 2018). The recent school closures that plagued the School District of Philadelphia were invariably those that housed mostly African American students, a trend well documented in the literature (Lipman 2011; Lipman et al. 2012; McWilliams 2019). In other words, African American students in Philadelphia are getting a "raw deal" when it comes to schooling, attending segregated, dilapidated schools that are more likely to close and be staffed by overworked and overwhelmed teachers (at best). Given these dismal conditions, it was not entirely surprising when the events at South Philadelphia High School occurred. On December 3, 2009, thirty Asian students were attacked by large groups of African American and Asian American students (Graham 2009). Victims reported being taunted daily and put into further danger by adults in the school who looked the other way regularly.

During my time at the refugee resettlement agency, I learned that the students who were attacked were refugees or the children of refugees, mostly Burmese and Bhutanese youth. In other words, this attack was not merely an interracial one but one that targeted those who were perceived as less American. A mere two years later, Mohamed, a recently resettled Iraqi refugee student, was placed in a school that was almost completely populated with African American students. One wonders what implicit and explicit messages the African American students were receiving about their communities, schools, families, and selves. What were the dynamics between the students and their teachers? How were their own bodies policed in and outside of the school? While there is no way to get to these answers in Mohamed's case, his experience does not leave me thinking of him as the sole target (of peer violence), but of his peers as victims of systemic, historic, cumulative dispossession and abuse that is both insidious and deeply damaging.

Rosenbloom and Way's (2004) study of circular discrimination points to the correlation between youths' experiences with adults in the schools and their relationships with other students, as well as their feeling of belonging within the school. An interview with Layla and Ayman revealed that youth experienced discrimination at the hands of adults at Liberty High, including teachers:

AYMAN: The teachers at the school, they all dislike Arabs. They are constantly giving us detentions and whenever we talk in the class, even when we are just trying to help each other understand what the teacher just explained. The other day the teacher was taking attendance, and then he called my friend's Adam's name. I raised my hand and told him that Adam was absent because it was Eid. The teacher yelled at me, and said, "Shut up!" The teachers hate the Arab kids. They always talk to us like this.

And they are constantly giving us detention for things that
other kids don't get punished for.

LAYLA: Yeah, the other day I walked into gym late because I
needed to go to the bathroom, which I had a hall pass for.
When I walked in, the teacher asked me, "Where were you?"
I told him I was in the bathroom, and he told me if I was late
again he would have me suspended.

SALLY: Suspended?!

LAYLA: Yes. That's how the gym teacher talks to all of the Muslim
girls, especially the ones who wear the hijab. He doesn't like us.

SALLY: Why do you think that is?

LAYLA: I think he doesn't like that we won't wear the "normal"
gym outfit which includes shorts. I also think it's because we're
different.

Both Ayman and Layla experienced their teachers as excessively punitive.
Especially interesting here is the response of the teacher to Ayman's seemingly "palatable" act, as he follows many of what one might observe to be
the rules of a classroom. Hearing his friend's name being called, Ayman
raises his hand—a sign of acknowledging the teacher's authority rather
than speaking out of turn. Next, the piece of information he shared is that
his friend Adam was absent for religious reasons—it was Eid Al-Fitr, the
holiday celebrated after the end of the holy month of Ramadan which is
one of the two most important religious events in Islam, comparable to
the importance of Christmas and Easter in Christianity. While the school
did not grant all students days off for Eid, it allowed Muslim students
who wished to observe the holiday to stay at home without being counted
as absent. They would still be expected to make up assignments and exams
they missed, but teachers were obliged to make alternative arrangements
with their students. Knowing this, Ayman wished to inform his teacher
that Adam was absent in observance of Eid, to ensure that Adam's absence
would be counted as such. Rather than making a note of this, the teacher
scolds Ayman and orders him to "Shut up!" Teachers' desire to exert complete control of the class is not necessarily surprising; Layla and Ayman
had already commented on this earlier. Teachers had made it clear that
"appropriate" behavior was the key to success at Liberty High. However, in
this instance, a student had raised his hand and was informing a teacher

of the absence of another student for religious reasons. What in this interaction would elicit such a negative response from the teacher?

Clues to this answer are to be found in Layla's account of her own experience with her gym teacher. In response to her (prearranged) tardiness, the teacher threatened her with suspension. In both cases, the students seemingly follow the rules set by the school and/or the teacher and yet encounter a strongly negative response by their teacher, arguably one out of proportion with their alleged "infraction." Ayman and Layla understand their teachers' reactions differently. Ayman attributes this to the fact that teachers "dislike Arab kids," citing the fact that they are punished at a higher rate than other groups in the school and never allowed to converse with each other in the class, even if it is to help each other learn or better understand a concept. In this conception, Ayman tied teachers' negative sentiments and actions to his ethnic identity as an Arab in the school, a group he argues is both visible and policed in a particular manner in the school. His experience is corroborated by scholarship that tracks the experiences of Arab youth in schools after 9/11 (Abu El-Haj and Bonet 2011; Bonet 2011). Layla, on the other hand, attributed her gym teacher's actions to her and her Muslim classmates' religious identities. As young women who not only wore hijabs but who also modified their gym outfits by wearing more modest clothing instead of the standard shorts that her classmates wore, they were marked as "other." Layla spoke of the negative feelings that the teachers had for the "Muslim girls." Teachers presumed that Muslim girls came from families and cultures that oppressed them, where they had little to no autonomy in important life choices such as higher education, sexuality, and marriage; the teachers framed them as submissive victims rather than agentic transnational subjects. Jaffe-Walter's (2016) work uncovered the implicit and explicit ways that feminist liberal teachers worked to "free" Muslim girls from their backward families' mode of thought. In other words, Layla and Ayman's experience in Liberty High confirms what we know to be true, that Arab and Muslim bodies are vulnerable in schools, even by the adults who are tasked with their care.

Just how vulnerable youth were was underscored by an interview with Ghada and her brother, Adam—Ayman's friend who was absent due to his observance of Eid Al-Fitr. In a family focus group, Adam shared that he was almost physically struck by an elderly substitute teacher who regularly "hit the Arab kids with his cane." Apparently the teacher struck the Arab and Muslim students when he became angry. Adam admitted that he was scared to report the teacher in fear of being punished or even suspended. Individual states began to ban corporal punishment in public schools in the United States as early as 1867, but the Supreme Court did not take up the case of corporal punishment until 1977. Officially, Pennsylvania permitted corporal punishment in schools until 2005, although it was not widely practiced. The state law had been in place for a decade by the time that this substitute teacher was hitting the students with his cane in Liberty High. In a school with over 3,000 students, it was presumably the case that the administration was unaware of the actions of this elderly teacher who was possibly "disciplining" his students in his own "old-school" manner. It must be noted that the reason behind the administration's ignorance of these deplorable actions was rooted in students' fears that reporting these actions might incur further wrath from teachers or administrators. In effect, this fear silenced students, and even worse, left them in harm's way.

The (Not-So-) Hidden Curriculum of Schooling for Refugee Youth

Over time, the aspirations of most of refugee youth changed, mostly following a downward trajectory. When I first met Ghada, she was adamant about becoming a journalist. By the end of her eleventh-grade year, Ghada was instead seriously considering cosmetology school. Adam said that maybe he "would work with cars," because engineering was "too much work anyway." In the spring semester of her senior year, Layla stated that she wasn't sure she wanted to be a pharmacist anymore. Instead, she told me that she would "take some classes at the community college and see." The cruelty, of course, was that she was graduating well beneath the reading and writing level required for college-level classes, so even this exploratory avenue would be cut off for her. Lian, an employee of the refugee resettlement agency, illuminated this problem:

> Most of the refugee students who enroll in community college don't take classes for college credit for a while. They take the English language placement test and then they are placed in remedial ESL classes there. Sometimes the students can be stuck in these classes for several years before they can enroll in college classes. A lot of the refugee students drop out of these remedial classes after a few years. It becomes discouraging for them, you know? So many of them are older students too, and by the time they begin taking

the courses for credit, they can be in their mid-twenties. They get discouraged because they know how long they have to go. And they have other pressures, like work and helping their family, so they drop out, which is a shame.

Refugee youths' hopes for inclusion and bright futures vis-à-vis a college education were becoming further out of reach. As a result, they began to adjust, to make their dreams smaller in order to minimize the cruelty of their fates. Through explicit and implicit messages communicated in their classrooms, combined with the real barriers they experienced in their schools, it seemed that refugee youth were being educated about their expected place in society, just as Willis (1997) long ago predicted. The students had learned their place—schooling had done its job. Through their encounters with the public school, an essential arm of the state, refugee students were learning the kinds of citizenship they were expected to enact and embody in the United States (Abu El-Haj 2015; Rubin 2007; Benei 2008). School is an essential site where youth experience and learn an embodied sense of citizenship. As Abu El-Haj, Kaloustian, Bonet, and Chatila (2018, 36) argue,

> Recognizing citizenship as an embodied experience means understanding that there are affective dimensions to one's understanding of, and relationship to, the practices of public life: for example, feeling a sense of belonging or exclusion, trust in or fear of authority, shame or pride in one's community are all constitutive of how one acts within and upon their society.

Refugee students were learning critical lessons about citizenship, and about their own place in their new contexts through their encounters and experiences in their public schools. This was visible in Ayman's attempt to question his grade, which resulted in severe scolding by the teacher and Layla's understanding that silence was the only option to success—a strategy that had won her glowing reports. These experiences underscore the ways that teachers might be more interested in behaviors such as obedience, silence, and stillness from students of color rather than evidence of real learning (Collins 2013; Shalaby 2017).

As social reproduction theorists have long argued, the hidden curriculum of schooling is to create disciplined, obedient, masses of skilled, low-wage workers to meet the capitalist demands of today's labor market (Anyon 1981; Bowles and Gintis 1976; Willis 1997). In other words, refugee youth were being molded into the types of workers they were expected to become (Anyon 1981). Seen through this lens, it is not surprising that Layla was being rewarded for "good" behavior rather than her academic prowess. Told by teachers to "shut up when I talk" and that their success was "all about their behavior," refugee students were learning to follow directions, take orders, and accept the total control of the teacher. They were being trained into becoming obedient, working-class subjects who submitted to the total control of their superior. As Anyon argues, the purpose of education for working-class students is the "reproduction of a group in society who may be without marketable knowledge; a reserve group of workers whose very existence, whose availability for hire, for example, when employed workers strike, serves to keep wages down and the work force disciplined" (1981, 31). Through their encounters with their public schools, refugee youth were being formed into laboring subjects, in a parallel manner to the ways that interactions with the resettlement agency and the welfare state disciplined their parents.

In this system, the only way to "succeed" was to be completely docile, submissive, and silent. Yet, as Layla's case demonstrates, that can lead to academic stagnation. She might have been lauded for her "behavioral excellence," but by the time she graduated, she was significantly underprepared for college. Furthermore, Ghada and Adam's troubling accounts of exposure to threats and violence further capture how Islamophobia interrupted their ability to be accepted members of the school community. The messages that were communicated by teachers and students alike situated Muslim refugee youth outside the boundaries of belonging, in the school but also the national imaginary. Unable to trust the school administration, refugee youth chose silence rather than calling out instances of threat and abuse, which put them in further danger. Through all of this, refugee youth were being dispossessed of their hopes of the promise of what education was supposed to espouse, namely, access to the "good life" (Berlant 2011) that they and their families had hoped for. They were learning what it means to be young and Muslim in America (Bayoumi 2008). But they are also learning their place in society, and in particular what they were permitted to dream and what they should realistically hope for.

Refugee youth identify education as their primary aspiration, envisioning it as a pathway to the "good life" that they hope to find in their newly resettled contexts (Berlant 2011). However, these young people come to their new contexts with complex pre-migratory histories that must be taken into account in order for their schooling to meet their unique needs, such as exposure to violent conflict and resulting trauma; educational interruptions that make learning in their new, English-only contexts difficult; and pressures to work to help support their families both before and after resettlement. Unfortunately, refugee students are subsumed into rigid educational systems that are further weakened by neoliberal reforms, exacerbating the vulnerabilities that students experienced before coming to the United States. Students' unique needs are not taken into consideration and become barriers to adequate learning opportunities that fit their needs. Refugee youth whose lives have been textured by violence are interpreted through a disability lens, rather than a holistic view of the student. Furthermore, schools cocreate identities for students, such as undesirable/dangerous Muslim bodies or deficient learners, through the biased and acritical tendency to collapse a range of signifiers—such as the absence of white, middle-class American schooling values coupled with a lack of English language fluency—into the criteria used to frame "ability" and "promise" in schooling. As a result, refugee youth are divested of their right to hope.

Students' negative experiences with schooling in America also impact their ability to imagine themselves as citizens with the right to full membership in their new contexts. Students look to school not only as the bridge for their lofty educational aspirations but also as a pathway to citizenship, which they define as belonging and inclusion. For these youth—who experienced the indignities of second-class citizenship in neighboring countries where they and their families fled—school is the key to the "good life" (Berlant 2011) they imagined: a college education and a meaningful career. More important, schooling would also provide youth with the opportunity, as Ghada put so simply at the outset of this chapter, to become "American like everyone else." However, the Iraqi Muslim refugee youth discussed here were regularly exposed to Islamophobic discrimination, verbal abuse, and physical threats by peers, teachers, as well as other adults in the school. Analyses of the troubling discourse lobbed at the students by their peers revealed that they were framed as noncitizens; allies of the ultimate enemy of the state, Osama bin Laden; and permanently outside of the imaginary of the nation-state. Teachers' actions and discourse uncovered a desire for complete control and discipline, including corporal punishment when students were "out of line." Through their encounters with urban public schools, students learn that they are outside the bounds of citizenship, framed as the ultimate other and as inherently "unassimilable." The next chapter will center the experiences of young people who are excluded from public schools, focusing on the ways that barriers to secondary education shape their future as well as their ability to become full citizens.

4

Young Adult Education

The Shaping of Laboring Citizens

America wasn't even on my mind when I was in Syria. I never even dreamed of it. I had never even thought of it, really. But when I came here, it was a surprise for me. I thought things would be different, but it turns out that everything is the opposite of what I thought it would be like. I was expecting life to be easy. I expected that there wouldn't be any difficulty in anything; that education would prepare you for a job, and that when you get a job, it would be good and really well paying. And I thought when I first came to the school, that the teachers would care, that they would help you, that things would be easier and smoother, you know? But I didn't find that at all. Everything is hard. And the teachers, they don't care. I try to get help, but I can't. I try to explain that I am new here, that I am a refugee, but it doesn't matter. I want to be an engineer someday. That is my dream. But how can I do this when every step is a struggle? America is not at all what I thought it would be. Sometimes, I wish I never came here.

—Heba

As Heba spoke the words above, my eyes fell on the large Iraqi flag that hung behind her, the one that she had purchased from a store near her home in Iraq before they left, that she carried in her backpack to Syria where her family fled in 2006 and then once again folded neatly into her luggage for the long trip from Damascus to Philadelphia. The first ten years of Heba's life had been happy. She lived with her family in their large, comfortable home located near the fruit orchards her family owned. For generations, Heba's family grew and sold several varieties of dates. The youngest of her siblings, Heba spoke of being spoiled by her father, who bought her all the toys and clothes that she wanted. After school and on weekends, Heba spent most of her time with her brothers in the fields. In spite of the financial difficulties brought on by the Iran–Iraq wars, the two

Gulf wars, and the international sanctions placed on the country, Heba's father had been able to keep his business afloat.

The "hard times" began when her father died of cancer in 2001. Without his business acumen and strong industry ties, the family began to flounder. To make matters worse, the sectarian violence, lack of security, interruptions of basic services including clean water and electricity, and the near collapse of state institutions including hospitals and schools that followed the American invasion of Iraq made life extremely difficult for Heba's family. The fact that the family lived in Basrah, near the border with Iran, made life for her Sunni family nearly impossible. Heba's brothers received daily threats, and Heba was confined to the house due to the rise in violence against women and daily incidents of kidnapping. As a result, Heba was forced to stop attending school, which broke her heart. She always dreamt of becoming an engineer and had a special interest in civil engineering. Heba had always struggled with math, but a caring, dedicated teacher in her school in Iraq had helped her tackle the subject. Heba worried that she would fall behind if she missed too much school. Meanwhile, the family business was near collapsing, and they continued to struggle to make ends meet.

In an attempt to support the family, Heba's brother Tarek purchased a truck and began to deliver cargo between Iraq and Syria. Due to the dangers involved with the trip along the road that he traveled, customers paid Tarek and his business partner and childhood friend Ali a high fee to move cargo between the two countries. Unfortunately disaster hit soon after Tarek established the business. Their truck was pulled over by a Sunni armed militia, and Tarek and Ali were asked to come out of the truck at gunpoint. Soon enough, Ali was identified as being Shia, and was detained by the group. Meanwhile, Tarek was told that he was free to go. At gunpoint, he was ordered to get into his car and leave the scene. Tarek begged the men to allow him to take his friend with him, but the militia men assured him that if he did not get in the truck and drive away, he would soon face the same fate that awaited his friend. Tarek got in the car, and saw, in the truck's rearview mirror, Ali being forced to his knees at gunpoint. Upon his return home, Tarek called Ali's family to inform them of what had happened to their son.

The family blamed Tarek for his friend's death. In spite of Tarek's many explanations of the situation, Ali's father was unconvinced. Soon after this conversation, Ali's father gave Tarek an ultimatum: either he paid a *diyya*, the payment of a sum of money by an aggressor to his victim's family, or face *qasas,* justified retaliation or revenge. The sum of money Ali's family placed on Tarek's life was more than Heba and her family could bear. Heba's mother was forced to sell her home, the land, the cars, and everything they owned, but it was only through borrowing money from her in-laws that she was able to make the full payment. Unfortunately, Ali's family, who had become increasingly hostile, demanded more money. The family who bought Heba's home informed her that Ali's family had come to the house, armed with guns, banging on the door, asking for Tarek and demanding "their son's right." It was then that Heba's family finally decided it was time to leave Iraq. In late 2006, Heba's family left for Syria.

Heba registered in public school in Damascus as soon as she arrived. Due to the educational interruption she had experienced in Iraq, she was required to repeat the grades that she had missed rather than be placed according to her age. This bothered Heba a little, but mostly she was grateful to be in school again. It took Heba some time to become accustomed to the schooling system in Syria. There she was required to learn French as a second language, and the Arabic and sciences curricula were much more dense and demanding. In spite of these challenges, Heba managed to excel there. Meanwhile, life in Damascus was proving to be very difficult for her family. Heba's siblings were forced into low-wage labor, in spite of their previous work experience. Damascus was an expensive city, and, as the family was growing in numbers, so grew their needs. In order to afford the high rents, the family lived together in very tight quarters. Heba shared a room with five of her nieces. Within a few months of arriving in Syria, Heba's brothers registered with the UNHCR with hopes of being resettled elsewhere. Nearly two years later, the family was informed that only Heba, her mother, and one of her brothers and his small family had been accepted for resettlement to the United States. The remainder of her siblings remained in Syria, waiting to be resettled.

Heba and her family arrived in Philadelphia in August 2010. During their first meeting with their resettlement agent, Heba inquired about her schooling options. She learned that she needed to be registered at Liberty High, her neighborhood high school. After a meeting with the director of Liberty High's ESL department, the school's vice principal, and a translator, Heba and her family were informed that she was placed in the ninth grade, despite the fact that she was already eighteen years old at the time. She had completed the eleventh grade in her Damascus high school, but due to her inability to procure transcripts proving her educational attainment, she was placed several grades behind her American peers. Furthermore, since Heba had been educated mostly in Arabic, both in Iraq and in Syria, she came unprepared to handle a high school curriculum taught entirely in English at her new school. When I met Heba, in the spring of her ninth grade year, she had already turned nineteen years old. In two short years, Heba would age out of public education, and would be unable to obtain a high school diploma. In her testimony, Heba articulated her educational aspirations— which were inevitably shaped by the hardships she and her family faced, textured by loss, threat, and flight in search of safety. Heba hoped that in the United States her schooling, which had taken place in fits and starts, would finally be smooth and accessible and lead her to the stability she craved. Unfortunately, Heba's dreams collided with the realities that she found in her urban public high school. She was learning that her education was in fact precarious, difficult, and moving quickly out of reach. More important, through her interactions with the public school and its agents, Heba was learning critical lessons about citizenship and belonging.

Like Heba, all of the youth in my study placed a great deal of hope of a "bright future" vis-à-vis a postsecondary education, which they would then leverage to secure stable and high-income careers. However, as Heba's story underscores, refugee youth came to their new contexts with unique challenges that shaped their educational needs, such as poverty, long educational interruptions, linguistic and foundational barriers, and lack of familiarity with the educational systems of their receiving countries (McWilliams and Bonet 2016; Stermac, Clarke, and Brown 2013; Taylor and Sidhu 2012). Upon arrival to their new contexts, they may face additional challenges, such as deficient or nonexistent program supports to assist them in their transitions to their new schooling environments and communities (Arnot, Pinson, and Candappa 2009; Jones and Rutter 1998). Despite the challenges they faced in schools, refugee youth continued to identify schooling in general, and higher education in particular, as their ultimate goal. Youth viewed higher education as a means to improve their financial situation, as well as a way to better care for family members. These hopes were not just a product of a longing for stability but are confirmed by bodies of research that highlight postsecondary education as increasingly central for access to gainful employment in the United States. Economists estimate that about two-thirds of all current jobs require at least some postsecondary education, up from 59 percent in 2008 and 28 percent in 1973 (Carnevale, Smith, and Strohl 2010). Furthermore, job availability projections in the next ten years limit high school diploma holders to work in jobs that are part-time, insecure, and transitional (Perna and Jones 2013). Refugees therefore recognize after arrival that access to postsecondary education is critical not just for stability but for survival in their new contexts.

This chapter takes on the discrepancy between the pre-migratory aspirations of older refugee youth and their lived experiences in their post-resettlement contexts. Here, I bring to the forefront refugee youths' disappointments, frustrations about their ability to access educational rights in their newly resettled contexts, and the resulting political analyses they engage in as they question the liberal ideals espoused by the promise of America. By homing in on the experiences of Heba, Ziad, Hussein, Seif, and Samah, as well as their parents, I explore how rigid educational policies at public schools, a lack of adequate education for young adults, and neoliberal reforms act as a pipeline to the low-wage labor force. I also investigate how the intuitional gap among public schools, postsecondary education programs, and the workforce disciplines young adult refugees into laboring citizens.

Anxieties and Realities of Inappropriate Grade Assignment

Problematic District Policies

Typical of many urban refugees[1] who have been educated in low-income neighboring countries, Iraqi refugee youth came to the United States with varying degrees of educational attainment (Dryden-Peterson 2016; Jacobsen 2006). Like Heba, many of the young people in my study came to the United States without school transcripts that documented their educational attainment, and as a result were placed in the ninth grade. A School District of Philadelphia employee explained the precise rationale behind this decision:

> So how the process works is that when we first get the transcript
> [for foreign-born students], we send it to translation services,
> which then sends it back to us. Then someone from the Chief Academic Office decides which credits transfer. Everyone who comes
> with six years of schooling from their country, they get two credits
> automatically. If some students come here with no transcripts, the
> only credits they will get are the two credits for having the six years

of schooling in their country of origin. Since those are the only credits they have, they are placed in ninth grade.

As the district official clarified, neither students' age nor their educational attainment prior to arrival in the United States were deciding factors in their placement, but rather only their ability to provide documentation of former schooling. Requiring refugee students to provide official transcripts in order to place them in an age-appropriate grade does not take into account the very nature of their pre-migratory conditions. More specifically, this problematic policy does not recognize the particular barriers that refugee youth might encounter in accessing and retrieving their transcripts, such as the nature of education in contexts of conflict or the complexity of the resettlement process. Students who come from countries afflicted with war and daily violence are often forced to abandon their schooling due to safety concerns. Additionally, due to the institutional collapse that often accompanies war, day-to-day operations at schools, including providing students with transcripts and other documents, are interrupted. Even when students flee to neighboring countries, the resettlement process can also prove to be a barrier to their ability to obtain the requisite documentation. Refugee families who are chosen for resettlement are often notified of departure dates within weeks and sometimes even days of resettlement. This does not give them adequate time to deal with the bureaucracies of public schools in low-income neighboring countries, which are typically underresourced, overextended, and struggling to meet the needs of their own citizens, not to mention refugees (Abu El-Haj et al. 2018; Dryden-Peterson 2015).

Even the few students who were fortunate enough to come to the United States with their transcripts often lingered in age-inappropriate grades, as a result of changes at the district level. Ms. Williams, a district official explained:

So, the process of having credits transferred is actually a centralized process. It used to be that every school in the district was doing this for their school, which was much faster, but each school was doing it differently, so the school district decided to do it to make it standard. It used to be six people who did this at the district level, but now only three people are doing this process this year. Unfortunately, because of this we have been *very* backlogged this year, so if you have been waiting on us to do this for you this year, we apologize for the wait.

The move to centralize the credit transfer process essentially nearly stripped the district's three hundred public schools of the capacity of handling this responsibility—a task that is critical to the lives of refugee students—and put in into the hands of *three* district employees. Of the 202,538 students enrolled in the School District of Philadelphia in the 2018–2019 academic year, (School District of Philadelphia 2018) approximately 13.1 percent or 26,532 students were foreign born. While there is no way to estimate how many of these students came to their schools with transcripts that needed to be processed, one can only imagine that *three* employees cannot begin to meet their needs in a timely manner. By removing authority from individual schools, in order to centralize and standardize school control, the district caused more harm to an already vulnerable population of students. Refugee students were placed in inappropriate grades as they awaited for their transcripts to be processed.

The Effects of Inappropriate Grade Assignment

I met Yasin through my year-long participant observation at the refugee resettlement agency. Yasin had fled Iraq with his wife, Hoda; son, Ziad; and daughter, Noor, to Syria in 2008. While in Damascus, Ziad enrolled in a public school and completed his high school studies in the liberal arts track, hoping to enroll in business school upon graduation. Unfortunately, violence began to break out in Syria, and Yasin's family was forced to search, again, for safety. Two years after they registered with the UNHCR, they were selected for resettlement to the United States. Before leaving Syria, Yasin was able to procure both Ziad's high school diploma and Noor's transcripts from her first year of college. In the family's first meeting with the school administrators, they were informed that Ziad would be placed in the ninth grade, even though he had brought his diploma with him and was eighteen at the time. Ziad and his mother Hoda spoke to me about his experience:

ZIAD: I finished high school in Syria. And so they said you need papers, you need papers to document stuff. So I brought them papers, papers from the school.
HODA: We have been waiting, and I am worried because Ziad loves school, and he wants to learn!
SALLY: So you brought them the diploma from Syria?
ZIAD: I brought all the paperwork, all of my records of my education

from Iraq, *and* my diploma from Syria. I had brought all of this so I can finally go from tenth grade to eleventh grade, and then maybe even skip that year and go to college. But I kept waiting, and nothing happened!

By the time I met Yasin, Ziad had been waiting for nearly two years for his diploma to be translated and for his Syrian high school credits to transfer, but to no avail. At a community meeting, Yasin shared his concerns with district officials about Ziad's grade assignment:

So, my son, Ziad, he was a twelfth grader in Syria. He graduated already, and we have his certificates all notarized from the Syrian Ministry of Education and everything. But they still have not processed those certificates. Now, he came here to Liberty High School, and they put him in ninth grade. He is very upset because all of his classmates are much younger than he is, and he doesn't want to come to school. He wants to go to college, like his sister. His sister, his older sister, when we came to Philadelphia, she began going to a local community college and he wants to do the same. Ziad is really giving us a hard time at home, I have to force him to come to school every morning. Is there any way for him to go to community college like his sister did?

Yasin spoke to me about his worries for Ziad as well. The combination of being surrounded by much younger classmates coupled with his desire to enroll in college had slowly chipped away at his former love of school. Ziad's refusal to attend school did not reflect a disinterest in education, but instead revealed a form of resistance against a system that arrested his aspirations for postsecondary education. Yasin's hopes for his son were dashed when he was informed by a district representative that Pennsylvania required a high school diploma (or its equivalency) for college enrollment. This left youth who had been assigned inappropriate grades little choice but to persist in their high schools, in hopes of someday attaining a high school diploma.

Some students, too frustrated with this age gap, did not persist at Liberty High. Layla's[2] brother Hussein—an eighteen-year-old student who had left Jordan in the middle of his eleventh grade year and was also placed in the ninth grade as a result of missing transcripts—shared his feelings about his placement:

I didn't see the point [of staying in school]. I was eighteen and surrounded by fourteen-year-olds! It was ridiculous. I had already done all of this! How long would it take me to finish high school? And then what? How long will it take me to finish college? How old would I be when I finish THAT? And what happens after that? It wasn't for me. I needed to work, to earn money, to be an adult. I already was an adult! But I was surrounded by these babies! I didn't have patience for that. So I left.

Hussein's narrative illustrates how the shame of being held back, combined with the infantilizing effect of this delay, can act as a real obstacle to educational advancement. As an eighteen-year-old, he perceived his grade placement as a barrier to his conceptualizations of adulthood, which were based in chronological age as well as access to higher education. Looking into the future and projecting the length of time required to earn an American high school diploma, a task he had already completed in Jordan, Hussein deemed American schooling unworthy of the investment. If Hussein were able to earn all his credits on time, he would earn his high school diploma at the age of twenty-one, and *then* begin his college journey. Not willing to wait until his mid-twenties to become "an adult," which he equated with earning a living, Hussein abandoned schooling at the end of his ninth-grade year, joining his father in minimum-wage labor, stocking shelves at a local grocery store. With his earnings, Hussein helped his family of seven survive and continue to afford the high rent of their three-bedroom row-home.

Ziad and Hussein's experiences highlight the problems that arise when schools do not respond to the unique needs of refugee students, including interruptions and foundational gaps in their educational histories. Furthermore, the district's policy of placing students in grades several years behind their peers has negative effects on students' educational aspirations and on their future life chances. Feelings of embarrassment and shame arise from being the eldest among their peers. The frustrations caused by moving backward rather than toward progress may eventually cause refugee students to lose their love of and motivation for schooling. Asking older refugee students—especially those who need to contribute financially to the survival of their families—to wait several years before they can access the benefits espoused by schooling is simply not feasible. Understanding the long road ahead, they simply cannot afford to put off the pressures that texture their lives in the present.

Aging Out of Secondary Education with Nowhere to Go
Exclusion from Public Education

Beyond placement, one of the most common experiences for refugee youth is an interruption in their educational trajectories. Refugee youth can go unschooled for many years in their own countries of residence due to the devastation of schools in their native countries (Bonet 2018; Boyden et al. 2002; Stevenson and Willott 2007; Winthrop and Kirk 2008). Even after they flee their native countries, refugee youth can experience a lag in their education due to repeated migration, a difference in educational systems between their country of origin and their interim countries of residence, and the need to work instead of attend school (McWilliams and Bonet 2016; Shakya et al. 2012). As a result, students can come to countries of resettlement like the United States having been unschooled for several years. This was the case for Seif Hassan.

I first met Seif (and his sister Layla) at the after-school arts program I ran at Liberty High. At the time Seif was a twenty-year-old high school sophomore. When I met him, Seif seemed like a jovial, outgoing young man, joking and laughing with his friends while he rehearsed a traditional Iraqi *dabke* (folk dance) with his friends for the school's annual Multicultural Day. In spite of his cheery demeanor, Seif had not had an easy life. He had spent the bulk of his adolescence in Jordan, where he was forced to drop out of middle school to join his father and elder brother in working as day laborers on construction sites in Amman. Upon arrival in Philadelphia, Seif was enrolled in Liberty High as a ninth grader along with his younger sister Layla and his younger brother Ayman, even though he was nineteen years old at the time. At first Seif resented his grade placement, but after some time, he eventually decided to make the best of it. He became involved in extracurricular activities, enrolled in an after-school tutoring program to improve his English, and made several friends at school. Seif was doing relatively well academically, particularly in his ESL class. Before coming to the United States, Seif could not speak any English, but in two years he was able to gain a rudimentary command of the language and served as his family's interpreter and mediator to the outside world. He accompanied his parents to their doctor's appointments, took and made calls on his parents' behalf, and wrote out checks for bills.

Near the end of Seif's eleventh grade year at Liberty High, he was called into a meeting with the assistant principal, Mr. Smith. In the meeting

Seif was informed that he could not return to school the following year as he had reached the age limit for public education in Pennsylvania—twenty-one years old: a process that teachers and administrators called being "twenty-one'd." Mr. Smith informed Seif that he could complete that academic year, but that he could not return for senior year. Seif pled with Mr. Smith to complete his last year, but Mr. Smith apologetically told him that this was school policy and that there was nothing to be done. Seif was forced to leave, only one year shy of a high school diploma.

Second Chances Program

The only help that Mr. Smith was able to offer Seif was by providing him with information about the Second Chances Program (SCP), an adult education program offered by the school district for adult students (above seventeen years of age) who wished to earn credits toward their high school diploma. Seif described the immense loss he felt when he was forced out of his school. Not only had Seif managed to build a community of friends and become a regular member of extracurricular activities at Liberty High, but he was also able to secure part-time employment that accommodated his school schedule. Seif operated a forklift at a local warehouse after school to help support his large family and to cover his own personal expenses. Due to the timing of the SCP classes, Seif lost his job at the warehouse, which put a financial strain on the family. Seif also reported feeling isolated at the SCP classes, where he did not know any one. At Liberty High, Seif had become familiar with his teachers and classes and was a part of a cohort of students he had become well acquainted with. In this new context, he was a newcomer, once again.

Seif also reported struggling with the academic content of the SCP classes, which was designed for adult students who had not completed high school and did not have an ESL component. The program was only available at four schools in the entire district and offered students six to nine credits a year. For students like Seif, whose former rosters were mostly composed of ESL classes (he spent three out of seven periods in ESL classes per day at Liberty High), transitioning to a learning context where he received no ESL instruction, and where he was expected to learn difficult subjects such as Algebra 2 and Biology without any ESL supports, would prove to be nearly impossible. In order to make adequate progress at SCP, he would have to earn the maximum amount of class credits in subjects—which, according to Seif, were well out of his reach. Seif reported feeling "lost in class" much of the time in SCP classes:

> The thing is that I am totally a mess in class, and completely confused. The teachers don't like to answer our questions. So sometimes, when the teacher is talking and explaining something, and I can't understand it, I ask someone, another student who speaks Arabic and English so he can translate and help me understand what the teacher is talking about. So the teacher sees me talking, and he looks at me, and he says "Well, you get a zero, that's it." . . . So now, I sit quietly in the class. I don't understand anything, but at least I am not getting in trouble.

Without any ESL support built into the program, and with teachers who seem suspicious when English language learners (ELLs) speak their native language in the class, even when they are simply seeking out assistance from bilingual students in the class, Seif was at a loss. Seif was effectively silenced in a class that was inaccessible to him and where he was punished for his attempts to learn. Interestingly enough, this was similar to his siblings' experience in their own ESL classrooms. Layla and Ayman had experienced similar silencing techniques in their own classrooms in Liberty High, where teachers required complete obedience and accepted no speaking from students, even if it was for the purposes of asking questions either of their teacher or their peers for clarification. However, unlike his siblings, Seif was embedded into a context where his linguistic needs were ignored, and as a result felt particularly vulnerable.

The Effects of Shrinking Adult Education Programs for ELLs

After several weeks of attending classes at SCP, Seif became increasingly concerned about his learning and asked me to help him. I called an SCP administrator on Seif's behalf, probing about his progress but also what his other options might be since the program did not seem to address his needs as an ELL. A SCP counselor informed me that it would take Seif at least three more years to earn the amount of credits required for graduation, and that is only if he earned full credits in each class he took— which she was doubtful about since SCP did not have adequate language supports. This meant that, in a best case scenario, Seif would be nearly twenty-six years old by the time he completed the program. The counselor recommended that Seif look into general educational development (GED) classes instead, as this would allow him to take the tests any time, without having to attend daily classes.

While there were several GED programs in Philadelphia, Seif could not find one near his home that would accommodate his language needs. Nancy, the director of the refugee resettlement agency that had resettled Seif and his family, confirmed this problem:

> A few years ago, in the Northeast—no, in Philadelphia in general, I want to say there were at least thirty-five state-funded adult education programs available to folks. That included GED classes, ESL classes, and other classes as well. So Iraqis would have had access to those, they would have found them, and they would have done it, and they could have done much of it on their own. Now there are only six classes in the whole city. So the likelihood of them being able to find one in their local community is . . . the odds there are not very good.

Eventually Seif found a GED center that catered to ELLs, but it was an hour away from Seif's house and required two forms of public transportation. Since Seif was still employed part-time to help support his large family to survive in Philadelphia, this commute proved to be a problem. Between his work commitments, the time that GED classes were offered, and the long commute involved, Seif could not make it work. Alternatively, if he chose to attend the classes at the center nearest him that offered programming in the morning, much of the content and subject matter included in the GED exams would be well beyond his reach as an ELL, basically replicating the problem that he was facing in the SCP. Seif's other choice was to stay in the SCP, where it would take him several years to earn a diploma.

Unfortunately, Seif did not have the opportunity to make a choice. Three months after Seif begun attending SCP classes, he was expelled from the program. Seif returned from a weeklong trip with his family to Michigan to visit his newly resettled relatives, only to be informed by the administrator of the program that he could no longer return due to his unexcused absences. When Seif tried to explain his absence, the administrator showed Seif the paperwork detailing the attendance policy, which clearly stated that only medical absences, substantiated by doctor's notes, would be accepted. The administrator showed Seif the student contract that he had signed upon enrollment, which included the program's stringent attendance policy. As it turns out, Seif had no idea what he was signing, as he was unable to decode the complex, high-level vocabulary in the contract. Seif tried to reason with the administrator, explaining that his extended family needed him, the only fluent English speaker, to help them settle into and navigate their new context, but the administrator would not budge. The SCP administrator told Seif that his "best bet was a GED class," echoing what the counselor had recommended before him. However, the scarcity of GED classes citywide and the absence of programs with an ESL component brought into question Seif's ability to ever earn a high school diploma (or its equivalency) and leverage that into his dream of a college degree.

Seif made one final attempt. He purchased the GED preparation materials, and attempted to prepare for the exams independently. After several failed attempts to pass the GED exam, Seif finally gave up. Fatima, his mother, told me that Seif was very depressed for a few months after he was expelled from the SCP. He spent all of his time in his room, lying on his bed, staring at the ceiling, barely eating, and chain-smoking all day long. Eventually, he emerged from his room and began to search for work. He secured a position as a forklift operator at the warehouse where he had once worked part-time while he attended Liberty High. Seif was paid minimum wage for this work, ($7.25/hour at the time) and did not receive health benefits.

Caught between Survival and Educational Aspirations

War, Displacement, and Resettlement

The responsibilities created by a resettlement program that prioritizes immediate financial self-sufficiency precluded refugee youth from secondary education altogether, including Samah Musa. I met Samah, a nineteen-year-old young woman, through her sister Ghada—a participant in the Liberty High programming offered by the local nonprofit where I was employed. Samah's family had suffered a great deal before being resettled in the United States. A few months after the American invasion of Iraq in 2003, Samah's father left the house for work one day and never returned. After several weeks, the authorities declared him *mafkood,* a missing person. This devastated the family and left them vulnerable. Due to sectarian violence and general lawlessness on the streets, Samah and her siblings stopped attending school. On days when Samah's mother, Baheera, needed to go to the market—which became an increasingly dangerous task since public spaces had become regular sites of violence—Samah and her siblings were forced to hide under furniture and remain completely silent, for fear of home invasions. Samah recalled, "One time, a man came and banged on the door, yelling, 'I know you're in there!' but we kept quiet, so he went away. Those times were the worst." The family also suffered financially due to Baheera's deteriorating health, which prevented her from working.

In 2004, Samah's family moved to Syria, but resettled in Yemen a few weeks later due to the high cost of living in Damascus. Life in Yemen was difficult for Samah, who worked at a hair salon every day after school to help support the family financially. Her Yemeni classmates derided her for being Iraqi and for being a refugee. Despite these challenges, Samah managed to become an excellent student and graduated from high school with high honors. Samah had hoped to earn a high school diploma in the United States and eventually pursue a degree in medicine to fulfill her dream of becoming a doctor. Seven years after she moved with her family to Yemen, Samah's family was granted resettlement to the United States.

Samah was thrilled with the news of their resettlement. However, the realities of the limited support her family received after their arrival in Philadelphia rendered her dream for higher education and a career in medicine untenable. Upon arrival in the United States, Samah met with a case manager at the resettlement agency who gave her grim news:

> When we came here, the case manager met with us and told us someone has to work to support the family because the money they gave us every month would be taken away after four months. My mother is an older woman, and you know how her health is. She has high blood pressure and diabetes, and has a hard time even walking sometimes, so I am not going to ever let her work! And my siblings are young, *too* young to work. They have to go to school. As a result, it fell on me to take care of everyone. I had to find work to take care of us.

Having been resettled without parents who could help shoulder the burden of supporting the family financially, it fell to Samah to do so. This meant that Samah would have to abandon her aspirations of attending school, to allow her younger siblings the opportunity to do so. School, college, and her dream of becoming a doctor would have to remain unfulfilled as her family's survival was her family's primary occupation now.

Obstacles to Employment in a Post-9/11 Context

Samah began searching for work the day after her meeting with her case manager, to ensure that she would be employed by the time the initial case management period and financial supports expired. The resettlement agency had agreements with a few employers in the city who agreed to hire refugees with limited English proficiency, including meat processing plants, fruit packing companies, and a superstore. However, even with the help of the resettlement agency, none of these job opportunities materialized for Samah. After weeks of failed job searches arranged by her case manager, Samah took matters into her own hands and tried to find work at big box stores and fast food restaurants near her home. She would leave the house in the morning and return several hours later frustrated and exhausted. None of the stores would even allow her to fill out an application:

> I have been to so many stores, and the thing is I *knew* that they were hiring. They all had signs on their stores! I would walk into the store and ask for an application and the person would just look at me, and especially at my hijab, and then say, "No, we don't have any work here for you."

Samah was quickly learning what it meant to be a Muslim in a post-9/11 U.S. context. As scholars have established, her identity as a Muslim proved to be an employment barrier (Derous, Nguyen, and Ryan 2009; Malos 2010; Yemane 2020), even in the northeastern region of Philadelphia, which has long housed generations of Arab Americans, including Palestinians, Moroccans, and Egyptians. While the male youth and adults in my study had no trouble procuring jobs in that community, Samah, the only female participant in my study who searched of a full-time job, was unable to access employment opportunities. Undoubtedly, Samah's language skills also affected this interaction. Samah had hoped to attend the language classes offered at the resettlement agency, but her job search interrupted her ability to make the ninety-minute journey on public transportation to get to class. Without access to public education or the English classes provided by the agency, Samah was unable to access any language instruction. As such, Samah's hijab and her limited English skills might have solidified her image as "foreign" and "an outsider," criteria that have long been linked to exclusion from employment opportunities in the United States (Quillian et al. 2019; Soylu and Buchanan 2013).

Painfully aware of the ticking clock of the dwindling support afforded to her family through their resettlement agency, Samah was becoming desperate. After two months of searching, the only work she could find was at a nearby Middle Eastern supermarket run by a Palestinian family, which only paid $5/hour—well below the minimum wage in Philadelphia at the time of $7.25/hour. The workload was heavy: Samah stocked shelves, carrying heavy boxes, and was a cashier sixty hours a week. Without access to a car, she had to rely on Philadelphia's notoriously unreliable public bus system to commute for three hours every day. Between work and commuting time, Samah was away from home almost eighty hours a week—a burden that began to wear on her quickly.

A Dream Denied

Prior to coming to the United States, Samah had envisioned a better life for herself and for her family, something she shared during our first interview:

> When I got here, I found that America was not at all what I had hoped or imagined. I had imagined that everything was in abundance and everything we needed would be here. My education, which is of course the highest priority, would be taken care of. Everyone would be comfortable and we won't be in need of anything. I thought that, finally, a country had opened its arms to us.

Like Heba, Samah articulated how the better life that she had imagined finding for herself and her family in the United States had evaded her. Unlike her siblings, who were too young to remember much about life in Iraq, Samah recounted witnessing violence on the streets the few times her mother felt it was safe enough to take the children out of the house. Samah was also old enough to remember her father. Samah rarely spoke of him, but when she did, tears often sprung to her eyes. Samah also framed Yemen as a space of endless suffering. It was there that she and her family were treated like second-class citizens; where she worked around the clock, the first half of the day at school, and the second half of the day at the salon to help support the family; and where she fought tooth and nail to stay on top of her studies. In light of all this, it should come as no surprise that America had come to hold such a place of hope for Samah. However, the realities that Samah faced quickly dismantled this vision:

> SALLY: How is the reality you see here in America different from what you thought?
>
> SAMAH: Look at what has happened to my education! I mean I am now nineteen years old, and in one or two years, I won't be eligible to attend high school here. So what am I going to do? How am I going to get my diploma and complete my college education? And it is just unthinkable for me not to complete my education. I mean it is the most important thing! And this year, I am working all the time, and I am never home. . . . It is driving me crazy that I am not going to school. Since I was in kindergarten, I was always interested in academics. I graduated high school with high honors! I wanted to go to college and become a doctor. But what can I do? There is no way out for me.

Samah's everyday lived reality, which was dominated by the struggle for her family's survival, affected her ability to realize her dream of continuing her education. In her Yemeni high school, she had chosen the more difficult Maths and Sciences route, rather than the Liberal Arts route, to ensure that she could prepare herself for a bachelor's degree in the sciences and then study medicine. She spoke of the countless sleepless nights she spent studying for her final exams and the struggle to maintain her status as an honors student while juggling her work responsibilities at the salon. It had been her dream, since she was in kindergarten, to be the first doctor in her family. It was this dream that got her through her most difficult days and what ultimately fueled her desire to come to the United States. However, in her American reality, her days were swallowed up by low-wage work, rendering her dream of attending Liberty High, the local high school, impossible. If she continued to work, she would inevitably age out of public education, but if she stopped working and attended school, her family's survival would be threatened. Faced with these realities, Samah saw "no way out" for herself.

Futile Attempts to Access Education

Samah's inability to access secondary and subsequently higher education was a source of much distress and anxiety for her, and for her mother, Baheera, who was concerned for Samah's future. During my weekly visits to the family, Samah would speak of the difficulties she faced at work and ask me if I could assist her in finding any educational alternatives. However, as a result of the reduction in adult education programs citywide, especially those with an ESL component, combined with the demands of her full-time job, Samah was unable to find GED classes that fit her schedule. The local GED testing center closest to Samah informed her that classes were held biweekly, for three hours at a time, and that they did not have any classes with an ESL component. After hearing about her time restrictions, they advised Samah to purchase the GED preparation book and attempt to study it independently, on her own schedule, and take the tests as many times as needed to pass. The test, which is composed of four modules— Science, Social Studies, Mathematical Reasoning, and Reasoning through Language Arts—required a varied and deep set of skills and knowledge that Samah would need to learn, and in a language that was almost completely foreign to her. In the few months that Samah had resided in the United States, she had managed to learn a few English words and phrases that she used on the bus and at work. Studying for the GED test independently would be a challenge even for a native English speaker, and hence nearly impossible for Samah.

Samah and I planned to work together, a few hours a week, in the attempt to prepare her for the GED exam. At the outset of our tutoring sessions, we met twice a week, preparing for these exams for two to three hours at a time, with the hopes that she could eventually sit for the exam. However, in spite of Samah's best intentions and efforts, our tutoring sessions were often postponed, and most times canceled. On several occasions, Samah would walk into the house after work, collapse on the couch, close her eyes, and soon thereafter fall asleep. Her mother would guide her to her bed and apologetically offer me dinner, and the planned tutoring session would turn into a visit with other members of the family. Other times, Samah would call a few hours before our meeting time and inform me that she had to cancel our session, telling me that after her eleven-hour day, she was simply too exhausted to meet. When we *did* actually manage to meet, Samah was often spent, agitated, and became easily frustrated with the material. She oftentimes lamented the fact that she had already completed her high school diploma in Yemen and could not see why she had to go through this again. Eventually, after a few months, I received a disheartening call from Samah. "It's just too hard, Sally. It's too much." She told me that she felt it was impossible to balance her heavy workload with her studies. The American refugee resettlement program, which prioritized financial self-sufficiency above all else, forced Samah to dedicate much of her waking hours to full-time, low-wage work. And as Seif had experienced, the structuring and programming of the few remaining GED classes available to Samah, none of which accommodated for her needs as an ELL, effectively excluded her from the opportunity to access a secondary education and subsequently her lifelong dream of a college education.

Effects of Exclusion on Youth Conceptualizations of Citizenship

Samah's Reevaluation of Refuge

Exclusion from education had a deep impact, not only on refugee youth's future life chances, but also on their relationship to the state. Samah shared:

> We lost so much—our home, our country—and life in Yemen
> was so hard. Finally, we were going to have a place, a new home.
> I thought America opened her arms to us, like a mother, and we
> could finally have a life here.

Samah had anticipated that the United States would be the "home" she had craved since her family's flight from Iraq. She had envisioned that in the bosom of this new mother, she and her family could finally find the settled life and stability in search of which they had fled from one country to the next. Her personification of America as a mother is a testament, not only of her hopes, but also to the transnational nature of the image of the United States as the world's police force. As an Iraqi citizen-subject who was forcibly displaced from her home after the American invasion made life impossible for her family, Samah was intimately familiar with the devastation caused by American military imperialism. Samah was also familiar with the image of the United States as a country imbued with liberal values such as freedom, democracy, and rights for citizens. There is perhaps no better testament to the power of these discourses than the buy-in from those, like Samah, who are displaced by their effects. Against all odds, Samah had faith in the promise of America as a welcoming mother who would take her in and finally make things right. However, the realities that awaited Samah in the arms of this "new mother" were sobering: eighty-hour weeks at a job that paid below the minimum wage, which prohibited her from attending high school and enrolling in college to become a doctor, her life's goal.

Approximately a year after Samah arrived in the United States and after she had given up her attempts to study for the GED exams, she shared with me: "If it were up to me, I swear, I would not stay here one more minute. America, it turns out that, she is a cruel mother and I would leave her if I could." Overburdened by work with no access to education or a meaningful career, it is not surprising that Samah had become intimately acquainted with the cruelty of the nation-state. What I had found particularly striking was Samah's persistent metaphor for the United States. Samah could have just as easily denounced America as a mother, understandably so after what she had been through. Perhaps Samah's choice to continue framing the United States that way was indicative of the ways that she found herself inextricably tied to the nation-state, much like a child is to a mother. Like a child, Samah was forced to be in an infantilizing relationship with the nation-state, with whom she could not break ties; a mother who provides for her child but, as she states, in the cruellest fashion. Samah is permitted to work, but only in the low-wage, no-benefit market, earning less than minimum wage. She is permitted to learn English, but only through the limited interactions between herself and the customers at the grocery store or other commuters on public transportation, learning just enough vocabulary to make do in those social situations. However, she is not permitted to pursue her dreams—an education—which will always be out of reach. A cruel mother indeed.

Samah's positionality as the provider for the family, which puts her in the role of the pseudo-mother of her siblings, also makes this metaphor particularly poignant. Perhaps as a mother of sorts herself, she looks at her own relationship with the United States through this lens. If she could sacrifice her own dreams for her family, why could America not provide for her? Every day, Samah witnessed her siblings Ghada and Adam live out her own dream of an education, and this was only made possible through her sacrifice. Her denouncement of America as a cruel mother might have been founded on the knowledge that motherhood could be, and perhaps should be, different, based on her own lived experience. In this light, it is not surprising then that Samah's exclusion from education permanently shifted her vision of the nature of the United States from a benevolent mother to a cruel one, and that it also led Samah to wish to abandon her as well.

Seif's Unlearning of the Promise of America

The experience of educational exclusion also affected Seif's former understandings of the nation-state. The following is an excerpt of an interview I conducted with him after his expulsion from Liberty High:

> So I left my country, lived in Jordan for a few years, and came as a refugee here. And how can a refugee be treated? I mean what does a refugee mean? You take someone in as a refugee and then throw them out in the streets?! Or do they take him all the way back to first grade?! They need to take him and place him where he belongs, in the right grade fitting his age and needs. And what would have happened if they would have done that, put me in the right grade? What would America have lost had it done that? What is America going to benefit when my future is ruined? I mean, America will benefit from me, right? So are they going to do this for free? No. I will end up paying them back times over. So where are the promises of this America, where is the democracy and where are the human rights?!

Invoking the category of "refugee," Seif perceived himself as deserving of particular rights, the least of which was the right to receive an education commensurate to his age and one that met his needs. Rather than receiving an American education that would pave the way to the settled life that he had hoped for, Seif came face to face with a reality marked with obstacles and repeated instances of exclusion. Seif critiqued the effects of the rigid school policy that caused him to be placed in the "wrong" grade, and the subsequent exclusion from Liberty High School and then *again* from the Second Chances Program—an exclusion that felt akin to being "thrown into the streets." Similar to Samah, Seif made a move to personify America, and in a sense depicted himself in a direct struggle with the nation-state. Rather than a cruel mother, Seif portrayed America as a tightfisted patron, one who refused to help him even though it was well within her ability to do so. Seif described America as one who has stood idly by and watched as his future imploded, even though she would benefit from his success. He articulated an expectation to "repay America back times over," presumably in the form of taxes and other duties expected of citizens. More fundamentally, Seif articulated a complex definition of citizenship, both as a set of rights and responsibilities and an interactive process that should address the particular needs of refugees. In exchange for fulfilling his duties and responsibilities as a citizen, Seif had expected America to invest in his education and future.

More important, Seif asked the question, "What does a refugee even mean?" The answer to this question has been at the heart of many philosophical queries, perhaps best captured in Arendt's seminal piece "We Refugees," in which she examines the fraught relationship between a refugee and their new contexts ([1943] 2009). While Arendt's essay centered the lives of Jewish refugees who had fled the Nazi regime and survived concentration camps, her work captures the struggles of Iraqi refugees within their new contexts. Arendt speaks of the various forms of loss that a refugee experiences, including that of one's home, which removes a person's ability to navigate their daily life; one's occupation, which robs them of the knowledge that they are useful members of society; and of their language, which removes one's ability to communicate and understand the simplest of feelings and gestures. Being a refugee also demands that one take on an almost impossible optimism. Those who have been forcibly replaced must somehow forget the very tragedies that transformed them into a refugee in the first place. Reminded that no one wants to hear of these tragedies, refugees instead try to look to the future, to what they might be able to achieve in their new homelands. Knowing that the past that haunts refugees cannot in fact be forgotten, Arendt critiques this optimism that she herself takes on, acknowledging that it can only mask so much. Death, rather than life, becomes a constant companion, and many of those who seemed the most optimistic attempt to end their unbearable lives—those textured by feelings of shame and degradation for being saved. In an attempt to make a new life, the refugee will try to remake themselves in a new image to become as close to the native as possible, going as far as pledging loyalty to their new country—a futile endeavor as they will always be marked as an outsider. Arendt urges the reader not to judge refugees for these attempts, as the alternative would be for them to be reduced from citizens of their new countries to stateless humans—a fate to be avoided at all costs since it was this very statelessness that robbed the Jews of their humanity, making them worthy of mass extermination without protest or objection from the rest of the world (Arendt [1951] 1979).

Much of Arendt's argument applies to refugee youth like Seif and Samah, who came to their new contexts with a similar optimism. Hoping to de-center their past life, marked by conflict, displacement, and financial insta-bility, these young people attempted to look to the future, in order to make a new life. Seif invested in his education, attending after-school classes, making new friends, and planning for a future. Samah desired to put the indignities of poverty and second-class citizenship behind her, hoping that America would finally give her the home she desired. Refugee youth were even willing to suspend disbelief in a country that had invaded, oc-cupied, and plundered their own, and came with unrealistically optimistic expectations—hoping to find rights that they believed the refugee label espoused. For Seif and Samah in particular, the promise of resettlement to America was, in essence, a chance at a new life, vis-à-vis educational opportunity. When that promise was broken, the optimism refugee youth once held, as well as their desire to belong, fell away, leading to an honest critique of the nation-state. In his testimony, Seif interrogates the liberal ideals espoused in the promise of America, such as democracy and human rights, and articulates the dissonance between his everyday experiences and his former conceptualizations of American citizenship.

Seif's account also attests to the power of the transnational myths about America. It is in his testimony that we can carefully track the ways in which American exceptionalism (Koh 2002; Lipset 1997; Madsen 1998; Tyrrell 1991) has successfully been exported, especially to those who have been dispossessed by its effects. *American exceptionalism,* a term that is be-lieved to be originally coined by Alexis de Tocqueville in 1831, refers to the historical perception of the uniqueness of the United States as compared to other developed nations, due to its distinctive origins, doctrine, history, and political and religious institutions (Shafer 1991). The American na-tional imaginary has long been anchored to democratic values, which are seen as essential to American principles as well as deserving of spread-ing on a global scale (Abu El-Haj 2015). In his testimony, Seif calls into question the values that he had assumed would be the basis for his inclu-sion, the very liberal ideals espoused by the "moral authority" of the world (Koh 2002). Specifically, Seif challenges the presence of democracy in the United States—the main justification for military intervention in Iraq. It is this very democracy, delivered by the military arm of American imperialism, that Seif comes to question when faced with the inability to access what he perceived to be the most basic of rights, an education.

The other value that Seif interrogates is human rights, on which the United States has long claimed to be an authority. The United States has had a leading role in promoting international human rights, evidenced by its leading role in the creation of the United Nations as well as the drafting of the Universal Declaration of Human Rights (Ignatieff 2011). The U.S. government has historically spearheaded legislation and tied funding to progress in human rights. The United States also boasts some of the most effective NGOs and nonprofits dealing with issues of human rights. That said, the United States also has an infamously checkered history with regard to human rights, both within and beyond its borders. This includes the maintenance of capital punishment in spite of the orders of the International Court of Justice, holding Guantanamo Bay detainees without Geneva Convention hearings, the Abu Ghraib prison scandal of 2004, and the assertion of the use of legality in self-defense. Scholars point to the multiple ways that American exceptionalism takes shape in relationship to human rights (Ignatieff 2011; Koh 2002; Moravcsik 2005). First, although the United States signs on to international humanitarian and human rights laws, it exempts itself through various means, including reservation, nonratification, and noncomplication. Second, the United States has and continues to maintain a double standard by holding itself and its friends to a more lenient standard that it does its enemies. Finally, by insisting on the tradition of self-contained authority, the United States denies the jurisdiction of international human rights law. This is perhaps best captured in the Bush administration's response to 9/11: the establishment of Homeland Security; the deeply troubling creation of extralegal zones such as Guantanamo Bay and extralegal persons who are considered as "enemy combatants" even if they are American citizens on U.S. soil; a new, top-down, military form of "promoting democracy"; and finally a policy emphasizing unilateralism—as perhaps the ultimate and worst version of double standards bred by American exceptionalism (Koh 2002).

As an Iraqi refugee, Seif had found himself displaced by the military machinery of "democracy" and "human rights," so it was not surprising that he came to question the nation-state. However, what is striking is that it was his experiences within the proverbial "belly of the beast" that had led him to do so. Both Samah and Seif, like most refugee youth, came with aspirations, not only for an education, but also for true inclusion and a settled life. Samah had described a hopeful relationship between her and America as one best captured by the imagery of herself as a weary daughter and the state as a mother who held her arms open wide, waiting to provide rest after a treacherous journey. Seif had hoped that America would be the patron, with whom he would have a relationship as an equal, where he would gain rights and in return "pay back times over," ostensibly in the form of being an upright citizen who pays taxes, follows the laws of the land, and lives a righteous life. And yet, for both Seif and Samah, it is not the hypocrisy, violence, and devastation of their native Iraq by American military imperialism that finally extricates them from their visions of becoming full members of their new communities—it is the stripping of their educational aspirations within its own borders. Their pre-resettlement optimism that had made life and suffering tolerable was laid bare, exposing its cruel nature (Berlant 2011).

Like their younger refugee counterparts in the previous chapter, young adult refugees come to their newly resettled contexts with similar pre-migratory challenges and educational aspirations. At the opening of this chapter we met Heba, a nineteen-year-old ninth grader at Liberty High. Heba articulated the hopes that many young adult refugees shared for higher education that would lead to stable careers, and yet were unable to achieve. Some students, like Seif, came to their new contexts with significant interruptions in their education, a typical refugee experience. These students were then placed in grades several years behind their native counterparts. This policy, as well as rigid maximum age limits, served to exclude them from public education. The family makeup of young adult refugees can also have significant effects on young people's ability to access public education. Resettled without parents who can serve as primary wage-earners, refugees like Samah were forced to prioritize work over education. The dearth of adult education programming in Philadelphia, specifically programs that accommodate the linguistic needs of refugees—which have been deeply affected by budget cuts at the state and local level—left students with nowhere to turn. Without any options, young adult refugees are forced to forego their former educational aspirations and instead are coerced into the low-wage workforce.

In spite of their direct experiences with American imperialism, these young people came to their new contexts with a great deal of hope for their futures. They had hoped to access a settled life vis-à-vis education and a high-paying career that would lift them and their families out of poverty. As those who had experienced second-class citizenship in neighboring Arab countries, they had bought into American exceptionalism. In the United States, they would finally access the "promises of America": stability, inclusion, and freedom. However, the realities that they faced there stripped them of their optimism and their dreams. In contrast to the settled lives they had envisioned for themselves, young adult refugees were saddled with daily lives that were textured with low-paying, hard work. These young people, who once hoped to become full citizens, were instead molded into laboring citizens—those whose futures would be defined by an endless struggle for survival. Faced with these obstacles and burdens, young adult refugees come to understand that the America they had believed in was but a myth, and were finally disabused of their hopes for the rights they once believed were owed to them. The next chapter takes on another basic human right that refugees had hoped to find upon resettlement: healthcare.

5

Healthcare

The Debilitation of Iraqi Bodies across Borders

I met Warda Mustafa at a community meeting hosted by the refugee resettlement agency for Iraqis. Warda, a fifty-six-year-old mother of seven, wore a black hijab to cover her hair and a black abaya, a full-length outer garment worn by some Muslim women. Her daughter Heba, whose story opened the last chapter, later explained to me that Warda had once worn colorful clothes, but had taken up wearing all black since the death of Heba's father, over a decade ago. Warda never wore makeup in public—another sign of grief and respect taken on by many Arab women after the death of a close family member. Warda had a ready smile, which lit up her round, pale face. She and Heba watched the latest Egyptian miniseries religiously, and Warda often teased me, saying, "Listening to you speak is like watching TV!" Warda loved to laugh, and had a light, cheery disposition. Warda seemed much older than her age, with her slow walk and slightly bent back.

Soon after we met, Warda enthusiastically agreed to take part in my study, and suggested that we meet at her home where we could speak in private. When I arrived at Warda's home, I was greeted at the door by Heba who whispered, "Don't be alarmed when you see Mom. She's OK." I nodded in agreement, and Heba walked me over to the living room where Warda was sitting on a low couch. Warda apologized for cuts on her cheeks and a big bruise developing under her chin, and explained that she had suffered a nasty fall the day before when her knees buckled as she walked down the stairs. Since then, her legs had become quite swollen, making it hard to move. Warda had not sought medical care for her injuries, even though she was still covered by state-funded insurance. She explained, "I have had a very hard time with doctors in America." Due to her limited English language skills, she was unable to call the doctor's office to make appointments. At the doctor's office, she could communicate with healthcare professionals through a city-funded phone service that provides medical interpretation, but had no linguistic support at home. Exasperated, Warda asked: "How can I go to the hospital alone when I am having a hard time even walking? . . . And I am in pain *all the time!* . . . You know, we were very grateful to be resettled here, but we need a medical system that works for us."

I had arrived for my first visit to Warda's home armed with a list of questions about Heba's schooling as well as Warda and Heba's overall resettlement experience, but the conversation quickly turned to Warda's health challenges. Warda suffered from Type 2 diabetes, hypertension, and chronic pain in her knees, making it necessary for her to use a cane to walk. Falling down the stairs had limited her mobility even further, making her stiffer and increasing her pain significantly. She was frustrated with her inability to access the medical care that she needed, even though she was still covered by the state-funded Refugee Medical Assistance program since she had been resettled only five months prior.

As our conversation progressed, Warda shared more about what she and her family had survived before her resettlement to the United States. Her youngest son, Samir, began to have seizures at the age of seven that did not respond to medication. Samir underwent surgery in an attempt to remove the part of the brain that was responsible for his seizures. As a result of complications during surgery, Samir became permanently paralyzed in the left half of his body. A few years later, Warda's husband was diagnosed with stage four cancer. Warda, who no longer trusted the doctors in Iraq, spared no expense and traveled with her husband to a reputable cancer center in Kuwait for treatment. The doctors informed Warda that the cancer had already spread, and that there was little to be done. Warda's husband died within a few months of his diagnosis. As detailed in chapter 4, Tarek, Warda's son who began a cargo transportation business in order to help support the family, was stopped by an armed Sunni militia on the road on one of his deliveries. The militia captured his Shia friend and business partner Ali, and forced Tarek at gunpoint to drive away. It was Ali's family's increasing financial demands escalating to threats of violent retribution that eventually led Warda to flee the country with her children.

During our conversation, it became clear that many of Warda's health problems emerged and were exacerbated by the difficulties that she and her family faced. The months that she spent caring for her husband and his death took a toll on her health, and soon thereafter she was diagnosed with hypertension. After her son Tarek began to receive increasingly violent threats, Warda's health began to worsen: her diabetes, which she once controlled through a strict diet, now required insulin. The pain in Warda's joints began in Syria, soon after she and her family fled under cover of night in an attempt to avoid further threat by Ali's family. At first the pain was manageable, but then it began to keep her up nights, making it difficult for her to move independently. She took the full safe dose of over-the-counter pain medication every day in order to manage. Warda was aware that she needed medical attention, but she struggled to access it for the decade leading up to resettlement to the United States. Samir's paralysis had shaken Warda's faith in the capability of Iraqi doctors. Still, desperate for relief from her symptoms, Warda sought out treatment in Iraq. However, healthcare in Iraq, once the envy of the Middle East, had all but collapsed. She tried once again in Syria, but the "good doctors"—those who practiced outside of the government hospitals—were expensive. She couldn't afford private care since she had spent most of the family money on her husband's treatment as well as paying off Tarek's debts to Ali's family. She had hoped that she would finally access high-quality healthcare in the United States, but that was not to be.

As a monolingual Arabic speaker, Warda struggled to make appointments with doctors for her various ailments. Heba was learning English at school but often could not manage the complicated automated instructions involved with attempting to reach a healthcare professional. Even when Warda *could* make an appointment with the help of an English speaker, such as a neighbor or friend, getting to the hospital proved to be another challenge. Her local subway station stop had only one elevator, which had been broken since she arrived, making it difficult for her to navigate the two steep flights of steps to the platform. The hospital, which was a subway and bus ride away from her house, was virtually inaccessible to Warda without the help of another person. Since she was resettled to the United States with Heba, who was in school during outpatient hospital and clinic hours, this left Warda with no means of getting to the hospital. When in dire need, Warda had depended on Heba to accompany her to the hospital, but this required Heba to miss school and later be chastised by her teachers for her absences, who informed Heba that her truancy could lead to repeating a grade. Heba, who was already several years older than her peers, simply could not afford to repeat a year as this could result in her aging out at twenty-one before achieving a high school diploma.

After learning this, Warda avoided relying on Heba as much as she could. This left Warda in constant pain and unable to get the medical attention she needed, causing her much anxiety and distress that further exacerbated her health problems.

Warda was not alone in her health struggles. Refugees are often exposed to long-term violence, persecution, and harassment, as well as economic and political instability stymieing their ability to access basic necessities including medical care—all factors that can have detrimental effects on their health. Research suggests that Iraqi refugees suffer from various health problems. In fact, a study conducted with five thousand participants found that 50 percent of Iraqis suffer from a chronic disease such as cardiovascular disease, cancer, arthritis, chronic pain, diabetes, frequent or severe headache or migraine, insomnia, neurological disorders, digestive disorders, and respiratory diseases (Al-Hamzawi et al. 2014). These health problems have also been confirmed among Iraqis who have been resettled in to the United States, as 60 percent of them reported suffering from one chronic health condition and 37 percent reported suffering from two or more conditions (Taylor et al. 2014). According to the Centers for Disease Control and Prevention (2014), 14.1 percent of Iraqi adult refugees had latent tuberculosis infections and 15.2 percent were hypertensive. The same review found that 7 percent of Iraqi refugees under five years old were severely malnourished, and 29.6 percent of women of childbearing age were anemic.

Given the statistics above, it might be tempting to hyperfocus on refugees' pre-resettlement experiences as the primary determinants of their health needs. Seen from this perspective, the health status of resettled refugees is framed as a static entity, shaped by the difficulties and suffering that texture their life before they arrive. While these conditions undoubtedly have dire effects on the health and well-being of refugees, this chapter puts forth two important perspectives that warrant further attention. First, we must consider the ways that the health conditions and debilitation of Iraqis has been shaped by the military machinery of U.S. imperialism (Puar 2017). This view pushes against the often depoliticized debilitation and slow death (Berlant 2007) of those whose bodies are intentional targets of war and occupation. Second, the health of refugees must be understood, not as a static entity, but affected by their post-resettlement conditions (Burnett and Peel 2001). As the previous chapters have underscored, Iraqi refugees are likely to face several chronic challenges in their new contexts, including inadequate financial supports, poverty, social isolation, and lack of access to adequate educational programming, to name a few. This chapter traces the ways that life in Iraq and in neighboring low-income countries has shaped the physical and mental health needs of refugees, while also documenting the ways that U.S. resettlement policies limit refugees' ability to access, navigate, and maintain adequate healthcare that addresses these needs. Shut out of an U.S. healthcare system that prioritizes profit over health, refugees begin to question their rights, citizenship, and indeed the nation-state.

The Debilitation of the Iraqi People

Suffering and Surviving

I first met Fatima Zaydoon in fall 2012 at a high school recital where her children Layla and Seif performed. After the recital, Layla introduced me to her mother, who smiled as she said, "So *you* are the Sally that Layla won't stop talking about!" Fatima, who stood at 5 feet 9 inches, had an imposing presence. She wore a brightly colored dress, a hijab that matched her outfit, and a full face of makeup, including bright red lipstick. Fatima exuded confidence and had a regal manner about her, speaking slowly and carefully. Fatima was the only mother in my study who held a full-time job. She had been resettled from Jordan to Philadelphia with her husband and four of her children. Her eldest son, Jawad, lived in Iraq with his grandfather. In our first meeting, Fatima asked me several questions about my study: "What was the research project about?" "Why was I interested in Iraqi students in particular?" "Who would read this report?" "Would it be confidential?" "Were there any foreseeable drawbacks or dangers that her children would experience if they participated in the study?" And finally, Fatima asked if she could be present during my conversations with her children. I answered all of her questions as thoroughly as possible, emphasizing that I actually preferred that she participate in the conversations, to get her perspective as well. After our nearly thirty-minute conversation, Fatima, who seemed satisfied with my answers, invited me to her home the following week, assuring me that she would have the consent forms for her and her children signed and ready for me upon my arrival.

When I arrived at Fatima's home, I saw that her long, dark brown hair was pulled back into a neat ponytail, and a strip of cloth was tied tightly around her forehead. After she greeted me, Fatima apologetically explained, "Pardon the silly Rambo-looking cloth. I have it there because of my horrible headaches." After drinking the sweet cardamom tea that Layla served me, Fatima and her children Seif, Layla, and Hussein sat down with me for our first family focus group. Like Warda, Fatima spent much of our first meeting together speaking to me about her health. Before coming to the United States, she had suffered from chronic daily migraines, which would often confine her to her bed for several days in a row. Fatima also experienced severe pain in her limbs, which resulted in difficulty standing for long periods, walking, and lifting heavy objects. This proved to be very limiting for Fatima as it affected her ability to do her job as a member of the housekeeping staff at a downtown Philadelphia hotel. Fatima took the job soon after her family arrived in Philadelphia to help support her family of six. Her husband found work at a local Middle Eastern grocery store two months after they arrived, but without her salary, the family simply could not survive. Seif and Hussein also worked to pitch in. Fatima searched for work for three months, and the only employment available was at the hotel. Fatima's chronic pain made an already physically taxing job more difficult. The scent and fumes from the cleaning supplies she was required to use triggered her migraines. Furthermore, the act of bending over to clean and lifting mattresses took a toll on her body, exacerbating the pain she experienced daily. She spent much of her evenings and days off in bed, with the curtains drawn, attempting to recover from the workweek. Like Warda, Fatima managed by taking over-the-counter pain medication every day. While this helped with her joints, her migraines were still frequent and severe.

One of my visits to the family occurred at the tail end of one of Fatima's worst migraines. This migraine had lasted an excruciating forty-eight hours, causing Fatima's vision to blur as well as difficulty speaking, known as transient aphasia. Her husband had begged for her to allow him to take her to the emergency room (ER), but she had adamantly refused. Her state-funded insurance had long expired, and her employer did not offer her any health insurance. Familiar with how costly ER visits can be, Fatima decided to just bear the pain. It was so intense that Seif had to call her employer, explaining that she simply could not make it to work on the third day of her migraine. She rarely called in sick even though she was constantly suffering from chronic pain, in fear of losing her job, but simply could not get out of bed this time. Fatima later explained to me that this had become her new normal, simply trying to cope with daily pain while attempting to do all that was required of her for her family's survival. When I asked about when she began to experience her symptoms, Fatima explained:

> Early on in my marriage, I got pregnant and was in a car accident. I was six months pregnant, and lost the baby. . . . I was just walking on the street, and a car hit me. The funny thing is that I was actually walking on the sidewalk, not on the street. Well that car . . . came all the way up to the sidewalk and hit me. Some luck I have, huh? [She laughs nervously.] When the car hit me, I flew up onto the car hood, and then I was knocked onto the ground, hard. When I landed on the concrete, I landed on my back and I hit the back of my neck on the sidewalk. . . . Since then, my body has not been the same. That is when the headaches and the pain started.

After the accident, Fatima was rushed to the hospital and treated for her injuries and her miscarriage, and released quickly. Fatima describes this time as one of the most difficult periods of her life. She had always wanted to have a large family and had lost her second child as a result of this accident, which was devastating for both her and her husband, Mohammed. Upon her release, Fatima felt unable to cope, take care of her son, or do her daily chores. Depressed and in pain, Fatima was bedridden for months, in spite of Mohammed's attempts to help her return to herself. Over time, her health problems began to increase. At first, she suffered from a migraine once or twice a month, but they became more incessant and acute. This was also the time that the chronic pain in her limbs emerged. Fatima's family grew more and more concerned about her health and were convinced that she needed medical attention. However, gaining access to adequate healthcare was nearly impossible, given the state of Iraq at the time.

Debilitation at the Hands of the U.S. Empire

Both Fatima and Warda are living examples of Jasbir Puar's concept of the "biopolitics of debilitation," defined as "the violent debilitation of those whose inevitable injuring is assumed by racial capitalism" (2017, xviii). Puar argues that capitalism, war, forced migration, and capital imperialism render some bodies as targets for injury (65). Puar also troubles the notion that populations debilitated by U.S. imperialism are "accidentally" harmed in the process of war. Imperialism creates disability in the global South while simultaneously diverting attention toward a liberalized understanding of disability in the global North, centering rights-based agendas and discourses (70). As a result, the focus is shifted toward the individual experience of disability and away from the ways that debility has been weaponized and unleashed on entire populations. Debilitation, Puar contends, is unique from "disablement" as it moves away from the exceptional event of becoming disabled to the slow wearing down of peoples who have been colonized and occupied. The biopolitics of debilitation not only acknowledges the higher numbers of disability among marginalized populations but also insists that debilitation is an intentional and strategic practice "deployed in order to create and precaritize populations and maintain them as such" (73).

All of Iraq's once healthy state institutions were devastated as a result of the two wars waged in Iraq and the severe sanctions imposed on the country. There exists no better testimony to the ravaging of Iraq than the country's healthcare system. During the forty-two days of the 1990–1991 Gulf War, more than ninety tons of bombs were dropped in Iraq by the U.S. coalition, specifically targeting civilian as well as military facilities (Dewachi 2017). Power plants, water sanitation systems, oil refineries, and communication networks were destroyed, as well as factories, bridges, and roads. In the months after the war, Iraqis lived with limited or no access to electricity, clean water, or telephone lines (Dewachi 2017). The war had undone decades of infrastructure building and put the lives of Iraqis at grave risk. The subsequent brutal sanctions, which triggered an era of "de-development" in Iraq, devastated its healthcare system—once considered the frontrunner of quality universal healthcare in the Middle East. The war and subsequent sanctions had transformed Iraq from a successful country to what development and relief organizations deemed a "place of death and sickness" (Dewachi 2017) and "social misery" (Puar 2017). Officially, the twelve years of sanctions were put into place to disarm the reconstitution of Saddam Hussein's regime from its biological, chemical, and nuclear weapons. Practically, the sanctions prevented the sale of oil, Iraq's number one export, and banned the import of various items that were deemed by the UN Security Council as potentially having both civilian and military purposes, including medications and vaccines that were critical for the well-being of Iraqi civilians (Dewachi 2017).

The effects of the war and sanctions on the health and well-being of the Iraqi population have been devastating. Hospitals lacked basic medical supplies and suffered from power outages, leaving doctors helpless to treat patients. Food insecurity and the lack of access to clean water were rampant, affecting vulnerable populations like children and the elderly disproportionately. UN agencies estimate that a third of Iraq's children are malnourished, a fourth are born underweight, a fourth have no access to clean drinking water, and 1 out of 8 children die before the age of five (Inhorn 2018). By 1999, only 41 percent of the population could access clean water, since the state could not afford to rebuild damaged water plants and pumps (Ismael 2008). By 2003, nearly 75 percent of the country's population was malnourished (Inhorn 2018). The sanctions induced one of the worst and most shocking increases in infant mortality in modern history (Dewachi 2017). These deaths were mostly caused by preventable and curable diseases such as malnutrition, diarrhea, and pneumonia, as well as measles and other diseases with effective vaccines. Maternal mortality was also on the rise. Iraqis also suffered from injuries sustained by electric shocks, falls in rubble, explosions, and gunshot wounds (Inhorn 2018). By the end of the sanction period, the Iraqi Ministry of Health reported that it was only able to meet 10 to 15 percent of the country's medical needs (Inhorn 2018).

The healthcare system was further destroyed by the U.S. invasion and occupation of Iraq in 2003. During this time, the United States destroyed medical infrastructure, breaking from nearly 150 years of adherence to medical neutrality, which prohibits the targeting of medical buildings and personnel, who are considered noncombatants (Puar 2017). This was rationalized by framing the Iraqi people as terrorists, which effectively blurred the lines between civilians and combatants (Dewachi 2017; Puar 2017). As Puar (2017) argues, the right to disable and maim is achieved through racializing civilians into insurgents. According to Hedges and Al-Arian's (2009) in-depth interviews with over fifty U.S. veterans who fought in Iraq, the war prevented soldiers from believing in the humanity of Iraqis. The war transformed Iraqis into objects that exist to thrill or destroy, and at times both. U.S. soldiers often "fell into a binary world of us and them, the good and the bad, those worthy of life, and those unworthy of life" (Hedges and Al-Arian 2009, xvi). In their testimonies, veterans confessed not only to killing but also denigrating, humiliating, and terrorizing Iraqi civilians. The term "haji" was used to demean Iraqis, similar to the term "gook" that was used to debase the Vietnamese and "raghead" for Afghanis. Soldiers regularly mocked "haji food," "haji music," and "haji homes." When U.S. soldiers raided Iraqi homes, they forced families to huddle in a corner at gunpoint while they ate the family's food and confiscated the family's possessions. Iraqi civilians were rounded up in indiscriminate and meaningless raids, and often stripped naked and left to stand in the brutal sun, all the while being physically and verbally abused. This framing of the Iraqi as nonhuman also resulted in the mass death of civilians. At the outset of the violence that followed the U.S. occupation of Iraq, approximately 1,000 civilians were dying weekly, 40 percent of those at the hands of U.S. soldiers (Gonzalez 2003). By 2011, the end of Operation Iraqi Freedom, the name given to the invasion and later occupation of Iraq, 162,000 Iraqis had been killed, 79 percent of whom were civilians (Iraqi Body Count 2013). As of this writing, approximately 200,000 civilians have been killed since the invasion and occupation of Iraq (Iraqi Body Count 2022). This number continues to increase on a daily basis.

The Iraqi healthcare system has been seriously affected by the flight of physicians from the country as a result of the attacks on medical personnel (Dewachi 2017). Hundreds of physicians were killed by militias and kidnapped by gangs for ransom, targeted as a result of their prior affiliations with the Ba'ath Party or as an intentional attempt to weaken Iraq's stability and infrastructure (Dewachi 2017, 3). Dewachi, a former medical doctor turned anthropologist, argues that the "mass exodus of Iraqi doctors . . . has been one of the central tragedies of Iraq's healthcare system" (25). Doctors have also suffered at the hands of patients' angry relatives who threaten physicians with violence if they do not pay reparations for the loss of their loved ones. As a result, many doctors refuse to treat very ill and dying patients, for fear of retaliation from their families.

The health of Iraqis has also suffered as a result of the toxic aftereffects of war. During the 1990–1991 Gulf War, the U.S. military experimented with the use of depleted uranium (DU), the waste product of the uranium enrichment process. While uranium is found in trace quantities in the Earth's soil and approximately one microgram is ingested by humans through food and drinking water over an average lifetime, DU is 60 times more radioactive than naturally occurring uranium (Inhorn 2018). DU is denser than lead, has a high melting point, and ignites when it fragments (Inhorn 2018). When DU explodes, it creates a respirable dust that then contaminates the site, which presents a grave hazard to the people in the vicinity (Inhorn 2018, 70). DU dust has a radioactive half-life of up to 4.5

billion years, exposing Iraqis to long-term and generational health risks. During the Gulf War, the U.S. military relied on DU for the destruction of enemy tanks and the strengthening of their own, and fired 90,000 DU shots at military and civilian targets (Inhorn 2018). During the invasion and subsequent occupation of Iraq, specifically 2003 and 2006, six *billion* rounds of DU rounds were fired by U.S. troops (Inhorn 2018). Effectively, the Middle East served as an experimental ground where nuclear armaments became normalized (Inhorn 2018).

This underacknowledged version of nuclear warfare has been correlated with an alarming increase in several diseases, including congenital birth defects, various types of cancer, and renal failure (Dewachi 2017). In Fallujah, a region of Iraq that sustained the worst damage by U.S. forces, reports have estimated a fourfold increase in cancer—particularly leukemia and lymphoma—as well as a twelvefold increase in cancer in children under the age of twelve. Approximately 15 percent of all births were of infants with congenital malformations. While researchers have debated the toxicity of DU, hair samples of mothers of children with malformations have shown statistically significant levels of uranium (Inhorn 2018). Alarmingly, these health effects are occurring at higher rates than those reported by survivors of Hiroshima and Nagasaki (Puar 2017; Inhorn 2018). Inhorn (2018) contends that "the future generations of Iraqis, living in places like Fallujah [are] the unwitting inheritors of the radioactive legacy of US military intervention" and that the use of DU may in fact be the "war's most lasting effect" (72). Basically, the debilitation (Puar 2017) of the Iraqi people has been achieved through the intentional targeting of medical infrastructure including healthcare institutions and physicians, in blatant disregard of medical neutrality; the maiming and death of civilians; and the use of nuclear munitions that will continue to shape the health and well-being of Iraqis for generations to come.

Access Interrupted: Fatima's Health Journey across Borders

Given the state of Iraqi healthcare in the late 1990s, it is no wonder that Fatima was unable to access adequate medical attention there. In fact, these precise conditions were what led Fatima and her family to leave Baghdad for Amman, Jordan, in fall 2000. By then, Fatima had five children—Jawad, Seif, Hussein, Layla, and Ayman—and she was adamant about keeping them safe. Jawad, who was already in secondary school, refused to leave with them, citing the importance of completing his education first. He begged Fatima to allow him to live with his grandfather, and after some time she acquiesced, after Jawad promised to move to Jordan after his graduation from college. Fatima and Mohammed sold their house and left Iraq searching for a better life, which included access to medical care.

Life in Jordan proved to be difficult for the family. Amman is an expensive city, and the money they had from selling their house was running out fast. Mohammed worked two jobs, but still could not afford to sustain the family alone. Seif was forced to drop out of school in order to help his father make ends meet. Fatima was willing to work, but her health simply did not allow it. Mohammed sought out medical attention for Fatima, but soon realized that without health insurance and the ability to afford private care, their only option was care by public sector doctors. Like many of the countries that Iraqis have fled to, the quality of care provided at public hospitals and clinics was grievously low. Unfortunately, she had no other option. After examining her, the doctors at a local clinic prescribed her painkillers for her migraines, and recommended that she begin physical therapy (PT) to address her knee pain. PT was beyond her family's financial reach, so Fatima relied on daily pain medication. Like Warda, Fatima had hoped that she could finally receive high-quality medical care in the United States, where her family was resettled eight years after arriving in Jordan. "America is supposed to have the best of everything," she exclaimed, "but not for refugees."

Gendered Dismissals

A few weeks after she and her family resettled to Philadelphia, Fatima had her initial health screening, a mandated aspect of refugee healthcare. Accompanied by Khaled, her bilingual case worker, she was able to communicate with the physician. She explained:

> You know Sally, when I first got here, I told the doctors all about my pain and my headaches. I tried to tell them that the headaches began when I had that accident. I know that is when all these problems started. I tried to tell the doctors that, but they didn't look into it. They told me I was fine, but of course I am not, as you can see. Maybe they didn't understand me? I don't know.

Similar to her experience in Jordan, Fatima felt that her ailments and pains were not taken seriously by the doctors who examined her. Given the scholarship detailing the challenges that women in the West experience in their attempts to procure medical care for chronic pain, this is not necessarily surprising. Women suffering from chronic pain, including migraines, face several obstacles to credibility and trustworthiness, including being framed as hypochondriacs, less rational, more emotional, and more likely to complain than men (Kempner 2014; Pryma 2017; Hoffmann and Tarzian 2001; Schäfer et al. 2016). As a result, women exert themselves in an attempt to gain the attention and interest of doctors, and work hard in order to prove that their invisible pain is real and physical rather than imagined or psychological (Werner and Malterud 2003; Werner, Isaksen, and Malterud 2004). Worrying about being perceived in a negative light, they attempt to strike the perfect balance of being assertive but not pushy, sick but not too unhealthy, strong but weak enough to be deserving of care, and articulate about their pain without seeming like "whiners" (Werner and Malterud 2003). Refugee women, especially those who do not speak the dominant language in their new contexts, experience difficulty in communicating their pain, fear of pain, and exact symptoms to their healthcare providers (Müllersdorf, Zander, and Eriksson 2011). Varying cultural and religious perspectives on pain, including its causes and one's responsibility to bear it, further exacerbate refugee women's ability to be understood by their physicians, which can have dire effects on their health (Campeau 2018; Morris et al. 2009; Müllersdorf, Zander, and Eriksson 2011).

Language and Care

Fatima also spoke of her experiences with healthcare in the United States in two distinct periods, the initial period of her resettlement, when she still had access to a bilingual caseworker, and what followed:

FATIMA: In the beginning, it was good, because Khaled, who was in charge of our case and who was Iraqi, helped us. He had come with us to our first couple of visits to the doctor and helped us tell the doctor about my pain, and that was very helpful. And then, after our time [resettlement period] was over, he told us, "I can't help you anymore. If you need someone from the agency from now on, they are going to have to send you someone else." After that time, they would send us these young people to help us, and none of them spoke Arabic.

SALLY: And how did you communicate with these people since they didn't speak Arabic?

FATIMA: That's exactly it! We couldn't communicate with them! When we were in the doctor's office, the doctor would use a phone interpreter, but that was not always good. Sometimes the interpreter couldn't understand our Iraqi accent, and other times the line would get cut off. It was so bad! And every time we went to the doctor, they sent us a different person, and none of them spoke Arabic. They would come with us to the doctor, but they couldn't speak with us, or tell the doctor what we needed. But then the agency stopped sending people altogether. The agency, they didn't help us very much. It was like, "Sink or swim. You go and find where you need to go on your own."

While Fatima's frustration with the resettlement agency was understandable, my time at the agency clarified that it was not that resettlement agency employees were being callous. Khaled—the only Arab caseworker at the agency—was responsible for all of the agency's Arabic-speaking clients. During an interview with Khaled, he described regret and discomfort with the fact that he could only assist families for a short period, but due to his long list of clients, he had to hold to the ninety days that families were allotted. As an Iraqi refugee himself, he knew that the assistance he provided did not fully meet the many needs of newly resettled Iraqis, but his roster of clients was simply too long.

The level and quality of care that Fatima received was seriously impacted by Khaled's withdrawal of services. Once the initial ninety days expired, the agency relied heavily on unpaid interns who were mostly undergraduate and graduate social work students from local universities who accompanied families to hospitals and clinics until the state-funded insurance expired. This practice proved to be quite frustrating to refugees like Fatima because none of these interns spoke Arabic. Additionally, due to the inherently unstable nature of volunteer labor, a different intern was sent to the family each time, creating a "revolving door effect." Fatima expressed feeling passed down from one person to another, which made creating any sort of connection with agency personnel impossible. Without a reliable, consistent Arabic speaker by her side, the quality of Fatima's care suffered. With Khaled's help, she had been able to describe her pain and tell her doctor about the accident, in hopes of being referred to a specialist. The eight months of her state-funded insurance passed without hearing back from the doctor. Fatima wanted to call her doctor and follow up, but after her ninety days were over, she was unable to do so as a result of the language barrier. Fatima had given up on trying to get medical attention, until she received a call:

> Almost a year after we first went to the doctor, the hospital called me. They wanted to try to do something about my pain, but by that time my insurance was gone. I couldn't go back there and do more tests because I had no insurance. And I continue to suffer from my limbs and these horrible headaches, and I don't know what to do.

Navigational Capacity Limitations

Fatima's problems were heightened by her inability to make sense of the ins and outs of the U.S. healthcare system. As Warda's testimony similarly underscored, refugees like Fatima often lack the background knowledge and skills necessary to navigate a system that was completely alien to them. Fatima explained:

> The whole system here is so strange. I knew what I wanted the doctors to focus on when I got here. I wanted them to check my bones, especially my joints, and I wanted them to check my neck and head. That is what is wrong with me. I have been suffering from these problems for many years now. But here they expect you to go see a general doctor first. Then he has to check you, and if he thinks you have a problem, he orders tests and scans, and writes you a paper that lets you make an appointment with the specialists. That process takes forever, and it drags on. It dragged on so long that my insurance ran out! In Iraq you make an appointment directly with the specialist. You know what is wrong with your body, and you can see a doctor who can attend to your needs!

This system here is backwards, and it is bad for people who are suffering. And *especially* bad for those who only have a few months of insurance!

This unfamiliarity with the medical process affects refugees adversely. Like all supports provided to refugees, health insurance was time constrained. The referral process, which is built into most U.S. healthcare plans, is particularly damaging for those on a tight timeline. It was several months after her initial screening that Fatima received a call from the hospital to come in for X-rays, and by the time it was time to see an orthopedist, her insurance had run out. Fatima, an outspoken woman who had been an excellent advocate for herself and her family, felt lost in the United States. The inability to navigate the healthcare system, coupled with the time-restricted nature of refugees' health insurance, can be highly detrimental to their ability to access necessary care. Fatima and Mohammed's experiences are consistent with other studies that have underscored the difficulties that refugees face in navigating the U.S. healthcare system (Salman and Resick 2015). Language and cultural barriers, conflicting expectations, miscommunication, and a lack of trust in the system stand in the way of Iraqi refugees accessing adequate healthcare in the United States (Worabo et al. 2016).

Successful navigation of the healthcare system requires an understanding of its complexities, one that transcends the barriers created by language. Nancy, the director of the refugee resettlement agency, shared:

It is really a navigational issue more than a language issue. These bureaucracies of poverty are incredibly complex and difficult to navigate, even for native English speakers. When you add culture and language to it, then it makes it almost impossible.

Navigating the healthcare system includes a wide variety of tasks like making appointments, communicating effectively with general practitioners, asking for referrals, and being able to make follow-up calls. As Nancy underscores, while this is a complex task for most, it can prove to be almost impossible for those who are new to the country and unfamiliar with the healthcare system, and do not speak English. In spite of these obstacles, it falls on refugees like Fatima to learn how to traverse this system independently after their access to refugee resettlement personnel expires.

Insurance Troubles

As time went by, things got progressively worse for Fatima. A few months after she was hired, Fatima suffered a fall at work and sustained a back injury that prevented her from performing the physical tasks involved in her job. The injury ultimately cost Fatima her job and forced her to stay home permanently. Now it was up to her husband Mohammed and her two eldest sons, Seif and Hussein, to earn enough money to support their family.[1] Since her health insurance had expired, Fatima had nowhere to turn for medical attention, even after her miscarriage, detailed in the introduction of this book. She was bedridden many days of the week due to her intense migraines and began to struggle to do everyday tasks such as cooking, walking, and praying (which required kneeling and bending forward five times a day) due to the pain in her limbs. Fatima suffered on a daily basis, without medical attention, for over two years, until her husband heard about the opportunity to purchase health insurance through his employer. Fatima stated:

> Mohammed wants us to go through his work for health insurance, which will be $160 for each of us. He keeps pushing for this because he wants the doctors to figure out what to do with my headaches and my pain, but I know that they are going to be useless like they have been before. All they did back then was offer me stronger painkillers than what I was already taking, and that's not what I want! . . . They should find the cause of this thing and deal with it! . . . I really want this insurance for Mohammed, not me. He is in desperate need of an operation. . . . They might actually do something for him. His condition is visible, so they can't tell him "You're fine" like they told me.

Fatima's negative experiences with doctors in the United States—who she experienced as inattentive and unwilling to take her chronic pain seriously—ultimately caused her to lose trust in the entire system. Mohammed, who shared his concerns about Fatima's health with me often during my visits, was more optimistic. He viewed the costly investment in health insurance as a worthwhile one, in hopes that Fatima would finally get the care she deserved. On her end, Fatima remained ambivalent about this high expense but agreed to it in the end for Mohammed's sake.

Mohammed had long suffered from severe hemorrhoids, which were a constant source of pain for him. He was seen by a doctor in Syria, who recommended surgery, but he and Fatima decided to wait until they came to the United States to address their medical needs—a decision they grew to regret. Unaware of the brevity of their health insurance, they had assumed that they would have access to high-quality healthcare, only to be extremely disappointed by the brevity and quality of care they received. While Mohammed was hopeful that this new health insurance would prove to be the key to better health for Fatima and himself, as it turns out, this too was a mirage.

Mohammed signed up for health insurance for himself and Fatima through his employer. The months before the insurance began, Fatima had been suffering more frequently from debilitating migraines. As soon as Fatima and Mohammed received their health insurance cards, they asked me to make medical appointments on their behalf and to accompany them to their first visit. We soon found out that this visit would not be covered by insurance, since their insurance plan no longer used a co-pay system but rather a deductible one. Mohammed and Fatima were responsible for the first $5,000 for their care, after which Mohammed's employer would cover 80 percent of the healthcare bills. Once they had reached their out-of-pocket limit, which was $10,000, the employer would then cover 100 percent of the medical bills. Unable to pay for the doctor's visit out of pocket, they decided to leave without meeting with the doctor. When we got back to Fatima's house, I called the insurance company on their behalf, only to discover that Mohammed's employer only offered this type of plan. Frustrated by this news, Mohammed exclaimed:

> So what is the point of having this insurance anyway? What do they think? That we have an extra *five thousand dollars* lying around?! I didn't know this of course, or I would have never signed up for it. They take over $300 out of my paycheck every month for *this*?! Really, Sally, what is the point, we might as well have no insurance!

Ultimately, Mohammed and Fatima agreed that the only course of action was to cancel their insurance, leaving them back at square one, once again without health insurance. Fatima would remain unable to seek medical attention and would continue to suffer from debilitating migraines as well as chronic pain that limited her mobility. Mohammed's health problems would also go untreated and continue to be a source of constant pain for him.

The Hope and Disappointment of the Affordable Care Act

Nora, the director of healthcare services at the refugee resettlement agency, confirmed the problematic nature of the insurance plans offered to most refugees. She was hopeful that the Affordable Care Act (ACA)—commonly known as Obamacare—could provide a good alternative for poor refugee families. The ACA went into full effect on January 1, 2014, ushering in health insurance reforms such as banning health insurance companies from turning away or overcharging patients with preexisting conditions, extending young people's ability to be on their parents' health insurance, and most important offering Americans with low incomes affordable health coverage options. Through the ACA healthcare marketplace, low-income families could pay low monthly premiums, which were based on their yearly income (Smith and Medalia 2015). Nora, who was charged with signing up as many refugees as possible for affordable insurance, explained refugees' healthcare options under the newly passed ACA to a room full of Iraqi refugees at the resettlement agency:

> So there have typically been three ways to receive healthcare in the past. One was through your job. This oftentimes depended on how many hours someone worked, and there was variability in who can be covered and how much a person paid a month. Another way to get insurance was through the welfare office, which covers different cases: SSI or disability; pregnant women and their infants/children; refugees, for eight months after their arrival; people above sixty-five or seniors; and children who are younger than eighteen years old. If you fall under any of these categories, then this law will not change anything for you. You can just keep the insurance that you have. But now there is a new option, which is through the health coverage exchange. Of course this depends on your income, and these aren't exact numbers, but on average, a person who is earning $25,000 would have the monthly cost of about $42 a month.

As Nora explained above, the ACA would allow low-income refugees to purchase health insurance at a low cost, and would eliminate the need to pay high deductibles. More important, the ACA would cover the "basic ten" services: doctors' visits; hospital care; trips to the emergency room; care for infants before or after they are born; pediatric care (including dental and vision); mental health including substance abuse counseling, psychotherapy, and psychiatry; prescription drugs and physical therapy (including any equipment needed due to a disability); preventative care (including lab tests, mammograms, blood tests, etc.); chronic diseases; and women's health. Nora shared that she was thrilled about the availability of the program for her refugee clients. She had been waiting for this legislation to be enacted so her clients could finally gain access to affordable health insurance plans. Nora and her team of interns sent out flyers to all of the refugees they had resettled in the past few years. The flyers (which were printed in several languages, including Arabic) highlighted the new plans available through ACA and invited refugees to come to the resettlement agency where a "healthcare navigator" would help them choose a plan that fit their needs.

Fatima received one of these flyers and showed it to me when I arrived to her house for a visit. She and Mohammed were ecstatic about the opportunity of receiving health insurance that was within their means. Nora's flyer stated that refugees could make an appointment to go see her at the resettlement agency, or if they had the linguistic means to make the call independently, they could reach out to the health marketplace via phone or online. I offered to make the call myself, and they readily agreed. I called the health marketplace, and explained to the male representative that I was a family friend who would act as a translator. Over the next forty-five minutes he asked for a variety of information, including social security numbers; green card numbers; employer information; whether either of them was disabled; whether either of them had been incarcerated; whether Fatima was currently pregnant; and what their household income was last year, as stated in their 2013 taxes. After collecting this information, the representative first asked a few questions to confirm that the information given was true and correct. After being placed on hold for several minutes, the representative came back on with some grim news. He informed me that due to their low income, Mohammed and Fatima did not qualify for ACA insurance plans. They *were* eligible for Medicaid, but as a result of Pennsylvania's limitations on the program, they would not be able to receive benefits. The "good news," he stated, "is that they are not going to have to pay fines for not having medical insurance." When I asked the representative what other options were available for Fatima and Mohammed, he informed me that they could purchase full-priced plans through the health marketplace. The least expensive of these plans costed $335 per person.

The fact that Fatima and Mohammed's family was too poor for ACA coverage seemed devastatingly ironic and cruel given the name of the legislation: nothing about this was "affordable" for low-income refugees. If they purchased these plans, one-third of Mohammed's salary would be spent on health insurance. It was simply not feasible. Fatima and Mohammed were not alone in this struggle to acquire health insurance. According to the Kaiser Commission on Medicaid and the Uninsured (Majerol, Newkirk, and Garfield 2015), prior to the implementation of the ACA, 1.2 million state residents, or 11 percent of Pennsylvanians, were uninsured. While the ACA was designed to offer affordable healthcare plans to middle-class and lower middle-class families, the poorest families in the state were never meant to be a part of this plan. Even after the implementation of the ACA, the responsibility for providing medical care to the state's poorest citizens was still meant to be delivered through Medicaid. While twenty-eight states expanded their Medicaid programs in 2013 to accommodate the needs of their poorest residents, Pennsylvania—under Republican leadership at the time—opted out of the expansion, leaving the poorest Pennsylvanians, including refugees like Fatima and Mohammed, with no access to healthcare.

After delivering the summary of my call with the healthcare marketplace representative, Fatima and Mohammed had much to say:

FATIMA: So what is the point of this Obamacare? We have nothing, and he said that he wanted everyone to have insurance, right? So what about us, why can't we get it? Don't we matter? Don't *refugees* matter?!

MOHAMMED: What are people supposed to do, Sally? That is my question!

FATIMA: I think the worst thing is that this flyer they sent us, it gave me hope, Sally. I had already lost hope. [She pauses, and tears fill her eyes.] It is wrong to play with people's feelings like this. It is worse than just saying no, you can't get health insurance. Hope is a dangerous thing. They give people hope, and then they make you follow these threads and tunnels that lead nowhere and waste people's time. [She pauses, and tears roll down her face. Mohammed holds her hand.]

Mohammed grew increasingly concerned for Fatima's health and implored me to help him find Fatima a doctor. After some searching, I discovered that the last available resource available to Fatima was her neighborhood Free Health Care Clinic. I called the clinic in her neighborhood to make an appointment on her behalf, but was informed that appointments weren't available at the moment as they were booked for the next ten months. The clinic had a few walk-in appointments every day, but the line, which sometimes ran around the block, was much too long for the clinic to meet everyone's needs. The clinic opened at 8 a.m., but she suggested that Fatima get there as early as 7 a.m. The representative advised that if Fatima was not seen on the first day she stood in line, then she should come back the following day. If that did not work, Fatima should come back several days in a row, with the hope that she would eventually acquire one of the coveted walk-in appointments. Fatima attempted this a few times, but due to the chronic pain in her legs, standing for several hours outside in the cold proved to be too difficult. After a few days, she gave up, telling me, "All this standing is making my legs even worse. When I got home my legs were so bad I couldn't even walk up the steps to my apartment! Mohammed had to carry me part of the way up. I had to stay in bed the rest of the day and could barely walk to the bathroom. I can't go through that again."

Returning to Iraq for Healthcare

Their inability to access the ACA left Fatima back at square one and desperate for medical care. In a later conversation with Fatima and Mohammed, I learned of some drastic plans they had made to mitigate their lack of access to healthcare. Mohammed stated:

Everybody else we know, they go back to Iraq for their medical care. My friend from work, Ali, he just came back last week. He went there for two weeks. . . . It's awful. . . . Cars explode every day. People die every day. Death and violence, people just have gotten used to it now. They have to live their lives, what are they going to do? He told me he went out with his friend two days before he came back. They were walking back to his friend's car, and his friend was shot, killed. Ali was standing right here next to him, and his friend was shot. Ali just began to pat himself down, to search his own shirt and his body for bullets, for blood. His friend's blood had splattered on his shirt, so for a few seconds he didn't know whether it was his own blood, or his friend's. This is how it is now in Iraq. And you have people choosing to go back *there*, to *that*, just to get to see doctors. Is this right? How can this be right?

Despite the dangers that awaited them in Iraq, which they were all too familiar with, Fatima and Mohammed's desperation for medical attention had driven them to consider returning there. Mohammed's comments underscored the desperation that drives people to return to a context where the fortunate ones are those who come out of the experience alive, albeit covered in the blood of their friends. This desperation reflects the severity of their suffering without access to affordable healthcare in the United States. Without health insurance, Iraqi refugees might resort to desperate measures to seek medical attention, putting their lives at risk. Of course, the medical care available to refugees in Iraq was not what it once was, but Mohammed explained that there Fatima could have an appointment with a specialist right away, and that he would be able to get the surgery he needed immediately as well. He explained that "the medical care might not be as good as America's, but that doesn't mean anything when you can't even see a doctor here!"

The Effects of (Ongoing) Debilitation on Refugee Mental Health

Effects of Post-Resettlement Conditions on Mental Health

Zeina and her mother Nadia were also deeply impacted by the post-resettlement realities she and her family faced. As detailed in chapter 1, Zeina, who had survived a mass shooting at her school when she was only nine years old, had suffered a traumatic brain injury (TBI) in the process. After the shooting, Zeina suffered from night terrors, severe depression (including suicidality and prolonged periods of catatonia), agoraphobia, anxiety, and fear of unfamiliar adults, especially security personnel, police, and other armed authority figures. Upon her arrival to her school in the United States, Zeina was diagnosed with the TBI and developmental delays by her school psychologist, and was transferred to the school's "resource room," the room where students with disabilities were taught by special education teachers, on a full-time basis. Zeina found this placement extremely demoralizing, and her mental health began to decline again. Zeina had begun restricting her food, refusing to eat anything, telling her mother that she was not hungry and that "there was no point." Zeina stopped eating solid foods for a few weeks and restricted her water intake. Nadia believed this was all connected with her daughter's longtime battles with anxiety and depression, which was triggered by being in the resource room all day long rather than in a mainstream class with her peers. A few months after Zeina arrived in the United States, she began cutting herself with razor blades, telling her mother when she caught her doing so that she felt nothing, that she was "dead inside."

Upon arrival to the United States, Nadia sought out mental health-care for Zeina. At the family's first healthcare screening, Nadia requested (through Khaled, who accompanied her to the appointment) that Zeina be seen by a psychologist as soon as possible. The doctor who examined Zeina informed the family that a new pilot program had just been funded by the state for young victims of violence, and thankfully Zeina was eligible to participate. Under the care of her psychologist, Zeina had begun to show real improvement—she stopped spending all of her time in her room, spoke to her family members, and according to her mother, was "finally re-turning to herself"—until she was placed in the resource room. This placement was difficult for Zeina, who had hoped to learn English and make friends. Instead, Zeina spent her days tasked with minimal assignments like coloring. Surrounded by students who had disabilities that required more of her teacher's attention, Zeina felt lost and ignored. According to Nadia, that was when many of Zeina's troubles began. She stopped par-ticipating in class and instead sat quietly, staring at the floor. This is also when Zeina's food restriction and cutting began. Soon after, Zeina refused to go to the psychologist and began to refuse to attend school. According to Nadia, her daughter was regressing to her former state, displaying even more concerning problems than those she suffered in Iraq and Syria. This time, Zeina's life was in danger.

A few weeks after Zeina began to restrict her food and water, Nadia called me in a panic. Zeina was in a great deal of pain. She was having a very difficult time urinating, and when she did, blood appeared in her urine. She appeared glassy-eyed, listless, and lethargic, and wasn't responding to Nadia when she spoke to her. I drove over to their house immediately, picked up Nadia and Zeina, and drove them to a nearby emergency room. I could tell that Zeina was not her usual self. As I drove to the hospital, she was slumped in her seat, staring at her shoes. By the time we arrived to the hospital, Zeina needed to lean on her mother in order to walk. I helped Nadia fill out the forms handed to us by the ER staff, and then we waited for nearly two hours before she was examined by a doctor. Zeina was diagnosed with severe dehydration and admitted to the hospital for the night. During the two days that Zeina spent in the hospital, she was seen by a general practitioner, a psychiatrist, and a nutrition specialist. They all recommended that Zeina join a two-week inpatient eating disorder program for young people, but the thought of leaving her parents for that long made Zeina very anxious. In the end, Zeina was discharged with the number of a nutrition specialist, an appointment to check back in with a general practitioner, and a full account of her diagnosis and treatment to share with her psychologist.

Navigation Troubles and Refugee Well-Being

Zeina's health was of great concern to her family, especially to Nadia. As Zeina slept in the hospital, Nadia wept and shared how devastating it was to witness this regression in her daughter's health while feeling helpless to help her. Even though Nadia had observed how Zeina's health "was declining" and "was going from bad to worse," she was unable to speak with her daughter's healthcare professionals in between appointments to communicate her concerns with them. Since the family's initial resettlement period had expired, she no longer had access to Khaled, her bilingual case manager at the refugee resettlement agency, or any of the agency's other personnel for that matter. He had assisted Nadia with making appointments for Zeina and with speaking to doctors during hospital visits. Without Khaled present, doctors and nurses used telephonic interpretation to speak with Nadia and her family during their scheduled visits, which didn't always go well. At times, the Arabic speakers, who came from a different region of the Middle East than Nadia, seemed to have difficulty understanding her and communicating effectively with the doctor due to their lack of familiarity with the Iraqi dialect. Furthermore, like Fatima, Nadia struggled with a lack of familiarity with the U.S. healthcare system. Nadia, who had successfully navigated healthcare systems in both Iraq and Syria, often found herself at a loss when it came to getting Zeina the medical attention she needed. None of her previous experiences in either country had prepared her for the procedures of emergency care in the United States. In both Iraq and in Syria, Nadia would have made a same-day appointment for Zeina to see a specialist, but now felt overwhelmed by the referral system.

Nadia's inability to navigate the healthcare system on behalf of her daughter was a source of a great deal of anxiety for her. It brought back memories of other times and places where caring for her daughters was out of her control. The horrific school shooting that Zeina had survived was not the only time that Nadia's daughters were in danger. Nadia's youngest daughter, Dima, was almost kidnapped as a young girl, only to be pulled out of the kidnapper's car by a neighbor who had witnessed the whole thing a few seconds before he sped off. Finding herself once again unable to provide her child with what she needed triggered terrible memories for Nadia:

> In Iraq there were constant death threats, and they would target the homes of people with young girls, because they would try to kidnap the girls and sell them as sex slaves. I never slept, I mean *really* slept. . . . I would constantly be worried about my girls and their safety. . . . I would hear worse stories, horror stories about how people would pay thugs and militia people to go in homes, kill the men, and then take the women. Women would see their husbands and sons slaughtered before their eyes and then they would have to watch their daughters being ripped away from them, and they would be taken and never heard from again. These kinds of stories became the everyday. They became what you heard and saw and were surrounded with. . . . Then we went to Syria and it was worse. The men on the street would make sure that I heard them when they said that they would come to my house and attack it first once the Assad regime fell. We lived in constant fear. I am still really scared for them, and still can't sleep. Even though I have left those places, all of those worries and fears, they still live inside me. They are in my brain.

Nadia's account underscores the mental health costs related to keeping her children safe in not only one but two active war zones—first in Iraq and later in the unrest in Syria. Her comments also speak to the particular psychological toll war can take on women and girls. Nadia—the parent and primary caregiver of two girls in a setting where female bodies were under constant threat and attack—was on continuous alert. This took a toll on Nadia's psyche, evidenced by her inability to sleep, which was not resolved even after her removal from the context of physical danger. Even after resettlement, Nadia suffered from insomnia, and when she did fall asleep was often awoken by her husband, who had heard her crying or even screaming in her sleep. The night terrors had subsided for some time after resettlement but reemerged once Zeina's mental health declined. Nadia also struggled with social isolation:

> The hardest about this is that you can't talk to anyone about what you have gone through. I spend all my time here, with my girls, and alone. My husband, he is practically gone all the time because he is always working. So I am either here alone, or with my girls. And I can't talk to them about this. They need me to be smiling, to be there for them, to be the one who is their friend, and mother and everything. And then when I *do* go out, I can't talk to anyone. I don't speak the language, and even if I did, you can't just talk to anyone about this. So I have nightmares every night. And sometimes I just close my door and sit alone in my room; that way the girls won't see me if I cry. It is hard, Sally. It's very hard.

Nadia's commentary reveals the emotional toll that the trauma of living under constant threat can have, especially on women. Since Nadia's health insurance had lapsed, she was unable to access mental health services. She had spent the first few months focused on Zeina's health and acquiring medical and mental health services on her behalf. As a result, by the time that Nadia's state-funded insurance expired, she was unable to see a psychologist or psychiatrist herself.

Survivors Support Network

The only other method of gaining access to mental health services was through the Survivors Support Network, a program housed at the refugee resettlement agency. This three-year program, funded by the Office of Refugee Resettlement to assist victims of torture as well as their families, offered eligible refugees with extended case management (beyond the initial four months refugees receive upon arrival), mental health counseling, and cash assistance. Even though the program was housed at the resettlement agency where I conducted participant observation, it accepted *all* eligible refugees, regardless of which of Philadelphia's three refugee resettlement agencies had resettled them. Heather, the director of the program, spoke with me about the challenges that Iraqi refugees faced:

I would say that their main struggle is with mental health issues. In particular, there seems to be a complex intersection of medical and mental health issues. They seem to present with some serious co-occurring somatic manifestation. Not surprisingly, many of our clients who have experienced trauma tend to also have major health issues and chronic diseases. Also, as can be expected, they are presenting with trauma levels that are much higher than other refugee groups in Philadelphia.

Heather's comments support the research that suggests the ties between exposure to violence, subsequent trauma, and chronic illnesses. Research on Iraqi refugees' well-being suggests that psychological problems, which can often have somatic representations, are often reactions to refugees' experiences of war, forced migration, and lack of access to basic needs (Burnett and Peel 2001; Gorst-Unsworth and Goldenberg 1998). Warda, who we met at the outset of this chapter, is a prime example of this. Warda's chronic pain, hypertension, and diabetes all emerged during or after moments of immense struggle or loss. Nadia's depression, anxiety, and sleep problems came about as a result of the traumatic events and tragedies that she faced.

Nadia would have benefited immensely from a program that gave her not only mental health assistance but also financial assistance and access to a bilingual counselor. However, she was not eligible for the Survivors Support Network, due to the restrictive eligibility requirements involved. According to the U.S. Torture Victims Relief Act, torture was defined as "an act which is intended to inflict severe physical or mental pain or suffering and committed by a person acting under the color of law upon another person who he has under his custody or physical control" (U.S. Department of Health and Human Services 2022). This new definition excluded many Iraqi refugees and their families, who had suffered a great deal of trauma loss as a result of the violence and lawlessness following the U.S. invasion but were not eligible for the program since the suffering they incurred was not done by those "acting under the color of the law," such as members of the government, military/militia, rebel group, police, or political groups. With this restrictive definition of torture as the basis for eligibility for the Survivors Support Program, Nadia and many other Iraqi refugees who presented with complex mental health problems were ineligible for the program. As a result, Nadia had no one to speak with about her trauma, a fact she assessed to be "the hardest thing" about her experience. With nowhere to turn for help, Nadia retired to her room, with her door closed, crying quietly and ruminating, where she could be alone and not be a burden to her children. She grew increasingly isolated, and her anxiety, depression, and resulting problems with sleep became more acute. Effectively, Zeina's schooling had triggered a steep decline, not only in Zeina's health but also Nadia's, which points to the ways that refugee's post-resettlement experiences negatively affect their health and well-being.

The experiences of Nadia and Zeina underscore the ways that the debilitation of the Iraqi people traverses borders. Wars, sanctions, and the resulting destruction of the healthcare system in Iraq has left a permanent mark on the lives of Iraqi refugees, compounded by forced migration and life as second-class citizens in neighboring countries. Studies conducted with Iraqi refugees indicate that they are extremely likely to be victims of discrimination, persecution, and harassment, and are often forced into exile or long periods of hiding (Gorst-Unsworth and Goldenberg 1998; Jamil et al. 2002). Reports estimate that nearly 50 percent of Iraqi refugees resettled in the United States suffer from emotional distress, anxiety, and depression, while 31 percent are at risk for posttraumatic stress disorder (PTSD; Taylor et al. 2014). Among Iraqi refugees who seek mental health treatment, 54 percent of the men and 11 percent of the women suffer from PTSD, and more than 80 percent present with symptoms of anxiety and depression (Jamil et al. 2007). While it is critical to understand how the nature of war and sanctions debilitate Iraqis (Puar 2017), I contend that it is equally important to recognize and appreciate the ways their post-resettlement experiences affect and shape their health and well-being. Poverty, which "may well be thought of as a form of debilitation" (Puar 2017, 73), the brevity of welfare supports including state-funded health insurance, and inadequate educational opportunities break down the bodies and souls of Iraqi refugees.

Healthcare Access and Citizenship

As the past few chapters have underscored, Iraqi refugees come to the United States with hopes and dreams for a better life. Many of them had expected to be provided with adequate welfare support, appropriate and high-quality educational opportunities, and access to healthcare to address what their bodies and minds had undergone as a result of war and forced migration. As Warda, whom we met at the outset of the chapter, stated:

What we're asking for is simple, and what we need is to just get our basic needs met. It doesn't make sense that they give a refugee health insurance for eight months and then cut it off. We need health insurance because we come here with many ailments. If they are going to resettle refugees here, then they need to ensure that we are OK, not just throw us in the deep end and then see if we will sink or swim. . . . As refugees, we didn't come here expecting much. We came here to live a simple, peaceful life. After all we have been through, this is all we want, and this is what we deserve.

Warda, whose health continued to decline to the point that even standing and walking brought on severe pain, outlines the hopes of refugees, particularly of those who suffered from chronic illness. Iraqi refugees like Warda, Fatima, Zeina, and Nadia, who had been debilitated by U.S. imperialism, come to the United States to find that they once again have few rights, including the right to access healthcare. This endemic exclusion has serious effects on refugees' hopes, as well as their view of the United States. In an interview with Fatima and Mohammed, they spoke of their disappointment with their experience with the U.S. healthcare system:

FATIMA: As a refugee, you would think I would have particular rights, but that is not the case. . . . The health system here has been just terrible. I mean maybe they have the best doctors, maybe they have the best hospitals, that's what everybody thinks, but how do you get to them?! They make it impossible to get the medical care you need. Those excellent doctors and fancy hospitals are reserved for other people, not for us.

MOHAMMED: We came from a country where we had access to the best medical care, and it was all taken care of for us. And then we come here, to the "most advanced country in the world" and we can't even see a doctor. What sort of health system is this? In Iraq . . . if you have an accident, you can rest assured that you will be taken care of and that you are not in danger of losing everything.

Fatima and Mohammed's testimony reveals the extent to which U.S. imperialism has debilitated Iraqi refugees, first through the destruction of the healthcare system in their native country and then by making medical care inaccessible in the United States. Wars waged and sanctions imposed by the United States on Iraq have left its once state-of-the-art and robust social medical system in tatters and its citizens with the burden of various chronic health problems. Like others in my study have done, Fatima invokes refugee rights, which have once again proven to be an illusion. She also points to the contradiction at the heart of refugees' experience: while they reside in the United States, where medical care is assumed to be top notch and cutting edge, refugees' lack of access to healthcare makes this point moot. As Mohammed posits, at least in Iraq, refugees would not be at the risk of "losing everything" as a result of medical bills—the reason behind two-thirds of all bankruptcy cases in the United States (Konish 2019). For all intents and purposes, refugees might as well be living in Iraq or the many low-income neighboring countries from which they fled. For the adults in this study whose state-funded insurance expires within months of their arrival, and those who work jobs with no benefits, their access to adequate healthcare is no better than it was before they came to the United States.

Nadia, Zeina's mother, also spoke of the contradiction of being resettled to the United States:

> You know, everyone in Iraq envies us being here. . . . They have no idea how we suffer, or what we go through. *This* is life in America?! . . . There is no compassion; there is no concern for the history of the refugee or what he has gone through. They pay your rent for a few months, then stop. Medical care is taken away after eight months. And when you ask for help, you can't find it. They say, "You have to take care of yourself now." [She pauses.] You know, the refugee is just like everyone else in this country. . . . The word *refugee* means nothing. And if a refugee has no rights, why does America bring him here? If America cannot provide for us, she should leave the refugee in his country! If he dies there, he will die once. But life here is like dying every day.

Nadia reiterates the irony of living in the United States. Nadia's family and loved ones who still live in the Arab world—who make assumptions about life in the United States based on transnational media and Hollywood portrayals of American exceptionalism—envy her for resettling there. It is this very view of the United States that probably informed refugees' expectations, stoking their hope for a better life. As Nadia reminds us, the realities that refugees are faced with in the United States could not be more different than what they had imagined. Nadia questions not only the rights she had assumed would be provided for refugees but also the U.S. refugee resettlement program. She challenges the broken system that brings refugees to contexts where there is so little for them, where life is like dying daily. While typical understandings of violence frame death as the ultimate assault and offence, Nadia's testimony illustrates that the daily indignities of life in the United States can be more harmful. For those who have suffered at the hands of U.S. imperialism, only to find that nothing awaits them on the other side of resettlement, theirs is a "slow death," defined by Berlant as "the physical wearing out of a population and the deterioration of people in that population that is very nearly a defining condition of their experience and historical existence" (2007, 756). Slow death flourishes, not in traumatic events such as military aggression, but in the everyday temporalities of ordinary living and activity. As such, populations like refugees are worn out by the burdens of living, particularly in inequitable environments that are marked by a disparity of resources, including a lack of access to healthcare. Accepted as a symptom of the neoliberal common sense, or "a problem the world can live with," refugees die slowly.

According to Nancy, the director of the refugee resettlement agency, other refugees echoed Nadia's sentiments. In her conversations with South Sudanese refugees from the Darfur region, Nancy learned about the toll that surviving in America took on them. She shared:

> It was really heartbreaking for me to hear them comparing the challenges they are facing here in Philadelphia to the genocide they faced in Darfur. But I think this makes sense in a way. They are new here, and everything is so hard, and they need so much more help than we can give them.

Refugees who had been systemically debilitated by the machinery of war are further damaged by a lack of access to healthcare in the United States. And as Nadia contends, refugees do not hold a special place in the United States, and in this sense "are like everyone else." Like other poor Americans and the historically disenfranchised, refugees are embedded in a context hollowed out by the neoliberal attack on the welfare state and all of its institutions, one where the debilitation and death of these peoples is a given rather than an exception. As a result, they are stripped of their former rosy visions of citizenship and rights, and articulate a critique of what really awaits them in the belly of the beast.

The accounts detailed in this chapter demonstrate that Iraqi refugees' premigratory lives—textured by conflict, violence, forced migration, and all sorts of instability—have negative effects on their physical and mental health. Refugees are debilitated not only by U.S. invasions, occupations, and brutal sanctions but also by their post-resettlement experiences, including chronic barriers to adequate healthcare. The brevity of the resettlement period, during which refugees have access to case management services from refugee resettlement agencies, leaves non-English-speaking Iraqi refugees without the ability to communicate with medical professionals. Refugees are left unable to ask for assistance, clarification, or guidance in dealing with this new, unfamiliar medical system—which has consequences on refugee health.

As Warda's opening testimony highlights, refugees come to this country hoping to have their "basic human needs" met. One of these basic needs is adequate, consistent access to comprehensive healthcare. This demand might seem unrealistic given that healthcare is not an entitlement for Americans but rather a responsibility turned over to individuals. In fact, nearly 15 percent of nonelderly adults living in the United States currently lack health insurance (Majerol, Newkirk, and Garfield 2015). This population not only experiences barriers to accessing care but also is at higher risk of suffering from medical debt. In this context, refugees are merely the latest wave of U.S. residents who live with this kind of precarity. Iraqi refugees—whose bodies, minds, and souls have been debilitated by the U.S. empire—are owed access to adequate and consistent healthcare, which includes care for their mental health needs. As Warda said at the opening of this chapter, "After all we have been through, this is all we want, and this is what we deserve."

Conclusion

Meaningless Citizenship

My ability to stay in contact with the families has been interrupted by the instability that textures the lives of Iraqi refugees in the United States. The challenges of building a new life in Philadelphia pushed half of the families to outmigrate[1] in search of better opportunities. In spring 2012, Samah's family moved to Connecticut to join relatives who had recently resettled there from Iraq. Her mother's nephew rented a house large enough for his and Samah's family to live together. Samah's younger siblings, Ghada and Adam, were quickly enrolled in a suburban school with plenty of resources compared to Liberty High. They were each given a laptop to take home, and had an immense amount of support within the school as English language learners. Samah, who no longer needed to work full-time to support the family, was enrolled in a GED program that accommodated her linguistic needs. A few months later, she met a young man, also an Iraqi refugee, in her class, fell in love, and got married. We lost touch a few months after the family left Philadelphia when Samah changed her phone number, but it seemed as though the move to Connecticut was a positive one for everyone involved.

A few weeks later, Seif's family left for Michigan. Seif's father, Mohammed, had found work with some longtime friends from Iraq who lived near Dearborn, a hub for Arab immigrants and refugees. Seif's mother, Fatima, was hopeful that she could find better healthcare there, as she was told by relatives that her chronic pain might help her qualify for Social Security Income as well as state-funded health insurance. Still unconvinced of the utility of a high school diploma, Seif's younger brother Hussein planned to work full-time alongside his father. Both Seif and his younger sister Layla were looking forward to pursuing community college options there, hopeful that a community rich with Arabic speakers would have better educational resources that could meet their needs. Ayman, Seif's youngest sibling, who was a tenth grader at Liberty High at the time, was unhappy with the move, since he had finally joined the school's varsity soccer team. Soon after the family left for Michigan, they also changed their telephone number, and we also lost touch.

As of this writing, only two families have remained in Philadelphia. Baheera's growing mobility struggles—which were exacerbated by her inability to access healthcare—made life in the second-floor apartment procured for her by the resettlement agency untenable. Baheera's family moved to another apartment on the ground floor, but the rent there proved to be beyond their means, so they had to relocate a third time. Each time the family moved, they would change their telephone number—an old habit that Baheera insisted on since her family was targeted in Iraq and Syria. After their third move, in fall 2014, I lost touch with the family when their telephone number was disconnected. I found out from one of her friends that Baheera's daughter Heba eventually graduated from Liberty High, but never learned whether she was able to enroll in higher education.

I lost touch with Zeina's family in winter 2015. At the time, Zeina was slotted to graduate Liberty High the following semester, and her sister Dima was going to transition from middle school to Liberty High. The settlement that her lawyer had won on her behalf (see chapter 3) would also cover postsecondary programs that taught students with intellectual disabilities life skills and trained them for work in service jobs. Zeina's options would be limited since she was reading at a second-grade level, but she was most interested in cosmetology. Zeina's father, Sayed, was still employed at a local branch of a superstore, earning just over the minimum wage. Zeina's parents eventually purchased a car, and her mother, Nadia, acquired a driver's license, giving her more confidence to leave the house. Nadia and Sayed still had no access to healthcare and like other refugees were seriously considering traveling to Iraq to address their health needs, in spite of the dangers involved.

In one of my last meetings with Nadia, we sat in her living room, sipping the cardamom tea we always drank together. The atmosphere in the house felt different somehow, in a way that I could not put my finger on at first. Gone was the usual music of Fairuz that filled the house during our visits. There was nothing cooking on the stove for the family upon their return from school and work; an aberration from Nadia's daily routine that I had come to know so well over the past several months. There were deep purplish bags under Nadia's eyes, and she seemed more distracted than usual. I asked Nadia if she was alright, and it took her some time to respond. "I've been thinking about the question you asked me last time, the one about citizenship."[2] I nodded, and asked her to go on.

> This whole resettlement process, and becoming an American citizen, it is a farce. . . . I didn't find any rights here. I only found the same suffering, the same hardship. And this is what is devastating, not only to me, but also to every refugee who comes here. . . . They just send me a green card and that is supposed to shut me up? I don't want the card. Keep it, and tell me, *show* me where my rights are. I want these rights they talk about.

For refugees like Nadia, life in the United States has proved that the formal process of becoming citizens bears little fruit. Echoing Somers's (2008) definition, Nadia frames citizenship as the right to have rights. Locked out of the ability to be a rights-bearing future citizen, Nadia questions her position as a refugee, as well as the American resettlement project. Struggling to make ends meet as her family's public assistance consistently declines, locked out of healthcare, and looking on as her daughter Zeina struggled daily in her public high school, Nadia rejects the prospect of legal citizenship, asking instead for the rights she once believed belonged to her and others who sought refuge in the United States. Refugees like Nadia have much to teach us. Ramsay (2018) reminds us that resettlement is a contested condition, not merely one of the three "durable solutions" put forth by the United Nations High Commissioner for Refugees (UNHCR) to address the refugee problem. Given that only 1 percent of refugees are resettled to third countries, typically in the West, resettlement is often taken up uncritically as the ultimate solution. However, as Nadia's critique above suggests, how can a life marked by poverty and barriers to basic rights such as education, healthcare, a living wage, and adequate support from the state be considered one lived in refuge? What good is resettlement when refugees are absorbed into a context where their very worth is evaluated by their ability to work and to avoid dependence on the state? These are the questions we must take on if indeed we seek a better life for refugees.

The refugees whose lives are at the center of this book had a complex understanding of the forces that limited their lives, and spoke of them with all who would listen—not only me, but with the agents of the state who they encountered in their daily lives, including teachers, welfare office agents, refugee resettlement case managers, and doctors. However, when Iraqi refugees shared their suffering and disappointment with those who were tasked with caring for them, they were often exhorted or even chided to be grateful, for in the United States, "at least they are safe." But for many Iraqis, their experience of life in a neoliberal America is, as Nadia put it, "like dying every day." For in the United States they are finally dispossessed of the "cruel optimism" that allowed them to survive unspeakable horrors to find the "good life" they had envisioned for themselves, which never really existed (Berlant 2011). As Ramsay contends, "After being resettled, refugees can be confronted with new—and for some . . . more devastating experiences of displacement" (2018, 188). For Iraqis, theirs was an experience of double displacement, a life removed from the stability they sought, first by American militarized imperialism in Iraq and then again by the neoliberal gutting of the welfare state that was theoretically tasked with caring for them (as well as other marginalized groups) within the United States.

The lives of Iraqi refugees are a testament to the myths that underlie the refugee experience, including universally accepted definitions of "crisis," "displacement," and indeed "refuge." As Ramsay contends, by framing it as a "refugee crisis," we suggest it is a "distinct problem that can be solved" (2018, 3). If we hope to better the lives of refugees, we must attend to the forces that displace them, as well as those that keep the lives that they hoped to find perpetually out of reach. Iraqis were not only displaced by the outright wars fought by the United States on their soil but also by the long and often invisible arm of American imperialism that began in earnest decades before the 1990–1991 Gulf War. Before dropping one bomb on Iraq, the United States supported military coups and buoyed the administrations of brutal dictators including Saddam Hussein—under whom tens of thousands were killed and millions were displaced—by providing munitions, chemical and biological weapons, and military intelligence. Once Hussein acted against American interests, the United States reversed its position and began to seek out regime change via any means necessary, all in the name of "peace," "democracy," and "freedom" for those who were threatened by a dictator who "killed his own people." For over a decade, the United States upheld the longest and most abominable sanctions that any country had ever endured, preventing the selling of oil to rebuild Iraq and banning the entry of essential goods, including life-saving medicines. Hundreds of thousands of children died from preventable diseases, infant mortality skyrocketed, and Iraqis struggled to access basic needs. The once middle-class country with the most robust medical and educational system in the Arab world fell to its knees. Then, in 2003, the United States terrorized the Iraqi people, destroying their homes, schools, hospitals, water and electricity plants, roads, and bridges—fulfilling the disaster capitalist requirements for creating a "new Iraq," where the only freedom prioritized was that of markets. Under occupation forces, Iraq was dismantled and sold off piece by piece, all while its people continued to suffer.

As of this writing, 20 percent of Iraq's population needs humanitarian protection and assistance (UNHCR 2019), 70 percent of Iraqis continue to lack access to clean water, and 80 percent lack access to sanitation, which can lead to cholera epidemics (WHO 2020). More than 9.2 million Iraqis are internally displaced or refugees who have fled the country; they represent a whopping 37 percent of the prewar Iraqi population (Watson Institute of International and Public Affairs 2020). Faced with these realities, some argue that in order to alleviate the suffering of Iraqi refugees, the United States might take more responsibility by opening their borders to them. Yes. The United States must increase, prioritize, and facilitate the asylum process for all Iraqis seeking refuge. However, as the experiences of Iraqi refugees within the United States have demonstrated, resettlement is simply not enough because it leaves intact the very forces that undergird the systems and forces that have fomented the suffering of Iraqis.

Real change for those displaced by American military imperialism requires an upending of the neoliberal logics that drive the destruction of countries in search for new markets and massive profits. In spite of American exceptionalist rhetoric, the United States has never made good on its claims to be acting in the interest of freedom and human rights. Instead, its military has invaded and/or supported ongoing wars all over the globe and in the Arab world—including Syria, Libya, Yemen, and Palestine, to name a few—ignoring the fact that a democracy "has never been imposed on governments or nations at the point of the bayonet" (Polk 2005, 187). Disaster capitalism has not only devastated Iraqi refugees' home country but also hollowed out the American state and its institutions, leaving refugees, once again, with nowhere to turn and without rights. Even though this neoliberal governance has become the new hegemonic common sense, it need not be so. We must remember that neoliberalism was once a fringe school of thought, one that we can fight against. The United States can take a different path, turning away from its current imperialist course by enacting laws and creating policies and programs that would center the public good. Examples of this would be a massive redistribution of wealth within its borders, the redirecting of funds into the renewal of social infrastructures such as education, and efforts to rebuild dilapidated infrastructures that place the most vulnerable among us in danger (Harvey 2003). The nation must face and find ways to address the ongoing legacies of racial, social, and economic inequalities, including committing to paying reparations to the descendants of BIPOC peoples whose lives were shattered by chattel slavery and genocide—and who built the wealth of this country. This can only come about by the dedication to buck neoliberal hegemonic ideas and policies and instead reinvest in the welfare state; impose higher taxation, especially for corporations; and return to a model of heavy state direction (Harvey 2003). For refugees in particular, there needs to be a reframing of the resettlement program, one that prioritizes the well-being and future life chances of refugee youth and their families over the creation of laboring subjects who are evaluated by their capacity to work and avoid dependency on the state.

The Current State of the Refugee Resettlement Program

Iraqis' experiences have become increasingly complicated since the beginning of the Trump administration. Refugee admissions[3] have plummeted since the first year that Donald Trump took office. While the number of admitted refugees has historically fluctuated with American strategic interests abroad as well as security concerns, between 1980 and 2017, the United States has set an average maximum of 95,000 refugees and admitted an average of 80,000 annually (Refugee Council USA 2019). As detailed in Table 1, beginning in January 2017, the Trump administration enacted a series of measures that essentially brought the numbers of refugees admitted to the United States down to a trickle. In fiscal year (FY) 2017, the Trump administration slashed the number of admitted refugees by more than 50 percent. Over the next several years, the Trump administration continued to set all-time low refugee admission numbers, arriving at 18,000 for FY 2020—the lowest number of refugees resettled by the United States in a single year since the creation of the nation's refugee program in 1980 and notably even lower than the year following the attacks of 9/11. It is important to note that this decline in refugee admissions comes at a time when the number of refugees worldwide has reached the highest levels since World War II. At the time of this writing, over 82 million people are displaced globally (UNHCR 2021).

TABLE 1.

Total Refugees and Iraqi Refugees Resettled to the United States: FY 2007–FY 2020

FISCAL YEAR	PRESIDENTIAL DETERMINATION OF NUMBER OF REFUGEES TO BE ADMITTED	TOTAL NUMBER OF REFUGEES RESETTLED TO THE U.S.	NUMBER OF IRAQI REFUGEES RESETTLED TO THE U.S.	NUMBER OF IRAQIS RESETTLED THROUGH SIV PROGRAM	PERCENTAGE OF IRAQI REFUGEES TO TOTAL REFUGEES RESETTLED
2007	70,000	48,218	1,608	0	3.3%
2008	80,000	60,107	13,822	438	22.9%
2009	80,000	74,602	18,838	1,557	25.3%
2010	80,000	73,293	18,016	2,000	24.6%
2011	80,000	56,384	9,388	618	16.7%
2012	76,000	58,179	12,163	3,203	20.9%
2013	70,000	69,909	19,487	1,460	27.8%
2014	70,000	69,975	19,769	3,084	28.3%
2015	70,000	69,920	12,676	890	18.1%
2016	85,000	84,988	9,880	2,049	11.6%
2017	110,000	53,691	6,886	2,455	12.8%
2018	45,000	22,405	140	605	0.62%
2019	30,000	29,818	465	189	1.56%
2020	18,000	11,814	540	177	4.57%
Totals	964,000	783,303	124,191	18,725	15.85%

In addition to the reduction in admissions, the Trump administration also drastically reduced funding for critical services for refugees, both pre-resettlement (including the interest-free travel loan that is provided to refugees for airfare costs) and post-resettlement (such as rental subsidies and access to public assistance programs).[4] These cuts were devastating for an already financially strapped system that cannot fully support the needs of refugees. These cuts have had an enormous impact on refugee resettlement agencies as well. Because voluntary resettlement agencies (VOLAGs) are funded per capita for refugee resettlement by the Bureau of Population, Refugees, and Migration (PRM), when arrivals are slashed, the very survival of local refugee resettlement agencies is threatened. Furthermore, the month after Donald Trump took office, the PRM announced changes that have impacted the network of local resettlement offices all over the country. Resettlement offices that expected to resettle fewer than one hundred refugees were mandated to close, and offices could only be affiliated with one VOLAG, ending a tri-agency model that allowed for several VOLAGs and local resettlement offices to work together. Prior to the Trump administration taking office, nine VOLAGs operated some 325 local refugee resettlement offices throughout the country, constituting a vast network of programs that supported refugees after their arrival to the United States. The Trump administration's policies and changes have resulted in the closure of 100 refugee resettlement offices nationwide, which account for one-third of the local reception and placement programs around the country (Alvarez 2019; Refugee Council USA 2019; Siegler 2019). In March 2019, the Trump administration released a FY 2020 budget request to dismantle the PRM, substantially decreasing funding for critical initial funding for resettled refugees and for overseas refugees.

At the outset of his presidency, Trump issued critical executive orders in 2017 that have had disproportionate effects on Muslim refugees and immigrants. Trump issued a halting of all refugees for 120 days, banned Syrian refugees indefinitely, and attempted to enact the first iteration of the "Muslim ban,"[5] which barred the entry of refugees from majority-Muslim countries based on the rationale that refugees from these countries required "enhanced vetting." Given Trump's presidential campaign promises to halt the entry of Muslims into the United States, to ban Syrian refugees altogether, and to create a Muslim registry (Krieg, Mullery, and Yellin 2017), these policy changes came as no surprise. The need for enhanced vetting is simply a fiction, since refugees undergo the most rigorous screening process of all those entering the United States, one that involves the Departments of State and Defense, Homeland Security, and the Federal Bureau of Investigation and the National Counterterrorism Center. This vetting process takes an average of eighteen months to two years (United States Citizenship and Immigration Services 2020). The administration's halting of the program for 120 days has delayed the entry of some refugees for several years, leaving them in limbo and in danger of repatriation to countries where their lives would be endangered (Refugee Council USA 2019; Golshan 2017). Refugees from the Muslim world continue to arrive in disproportionately low numbers, with an overall 90 percent reduction of Muslim refugees (Refugee Council USA 2019).

The Trump administration's drastic cuts have had a disastrous effect on the numbers of Iraqis resettled to the United States—the number of Iraqis dropped from several thousand per year to mere hundreds.[6] As Table 1 details, Iraqi refugees admitted to the United States belong to one of two groups: those who had assisted U.S. military missions in Iraq and refugees unaffiliated with the United States. The former group has historically entered through the United States through the Special Immigrant Visa program (SIV), which has allotted approximately five thousand visas annually.[7] Trump's various executive orders have caused several delays that created a backlog of more than one hundred thousand U.S.-affiliated Iraqis (Human Rights First 2019). Interpreters face daily harassment and death threats from the Islamic State, armed militias, and others that consider them traitors for working with U.S. forces (Gearan 2020). Many have received inexplicable rejections, but most wait for an average of two years to have their applications processed, not including the time it takes them to procure all of the proper paperwork and submit it through the rungs of the bureaucratic ladder. The Covid-19 pandemic has brought an already slow process to a near halt, since applicants are not able to be interviewed at the Baghdad embassy—a requirement of the process. It is important to prioritize the asylum of *all* Iraqis, not only for those who assisted U.S. forces in Iraq. A hyperfocus on this group—advocated by some in Washington based on the rationale that these Iraqis helped the United States on the ground while putting their own lives at risk and are owed safety in return—disregards America's role in the displacement of millions of Iraqis. The United States must take responsibility for its imperialistic actions in Iraq.

Since his inauguration, President Biden has vowed to raise the number of refugees to be admitted to the United States to 65,000 in FY 2021 and 125,000 in FY 2022. Unfortunately, only 11,411 refugees, 18 percent of the announced target, were resettled in FY 2021. The Biden administration cited the restrictive refugee policies set by former President Trump, which curtailed admissions and changed eligibility requirements, as the reason for the low admission rates. As of March 2022, less than 8,000 refugees have been resettled in FY 2022. The Biden administration has vowed to admit 100,000 Ukrainian refugees to the United States due to the Russian invasion of Ukraine, although not all will be resettled through the refugee program or in this fiscal year. While this commitment to aid Ukrainian refugees must be lauded and supported, the fact that the administration did not think that this new commitment warranted a change in the number of the refugees to be admitted in 2022 is worrisome. This leaves the fate of Iraqis and other Muslim refugees unclear, as the priorities of the refugee resettlement program shift to deal with the crisis in Ukraine.

Implications for the U.S. Refugee Resettlement Program

The experiences of Iraqi refugees within the United States speak to the specific role that its various institutions play in their double displacement. Their lives and stories have much to teach us about the ways that these institutions must change to serve them, as well as other marginalized communities, better, particularly in terms of remedying the broken nature of the American resettlement program. Even though the Trump administration's policies and restrictions have whittled away at the American resettlement program, the fundamental problem of the resettlement system is its adherence to the neoliberal project. A clear example of this is the notion of self-sufficiency, a central pillar in neoliberal framings of the welfare state and one of the most damaging aspects of the resettlement program. One way to assist refugees would be to turn the current notion of self-sufficiency on its head. As it stands, self-sufficiency is defined as ceasing to be a financial "burden" on the state, which can only be achieved through immediate work. This was not always the case. Though the Office of Refugee Resettlement (ORR) has explicitly and long stated that self-sufficiency is one of its major goals for refugees, it has not always emphasized immediate employment as the way to achieve that goal (Eggebø 2010; Sainsbury 2006). It was in the context of the Reagan administration, when notions of "welfare dependency" began to seep into the refugee program, that the concept of appropriate employment became synonymous with immediate employment, regardless of whether the jobs refugees found were commensurate with their experience in their home countries (Bean, Van Hook, and Glick 1997; Haines 2010; Halpern 2008; Nezer 2013). The current definition is detrimental to refugees' ability to truly realize the rights of full citizenship, or the right to have rights (Somers 2008). The pressure to procure employment as soon as they arrive in order to avoid homelessness robs refugees of the right to have rights. We must redefine self-sufficiency, understanding it as a project of providing refugees with all they need to succeed in their new contexts. What is needed is a program that prioritizes refugees' long-term well-being rather than the bottom line.

In their critique of the resettlement program, adult refugees in my study bemoaned the ways that the pressure of dwindling supports robbed them of the time they needed to *actually* become self-reliant. One of the most consistent critiques that refugees leveled at the current resettlement program was the lack of time and opportunity to learn English. Even though the ORR's second priority is language learning, it has long been outweighed by the emphasis on self-sufficiency, defined as immediate employment. Refugees in my study, particularly those who do not speak English, have expressed a deep desire to learn the language. This would not only allow them to acquire better jobs but also give them the ability to better navigate their new context and interact socially with those around them, reducing the social isolation that refugees, especially women and mothers, face. The refugee program should give refugees access to organized, stable, and accessible language learning, while simultaneously supporting them financially as they do so. This time could also be used for refugees to retrain or become recertified in their former employment fields, allowing them to build on their existing skills and expertise, rather than forcing them into low-wage work that offers neither healthcare benefits nor stability.

Refugees need comprehensive and adequate financial support from the ORR. Rather than providing refugees with a minimal, one time resettlement fund,[8] they should provide long-term support that can be used to subsidize refugees' housing while they acclimate to their new environments. The brevity and inadequacy of financial supports available to refugees from the ORR have serious effects on refugees' lives. If "the intention of the [resettlement] program is to provide 'sufficient support' to newly arriving refugees it must not be capped at a figure that falls short of achieving that goal" (Thomas 2011, 203). As it currently stands, the resettlement fund does not take into consideration the particular needs of refugees. For instance, Philadelphia's cost of living is relatively high as compared to other U.S. cities, and yet the cash assistance received by refugees is a fairly standard amount nationwide. Another example is the insensitivity to the needs of disabled refugees (Bonet and Taylor 2020), whose needs "should not be punished by a system that treats their needs and those of a healthy refugee equally" (Thomas 2011, 203). Refugees need to find adequate financial support to meet their needs as they attempt to build better lives.

Finally, refugees are in need of long-term navigational support. They should not be cut off from their case managers, who are their first point of contact upon their arrival, within a mere ninety days or less. Many participants reported feeling lost and unable to navigate the multiple institutions that they deal with on a daily basis after their short resettlement period is over. These suggestions are not that far removed from the former supports given to refugees in the United States. Prior to the Reagan-era welfare reforms and the passing of the Refugee Act of 1980, there existed programs that allowed for refugee professionals to access retraining in order for them to work in positions similar to the ones they held in their native countries and/or in countries where they sought refuge before arrival to the United States (Haines 2010; Thomas 2011). Refugees once received an average of three years of financial supports, which facilitated their opportunity to pursue language learning as well. If we are serious about supporting refugees, we must resist the neoliberal agenda that undergirds the current program, allowing them to eventually acquire what they need in order to stand on their own two feet. We need to remember that we need to provide refugees with the resources that they need to not only survive, but to thrive in their new communities.

Below, I provide suggestions for policy changes, which are informed by the lives of those whose stories are at the heart of this book.

Supporting Refugee Youth Transitions: Samah's Insights

In order to improve the lives of refugees, specifically of young adult refugees, the very nature of the American refugee resettlement program must change. While many refugee youth in my study worked part-time to support their families post-resettlement, Samah's position as the eldest child resettled with a widowed mother and younger siblings put an unduly heavy burden on her to provide for her family. Her mother—who suffered from several debilitating, chronic illnesses—was unable to work, leaving it up to Samah to take on the responsibility of becoming the primary wage earner. Samah's family was considered by the UNHCR as being in the "priority one" category, which puts them ahead of other populations for resettlement. Since Samah's mother was a widowed "single head of family" who was resettled without another head of household, the family was classified by the UNHCR as falling into the "women/girls under risk" category (UNHCR 2018). Since Samah's mother's medical records had been included in her file with UNHCR, Baheera had possibly qualified as a refugee with urgent "medical needs"—another priority one category. While this policy undoubtedly helps to prioritize the resettlement of the most vulnerable people[9] to countries of third resettlement, these considerations seem to matter only for resettlement purposes. This raises many questions: What happens to these vulnerable populations after they are resettled? Will they find the necessary supports on the other side? In other words, does resettlement alone relieve Samah and her family from vulnerability? In what ways do we stop attending to vulnerable refugee populations once they are resettled? Led by a widowed mother with medical problems, what will happen to her family of four if they rely solely on Samah's minimum wage earnings? What of Samah? Shouldn't being locked into a no-benefit, low-wage job that led to the abandonment of her educational aspirations *also* count as vulnerability? Samah and her family's experience calls into question American refugee resettlement policy. It implies that resettlement *must* include better supports for youth and their families vis-à-vis financial supports, rather than simply "allowing" them to partake in a capitalist system that chews them up and spits them out, locking them permanently into poverty.

Implications for Public Assistance Programs

All of the adults in my study unanimously voiced a need for longer and more adequate support from their welfare office. Many voiced the feeling that they had been "thrown into the deep end" and were expected by their welfare office agents to "sink or swim." As refugees struggled with the need to find immediate work before the end of their resettlement period, they faced the reality of dwindling cash assistance and food stamps. The problem that refugees face in accessing longer and more adequate support lies in the decision to bring post-resettlement supports under the larger umbrella of mainstream public assistance in the United States. Rather than having a set of stable, federally funded supports that are earmarked specifically for refugees, the Refugee Act made access to financial assistance subject to local and state implementation of programs such as Temporary Assistance for Needy Families (TANF) and the Supplementary Nutrition Assistance Program (SNAP). Refugees' access to financial support has thus been indelibly marked by the neoliberal reframing of public assistance that repositioned welfare programs from a social virtue to a social vice that damages society by encouraging dependency. Under neoliberal control, the number one goal of welfare programs is the reduction and eventual elimination of recipients from welfare rolls. Despite the increase of poverty among welfare recipients—a result of new measures that limited support periods, prioritized immediate work, and disallowed education and training—neoliberal welfare reformers consider the reforms successful simply because the number of recipients has been reduced. Nearly three decades after the reframing of the TANF program, poverty has *increased* among recipients, a fact that is rarely recognized in public discourse about welfare programs. Rather than acknowledging that it is *poverty* that leads people to turn to public assistance, the neoliberal paternalist view frames those who depend on welfare as either lacking personal responsibility or simply refusing to work, and instead desiring to be a burden on others (Somers 2008). Furthermore, research suggests that welfare benefits are *far* from generous. Public assistance benefits are not adequate enough to meet the needs of low-income families, and need to be expanded in order to do so.

One seemingly straightforward strategy might be to divorce refugee assistance from generalized public assistance programs and ensure that refugees get long-term, adequate financial support. Along with the earlier suggestion of removing the pressure to find immediate work rather than appropriate work, the ORR should also provide long-term financial assistance to refugees as they receive training in their former fields or new ones that interest them, learn English, and find gainful employment. Like other Western countries, the United States could provide for refugees' housing costs for several years, encourage them to enroll in language classes that are stable and accessible, and provide state-funded healthcare for as long as they need it. The problem with this solution is that it leaves the current status quo of public assistance unquestioned and the inequities built into the system unaddressed. We cannot be content with answers that benefit refugees, while ignoring the plight of millions of marginalized people within the United States whose fate is decided by problematic neoliberal framings of welfare programs.

Feminist scholars remind us that in order to achieve justice, we must reveal and alter the very building blocks of the current welfare system, rather than merely be satisfied with changes in redistributive policies (Fraser 1994; Smith 2008; Young 1990). First, to build a new and equitable understanding of justice, we must bring the oftentimes neglected voices of those served by these programs to the fore (Smith 2008). We must move away from relegating decision-making to a small group of so-called experts and a bureaucracy that is protected from political contestation and use the social knowledge of those whose lives are on the line to inform policy and practice (Young 1990). Second, in order to change the experiences of those who depend on public assistance programs, we must correct the assumptions and principles that undergird the current system. Many households in the Iraqi refugee community are headed by widowed mothers, leaving them vulnerable in a welfare system that was built on the notion of the ideal industrial-era family, which theoretically supported the male breadwinner during instances of disability, unemployment, or old age, while women were uncompensated for their labor in the home. Those who fell outside of the boundaries of this family constellation—such as female heads of households and single women—never met this criteria, and as such continue to struggle without the financial support of a male breadwinner. Simultaneously, as the testimonies of refugee adults reveal, the current postindustrial labor market is rife with low-wage, temporary, and unstable employment that does not offer standard benefits such as healthcare or pensions (Fraser 1994). The current welfare system does not offer insurance against the precarity that is embedded into this neoliberal labor market. Finally, the ideals that should guide welfare reform efforts should be rooted in the prevention of poverty, protection from exploitation, a quest for equality, combatting marginalization, and anti-androcentrism—women should not have to lead male-like lives in order to receive support. Refugee women such as Baheera, Fatima, and Nadia should not have to find work, but be supported in their efforts as mothers. Authentic welfare reforms must aim to "overcome gender division of labor, to soften the public–private distinction, and to scramble the care–work distinction" (Fraser and Bedford 2008, 229). We need a welfare system that overturns problematic notions that have long vilified the most marginalized among us.

Implications for Public Education

Rather than following through with its current course of action, which has been characterized by the neoliberal project, such as closing of neighborhood schools, favoring charter schools, laying off teachers and essential staff, and threatening the health benefits of school personnel (Lipman 2013; McWilliams 2019), cities like Philadelphia *must* reinvest in public education—one of the last vestiges of the public good owed to U.S. citizens. These policies and practices, shaped by market logics, have had deleterious consequences on students attending Philadelphia public schools. For instance, district-wide budget cuts eliminated 40 percent of the school nurses. As a result, it was typical for one nurse to provide care for multiple schools, leaving many schools without a nurse for three or four days a week. Between September 2013 and May 2014, two elementary-aged children, twelve-year-old Laporshia Massey and seven-year-old Sebastian Gerena, died within hours after collapsing in their classrooms, where there was no school nurse on duty at the time (Lee 2014). Ann Smiegel, the once full-time nurse of Sebastian Gerena's school, stated, "the benefit of having immediate medical care, immediate response, [and] clear decision-makers"—all services provided by school nurses—can be the difference between life and death in attending to children who undergo health crises at school (Denvir 2014). In other words, these neoliberal policies not only threaten the academic futures of children but put their lives in danger as well.

How Zeina's Story Troubles Special Education

Refugee youth's testimonies highlight how special education policies can hollow out the educational futures of refugee students, as well as their ability to access citizenship rights. Zeina's story in particular brings forth two important ways that special education programs within her urban, public school need to change. First, the pre-migratory histories of refugee youth may present in complex ways, and these students need schools that can respond to their unique needs in flexible ways. In spite of the fact that Zeina suffered a traumatic brain injury—the basis of her special education designation—she also suffered as a result of being a survivor of a school shooting and living in a war zone. The trauma from these incidents kept Zeina out of schooling for several years, isolating her from peers for the duration of this time. She came to her American schooling with almost no literacy in her native language—making school and especially language learning quite difficult for her.

Even though Zeina's experiences in Iraq and then in Syria had a specific effect on her academic needs, the school initially prescribed a one-size-fits-all response to her case. Placing her in the resource room full-time, segregating her from her peers, was the farthest thing from the solution. Furthermore, as disability scholars argue, segregated special education classrooms are not the place for Zeina's special education peers either, who should have never been sent to the resource room where they might languish for years (Baglieri and Knopf 2004). Zeina and her resource room classmates belonged in the mainstream classroom. There, Zeina would be in a setting where all of her needs could be met, as an English language learner and as a student with specific learning needs that were also textured by trauma, violence, and the resulting complexities that caused her interrupted educational experience. More important, through true inclusion—which goes beyond simply mainstreaming students with disabilities—refugee students like Zeina (as well as her classmates) can access citizenship rights and become full members of their communities (Taylor 2020). According to disability scholars, this process cannot begin until difference is constructed as natural, acceptable, and ordinary, and inclusion is perceived as a moral imperative (Stiker 2019). A school that is truly inclusive values all of its members equally, normalizes difference through the provision of differentiated instruction, and fosters a school culture that centers care and community (Baglieri and Knopf 2004).

Second, while Zeina's improvement can be traced to the exceptional interventions made on her behalf—such as the pro-bono lawyer who procured a large settlement from the school district—what is needed is a system that works without these types of interventions. I must clarify that this is in no way meant to imply that Zeina was not an agentic subject, nor that her academic gains and overall success were not connected to her hard work in the process of learning and growing. On the contrary! In my double role as her tutor and as an ethnographer, I saw, on a daily basis, the incredible effort that Zeina put into her learning. She never missed a day of school, did her homework religiously, and was an avid reader. It was not surprising that in the span of three years she went from being preliterate to reading and writing at a second grade level. I was also a witness to Zeina's incredible tenacity and strength. On her "bad days," when she was flooded with bad memories, she did the "emotional homework" her psychologist had suggested and made art, listened to music, or watched TV instead of ruminating alone in her room. Zeina went through the unthinkable and had proven her incredible strength.

However, that Zeina was eventually transferred out of the resource room, that she could work with a tutor for three periods a day on a curriculum that met her specific learning needs, and that upon graduation she had several paid options for postsecondary programming were all opportunities that were made possible by the settlement procured by her lawyer. Without his intervention, it is likely that she would have persisted in the resource room and that she would have continued to struggle both academically and emotionally. Before the lawyer took on Zeina's case, Nadia's attempt to speak to her daughter's teachers and advocate for a change of placement had been rejected. Zeina's struggles were explained away as a part of her diagnosis, and, as usual, the school psychologist's diagnosis prevailed over Nadia's knowledge of her own daughter (Mehan 2000). In the end, it was Nadia's social capital that proved to be the key to Zeina's success. Had the lawyer not intervened on her behalf, Zeina's fate would have been very different. According to the scholarship on social and family capital, refugee families have less social capital than their native counterparts (D'Addario, Hiebert, and Sherrell 2007; Morrice 2007). Accordingly, they often lack the ability to make the types of interventions on behalf of their children that Nadia was able to procure for Zeina. In that case, most refugee students remain stuck in classrooms that do not meet their complex needs. Furthermore, the removal of Zeina from the resource room did little to change or challenge the rigid, ableist system in place that resulted in the labeling, placement, and persistence of her classmates there. In this case, there might have been a somewhat "happy ending" for one student, but it left an entire system unquestioned and unaddressed. What is needed is a system that carefully considers students' needs and prioritizes inclusion without the need for extraordinary interventions.

Layla's Story and ESL Policy and Practice

Layla's experience of being socially promoted regardless of her literacy level brings forth questions about current policies regarding English as a second language instruction. Language acquisition scholars have long argued that English language learners (ELLs) are expected to transition to full-time instruction in English in monolingual mainstream classrooms far too quickly (Harper and de Jong 2004; Fillmore and Snow 2000). Without the necessary supports such as trained ELL/bilingual teachers, instructional accommodations, and professional development for mainstream teachers, ELLs can "disappear" in their mainstream classes (Coady, Harper, and de Jong 2016). This practice finds its roots in the long-debated history of English-only teaching practices, which stemmed from several legislative initiatives nationwide. These prioritized the rapid transition of ELLs into mainstream classrooms while cutting language support programming (Harper and de Jong 2009). These programs problematically assume that the needs of ELLs are not significantly different from students who are proficient in English, and that ELLs will learn through social interaction with their peers.

The practices of mainstreaming ELLs too quickly also stems from the pressure to quickly prepare them for high-stakes testing demanded by the

No Child Left Behind Act of 2001, needed to keep public schools accountable and safe from closure (Menken 2010). By hurrying students into mainstream classrooms without structured English immersion, students do not have time to gain the academic skills needed to succeed. Older refugee students like Layla, who begin their academic journeys in later grades, face larger challenges as they have less time than their younger counterparts to develop academic language, which is further exacerbated by these pressures to move them out of their ESL classrooms. Without comprehensive linguistic support, it is no wonder that Layla was struggling academically. Policies are needed that take into account the linguistic needs of refugee youth and other ELLs. This includes providing students with ample time and support as they acclimate to their new contexts, schools, and the English language. Schools that have been particularly successful with refugee students have accomplished this through the emphasis of a language curriculum that views all teachers as language teachers (rather than only perceiving ESL teachers as responsible for this task), encourages the use of students' native languages, and relies on team teaching, which includes school counselors in designing learning for students (Mendenhall, Bartlett, and Ghaffar-Kucher 2017; Bartlett, Mendenhall, and Ghaffar-Kucher 2017).

Addressing Islamophobia in Schools

The negative experiences and barriers that many refugee students shared and attributed to Islamophobia further emphasize the need for schools that are safe and inclusive for Muslim refugee youth. Scholars have long documented the challenges that immigrant and transnational Muslim youth face in their schools in a post-9/11 and post-Trump era, including being overtargeted by measures of surveillance, securitization, and investigation, as well as being subjected to many forms of harassment including constant taunting, physical violence, and even death threats, which they experienced in their communities and their schools (Abu El-Haj and Bonet 2011; Bayoumi 2008; Bonet 2018; Wingfield 2006). These realities have become more acute due to rising Islamophobic political rhetoric and policies that situate Muslim refugee youth as the permanent "other." Schools, which have always been key sites for nation building, are at the heart of the battle for defining "American-ness" as the oppositional identity to the cultural and political values that are associated with Islam (Abu El-Haj 2010; Abu El-Haj and Bonet 2011) As such, education is framed as a form of liberating Muslim youth from "backward" traditions and beliefs, and disciplining them into becoming free, Western subjects (Abu El-Haj 2015; Jaffe-Walter 2016). To mitigate these experiences, teachers need to come to terms with and critically examine their assumptions about national belonging, and become better educated about the role of the United States as a global power (Abu El-Haj 2010). In this case, it would be especially helpful for teachers to become educated in the role of the United States as an invading and occupying force in Iraq, and in the realities that have occurred in their students' lives as a result.

Muslim refugee youth deserve safe schools, where diversity is not only represented within the student body but appreciated, fostered, and celebrated. The youth in this study attended Liberty High, one of the most diverse schools in the district, evidenced by a student body that spoke over sixty languages—a reason that the teachers proudly referred to the school as a "mini-United Nations." However, in spite of the various flags hanging in the school cafeteria and the annual multicultural celebration, Muslim refugee youth were not safe from everyday instances of discrimination and harassment. What Muslim students need is a school culture where all students are actually held in equal value rather than one that merely makes surface-level nods to aspects of their identity, such as flags and dances. Instead, the school can draw on the diversity of the students in a meaningful way through transforming the curriculum, allowing students to make decisions on important social issues that texture their daily lives and to take action to solve them (Banks and Banks, 2019). Furthermore, teachers need to view students' various backgrounds, experiences, and perspective as an asset, which they can draw from and build on (González, Moll, and Amanti 2006). Refugee youth have much to contribute about the state of the world, such as current international politics and how global migration policy manifests on a local level. Furthermore, students, their families, and communities bring with them a vast array of ways of knowing that are often untapped in schools. Drawing from these various funds of knowledge, rather than viewing students as subjects to mold and shape into Western subjects, would be a good place to start.

A Note about Educators

As a former K–12 teacher, I am and have always been wary of research and discourse that criminalizes teachers without paying heed to and under-

standing the context in which teachers and staff find themselves. The closure of neighborhood schools combined with the layoffs of teachers and
staff put pressure on schools to do more with less. Philadelphia teachers,
who reportedly have upwards of forty students in their classes after the
budget crisis (McWilliams 2016) cannot possibly meet the needs of all of
their students. Refugee youths' testimonies above were rife with critiques
of their teachers' actions and attitudes toward students, with the particular
complaint that teachers simply "didn't care" about them. We must keep
in mind that teachers are asked to care for multitudes of students with
varying needs, including refugee students, while their jobs and livelihoods
are under attack. How can we expect teachers to show care for refugee
students and for their unique needs, when we do not extend the same
courtesy toward teachers themselves? I say this not to excuse the deplorable actions of some teachers against Iraqi refugee students, but rather to
remind us that teachers are often at the nexus of neoliberal reforms and
blamed for the very conditions that spurred these reforms to begin with.
Before we become quick to indict teachers, we must think critically about
the broader systems that place them at the center of the current market
fundamentalist attack on education. Furthermore, the conditions of the
school district, and the pressure cooker environment for both students *and*
teachers, communicates deficit-minded ableism, reinforces anti-Blackness,
and normalizes discrimination against Arab and Muslim youth. In other
words, circular discrimination is at work across structural hierarchies
in schools.

Implications for Young Adult Education

In the search for ideas of how to support the educational needs of older
refugee youth, we need not look further than the refugee community itself. Refugee parents, who were concerned with the educational trajectories and barriers that their children faced, regularly offered up suggestions
and possible solutions during my conversations with them. Fatima argued
that programs need to be made available for refugee students who have
aspirations for secondary and higher education, but who like her son Seif
were too old, or who like Samah were simply unable to attend school as
a result of being the primary wage earner. Since the vast majority of the
existing adult education programs in Philadelphia primarily target native
English speakers, young adult education must exist within the realm of

public secondary education. The first necessary change, Fatima argued, was the rethinking of state limits on public education, which in many states, including Pennsylvania, is set at twenty-one years of age. Young adult refugees who come with significant educational interruptions—a hallmark of the refugee experience—are placed in younger grades and then excluded from public schools when they age out. The method of placing students must also be reexamined. Rather than basing students' placement merely on the number of credits that have earned, their age and prior education (or lack thereof) must also be taken into account. If current policies and procedures remain unchanged, many young adult refugees will continue to be excluded from public schooling with no place to turn for an education. School districts that serve refugee students need to be more flexible and add more programming that meets the unique needs of refugee students. Refugee parents suggested after-school programming for students who could not attend during the traditional school day. They stipulated that this programming needed to be offered at neighborhood public schools, to ensure that it was within reach via public transportation and that it employed ESL teachers who understood the linguistic needs of refugee youth. Otherwise, districts will continue to exclude refugee students, robbing them of their imagined chance at the "settled life" they had hoped to find in their new countries.

By excluding refugee youth from higher education, school districts are inadvertently funneling and locking young adult refugees into the low-wage labor market. When we fight for a quality education for refugees, we guarantee the rights of all students. As captured by the various testimonies of young adult refugees, it is clear that they deserve an education that responds to their unique needs where they are placed in age-appropriate grades, includes flexible programming that accommodates for their educational delays, offers adult education programs that fit their language and schedule needs, and provides meaningful pathways to higher education. In order for this to be a reality, we need to continue advocating for a bolstering of public education in ways that make the needs of marginalized students visible.

Implications for Healthcare

Most of the adult participants in my study presented with various health needs, including heart disease, diabetes, chronic pain, and chronic daily migraines, as well as various mental health challenges including depression, anxiety, and posttraumatic stress disorder. Once their federally funded health insurance lapsed, typically eight months after their arrival, many refugees lacked access to healthcare. Refugees were expected to purchase health insurance through their employers, but many of them were unable to do so as a result of unaffordable premiums and/or high deductibles. The enactment of the Affordable Care Act (ACA) had brought some semblance of hope, but this was dashed when refugees discovered that they were in fact *too poor* to qualify for ACA coverage and yet were also shut out of Medicaid due to the restriction of the program in the state of Pennsylvania[10] at the time. Refugees' ability to access healthcare is severely interrupted and perhaps permanently blocked once their federally funded health insurance lapses. Many Iraqi refugees reported that their first several months in the United States was a time filled with confusion, instability, and uncertainty as they grappled with a cultural and linguistic context that was far removed from their own, while also attempting to acquire gainful employment before their financial supports expired. By the time refugees began to have time to address their medical needs, many of them were shocked to find that their medical benefits had already lapsed. Even for those who prioritized seeking out healthcare, the slow nature of the U.S. healthcare system, which often requires referrals from a primary physician for labs, tests, and specialist visits, limited their ability to receive adequate healthcare before their state-funded benefits lapsed. Refugees also come to their new contexts with more than physical health needs. As a result of living in homelands ripped apart by war, violence, and various forms of instability, refugees often arrive in their new contexts with mental health challenges. While some help exists for those who have survived torture at the hands of a government official via the Survivors Support Network, many of the refugees in my study did not qualify under that program and thus had no access to mental health services once their federally funded health insurance lapsed.

An obvious solution for this problem lies with the Office of Refugee Resettlement (ORR). Rather than providing state-funded health insurance for a mere eight months, the ORR should provide refugees, particularly those who are living in poverty, with long-term access to healthcare. However, this would leave the larger problem—how healthcare functions in the United States—unaddressed. The U.S. healthcare system is in desperate need for an overhaul. The United States remains the only high-income country without universal healthcare, treating health as a commodity distributed only to those who can pay rather than a social service to those who are in medical need (Woolhandler et al. 2003). In spite of the fact that the United States spends more[11] on healthcare than comparable countries, Americans have a lower life expectancy (Christopher 2016; Fuchs 2018). Our current, complex system of network insurance is not only wasteful and inefficient but also deeply inequitable. The highly contested enactment of the Affordable Care Act made some progress in improving and expanding healthcare, but it was never meant to provide universal healthcare. Refugees whose healthcare benefits have lapsed are among the nearly 11 percent of Americans, more than 31 million people, who are uninsured (Tasha 2021). The number of uninsured Americans is rising every day due to the devastating effect of the Covid-19 pandemic, which has caused unprecedented rates of unemployment in the United States (Tolbert, Orgera, and Damico 2020). Nearly 75 percent of uninsured adults cite the high cost of insurance as the main reason they lack coverage (Tolbert, Orgera, and Damico 2020). Families with low incomes and people of color are overrepresented in this group, which points to the inequity embedded in the current healthcare system (Tolbert, Orgera, and Damico 2020). In 2019, three in ten uninsured adults forewent much-needed medical attention (Tolbert, Orgera, and Damico 2020). Study after study has confirmed that the uninsured are less likely than the insured to receive preventative care as well as services for chronic diseases and major health conditions (Christopher 2016). In comparison, Canada's healthcare system covers a series of medical treatments and exams, and supplemental insurance plans are required for additional services (Tasha 2021).

According to many scholars, activists, and physicians, the best possible way to address the inequity is the creation of a national health insurance system. Under this plan, all American residents would receive insurance under one health insurance plan and could access all necessary services, including doctors, hospitals, prescription drugs, dental and vision care, and long-term care (Christopher 2016; Fuchs 2018; Woolhandler et al. 2003). This system would essentially be an expanded and improved version of the existing Medicare program, which is nicknamed "Medicare-for-all" (Woolhandler et al. 2003). A universal healthcare system would address the needs of the uninsured and the underinsured, lower administrative expenses,[12] and counteract the monopoly power of pharmaceutical companies, health device manufacturers, hospitals, and physicians (Fuchs

2018). The current obstacles to universal healthcare are mostly political, including the immense lobbying efforts of those who have the most to gain from this system. Some advocates suggest rolling out universal healthcare at the state rather than the federal level, as a way to demonstrate feasibility (Christopher 2016). Others argue that similar to Canada's provincial control of national healthcare, universal healthcare should be managed at the state level due to the population size of the United States (Fuchs 2018). Regardless of the implementation method, universal healthcare is needed so that all U.S. residents, including refugees, can access healthcare more equitably. Access to healthcare is a universal right, not a privilege that is limited to those who can afford it.

At the outset of my research, the tide was turning, both nationally and globally, against refugees. The ongoing Syrian crisis was unfolding, and the world began to witness the worst refugee crisis in recorded history (UNHCR 2021). Masses of refugees made perilous journeys in rickety boats to escape the horror in their home countries, as discourses that framed Muslim refugees as a threat to national security and identity gained traction in both Europe and the United States. Photos of Alan Kurdi's small toddler body washed up on a Turkish beach went viral, bringing attention, if ever so briefly, to the enormity of the refugee crisis. At the time of this writing, the most recent wave of the ongoing Afghani refugee crisis has been the subject of international news coverage. Thousands of civilians clamored in already overrun airports, begging to be put on flights leaving Kabul after the Taliban took control of the country upon U.S. military withdrawal in August 2021. U.S. airlifts evacuated only 80,000 Afghanis, Americans, and other foreign nationals, leaving the vast majority of the 300,000 Afghanis who have been affiliated with U.S. operations as well as millions of vulnerable others in the hands of the brutal Taliban government. Afghanis have long been forced to flee for their safety, with 2.2 million Afghanis displaced in other countries and 3.5 million internally displaced within Afghanistan. In 2021 alone, over 550,000 Afghani refugees fled the country (BBC Visual Journalism Team 2021). The United Nations has called on neighboring states to open up their borders for refugees, but many have refused, claiming security reasons and oversaturation of existing refugees in their country.

Those concerned with refugees have demanded that Western countries open up their borders rather than set up fences, detention camps, or even deport refugees back to the deadly contexts they had fled from. Rightfully so, refugee activists and advocates have implored the United States to take responsibility for humanitarian crises caused by its military imperialism in countries like Afghanistan and Iraq. In this framing, the proposed solution to the horrific injustices perpetuated by the United States in the name of the War on Terror is the resettlement of refugees within its borders. Undergirding this proposal is the assumption that once resettled, those who have been displaced will in fact find refuge. However, the lives of the Iraqi refugees whose stories have been at the heart of this book reveal the cruel fallacy at the heart of this notion, as they have been doubly displaced by neoliberal imperialism, first in their home countries and then again in the very country that destroyed their homes and lives. While resettlement is indeed a necessary first step, it is by no means a comprehensive solution. Creating actual refuge for those who have been displaced by American imperialism requires the courage to change course. The United States must consider how its own actions have created humanitarian crises worldwide. The U.S. government and people must come to terms with the ongoing legacies of its global neoliberal imperialist ventures, including the devastation of whole nations such as Iraq and Afghanistan. Leaders, often afraid of the political ramifications of suggesting and implementing policies that prioritize the public good, including those suggested above, must face up with their responsibility to do so. This might seem to the reader a naïve or even impossible dream. However, as the testimonies of these Iraqi refugees suggest, refugees' lives cannot be improved unless we upend the systems that have wreaked havoc on them. As difficult as it is to imagine a reversal of the current neoliberal present, we must continue to advocate and fight for a different world. Nothing less will do.

Acknowledgments

This book owes a great deal to so many who helped me along the way. First and foremost, I owe a great debt to the refugee families who opened up their homes and lives to me, and whose stories are at the heart of this project. What you have taught me about resilience, love, and what it takes to make a new life after so much loss will stay with me forever. Thank you also to Rasha, Nancy, Susan, Mary, and Lian, and all of the other employees of the refugee-serving organizations who allowed me to observe, firsthand, the difficulties of supporting refugees with ever-dwindling supports. Though I have used pseudonyms for you here, your input and perspective have been so important. Thank you to Thamer Dawood Al-Sudani for allowing me to use your gorgeous piece "Baghdad" as the cover art for this book. I am truly grateful.

Thank you to my mentor Thea Renda Abu El-Haj for her constant encouragement and for teaching me by example about the joys and frustrations of writing. I am grateful to her, Beth Rubin, Ariana Mangual Figueroa, and Shahrzad Mojab for the close reading of my dissertation, which inspired this book. I will also be forever grateful to Thea for starting a "social nearing" remote writing group a few weeks after the outbreak of the Covid-19 pandemic. This wonderful group brought me into the orbit of incredible women who were always generous with their advice and time. I have since started several other writing groups, a practice that made a potentially isolating time of the pandemic shutdown rich with community and friendship. Thank you to Ashley Taylor and Rosemary Ndubuizu for being my writing partners during this process and holding me accountable simply through your loving presence during a difficult time for us all. Without the energy, support, and care shown to me during these writing groups, this book would have never been completed.

I am extremely grateful for the guidance and help of so many mentors. Thank you Reva Jaffe-Walter and Sarah Dryden-Peterson for giving so generously of your time to review earlier drafts of this manuscript. Your insights, comments, and suggestions shaped and strengthened this book immensely. To my dear mentor Kathy Schultz, thank you for all of your encouragement and guidance throughout my graduate career and beyond, and for encouraging me to write this book. I will always be grateful to you for demonstrating with humility and kindness what being a mentor really meant. I carry this lesson with me as I mentor my own students. To my gracious mentor Lesley Bartlett, thank you for the guidance, grace, and kindness you have shown me that went well beyond the confines of the CAE Presidential Fellows program. To Catherine Lugg, thank you for encouraging me to submit my first article and for guiding me through that process. Thank you for showing me how those of us on the margins can make a place for ourselves in the academy. To James Giarelli, thank you for your care and concern during one of the most difficult times of my life. This research would not be possible without your support. Thank you to my editor, Pieter Martin, whose patience and understanding made this book possible. Finally, I thank the Ford Foundation, the Spencer Foundation, and the Roothbert Fund for their financial support of my research, which made this manuscript possible.

I owe a great deal to the wonderful women in my life. To my dearly departed mother, thank you for blazing the path to the academy for me. Your brilliance, resilience, and quiet resolve in the face of the many struggles that textured your life have been and will remain an inspiration to me. Thank you and Baba, for your dedication to my education and for investing so much in me. To my late but never forgotten Teita Daad, thank you for the pride that shone on your face every time I hung another diploma on the wall of our little apartment in Cairo. You taught me that *al-qalam ma biyzeel al-balam,* that education does not necessarily remove ignorance. Though you left school early, you were the brightest person I knew. I miss you every day. To Rebecca Atallah, Mom, whose love, resolve, and care for the most vulnerable in society have been an inspiration to me since childhood: thank you for making me a part of your family. My dearest sister Rhanda, thank you for painstakingly editing every draft of the grant applications and articles that led to this book. I would not be who I am without your tireless support and constant cheerleading. Thank you for being my sister and best friend. To Leila, my tree friend and soulmate, thank you for being my biggest fan, the first one I want to talk to about anything, and my favorite travel partner. Your loyal and steadfast friendship has made me who I am today. To my dearest friend Julie McWilliams, thank you for graciously giving of your time to read and edit earlier versions of this manuscript. My book, and my life, have been made better by having you in it. Thank you for paving the way and writing your book first and teaching me about discipline and dedication. You are my heart. To my brilliant friend and soul sister Mara Hughes, thank you for giving me a home, not only during the year that I undertook writing this book but always. This entire manuscript was written on your Mimi's little table, and I know that both she and Teita were watching over me. Thank you not only for being the wonderful person you are but also for reading and strengthening this book with your deep insight and perspective. Without you all, I would not be where I am today.

Appendix

A Note on Methods

The Study

On an unseasonably warm fall afternoon of 2011, I sat at an empty student's desk in Liberty High, watching Seif, Ghada, Heba, Layla, Ayman, and Adam rehearse for the upcoming concert with their classmates. In a few months, they would join students from several other schools in a performance of Arabic songs, organized by a local educational nonprofit where I was employed at the time. Liberty High, a public high school with a population of nearly three thousand students, had been selected to participate due to the high proportion of students of Arab descent: second-generation Palestinians, Egyptians, and Moroccans, as well as a growing body of Iraqi refugee students. These Arabic-speaking students would lead the choir of non-Arabic-speaking students from other schools. As usual, the biweekly rehearsal became rowdy as the students began to tease and laugh with each other. On this particular day I was nervous because I planned to hand the Iraqi students a consent form, asking them to take part in my dissertation project—a qualitative inquiry about the educational experiences of Iraqi youth in the United States. Once I received their consent, I would muster the courage to speak to the assistant principal to conduct daily observations in the school. Knowing that many of the recently resettled Iraqi students and their families were monolingual Arabic speakers, I was sure to provide them with consent forms in Arabic.

What happened next surprised me. Without exception, all of the students brought their consent forms back unsigned, informing me that their parents were uncomfortable signing anything without meeting me first. As an Arab immigrant to the United States whose research has centered the surveillance, policing, and discrimination that Arabs and Muslims faced in the United States after 9/11, I must admit I felt rather foolish for not predicting this outcome. I apologized to the students, who were gracious and understanding, and eventually I received invitations to their homes, to meet their families. After offering me sweet cardamom tea and homemade baked goods, refugee parents asked me many questions about my own immigration history to the United States, my family in Egypt, and my interest in their children as participants in my doctoral study. In some families, these conversations took place over several visits, but eventually, all of the parents I had approached signed the consent form. Meeting the parents of the refugee students that I had gotten to know at their school had an unexpected effect on my work. I learned that refugee parents had stories to tell, and many, especially the mothers who were often socially isolated, were eager to tell them. I quickly realized that in order to understand the refugee experience, one cannot disembody youth from their families. Iraqi refugees lost their homes and livelihoods, and were forced to leave behind all that they had known. The family unit was all they had left. It became clear to me that a study that aimed to capture the experiences of refugees in the United States *must* make the family its unit of analysis. My study took an unexpected turn and became an exploration of the lives of four focal Iraqi refugee families and the American institutions that indelibly shaped their future in this new context. It was this new focus that allowed me to meet adult refugees and seek to gain an understanding of their worlds. The study that I had anticipated would last one year became a four-year ethnographic study, spanning 2011–2015.

As an ethnographer, my goal was to achieve a "thick description" (Geertz 1973) of participants' day-to-day lives and their understandings of their lived experiences. Many questions fueled my research. How did Iraqis, refugees who would eventually be eligible for legal citizenship, understand themselves in relation to the American nation-state? What did it mean for them to be living in the proverbial belly of the beast, in the very nation that had caused their displacement as well as endless destruction to their home country? How did poverty and the subsequent need to depend on the various institutions of the welfare state texture their lives? How did they interpret their interactions with these institutions? And finally, how did these encounters inform their notions of citizenship? To answer these questions, I spent countless hours with refugee families, mostly in their homes.

At the outset of my research, I conducted one-on-one interviews with refugees, as well as family focus groups where all family members were invited to discuss a particular topic and/or answer semistructured questions based on topics that they had shared with me prior to that time. These discussions were especially rich because they captured the ways in which participants' experiences were negotiated and co-constructed in the context of the family. Over time, the nature of my research with the families changed in a few key ways. First, the planned and audiotaped interviews gave way to a comfortable embeddedness within the families. Gone was my audio recorder and my sole role as a researcher. In their place was an eventual understanding of me as *waHda min il'ayla,* or a member of the family—a mutual feeling that I shared and cherished. Like all members of the refugee family, I did my part to ensure their survival in this new and unfamiliar context. Within the home, I became the tutor for the young members of the household, who, as recently resettled refugees whose prior (and often fragmented) education had been in Arabic, needed all of the academic help they could get. While visiting refugee family homes, I also made phone calls, interpreted mail, and helped make sense of documents that came from the school. Any fieldnotes that I jotted down were often scribbled hastily in my car after these visits, or as soon as I got home. Daily life in a family, with its duties and natural rhythms, was not conducive for traditional forms of ethnographic practice, typically referred to as "participant observation." As Altorki noted in her own fieldwork among Arab families, I became an "observant participant"; "My primary duty was to participate. To observe became an incidental privilege" (1988, 56).

A second way that my research changed over time was the site of my study. As I grew increasingly close to families, I was asked to accompany them to the various institutions of the state—including public schools, resettlement agencies, welfare offices, free clinics, doctor's offices, and hospitals—assisting them with interpretation and navigating these often-unfamiliar spaces. I was also asked to tag along to the bank, DMV, grocery store, discount clothing stores, and the mall. I had hoped to conduct my research in schools, to see firsthand the everyday lives of Iraqi refugee youth in the classrooms, hallways, and cafeterias of their school. However, having recently been "burned" by many educational researchers who came before me, the administration of Liberty High, the public high school that housed all of the refugee youth in my study, ultimately refused to grant their permission for my study. Over time, I have made my peace with this limitation of my study. While I was unable to conduct my study on school grounds, my research in refugee homes allowed me to document the way that the school penetrated the home in many forms: school documents, telephonic communications with the family where I acted as a translator, individualized educational plans sent home for parents' signatures, school assignments, and more. Ultimately, I was also able to interview a few Liberty High teachers and School District of Philadelphia administrators during public community meetings hosted by the refugee resettlement agency. Soon after I began my research, a topic that came up time and time again in my conversations with refugee adults was their disappointment with the refugee resettlement agency—the first state institution that they interacted with upon arrival. To better understand this phenomenon (and in an effort to triangulate my data), I spent a year volunteering and collecting data at a local resettlement agency. As an Arabic speaker, I was welcomed at the resettlement agency—with only one Arabic speaker on staff, it was struggling to communicate with its growing population of Iraqi clients. At the agency, I was able to interview and observe agency employees, including resettlement caseworkers, the director of case management, and the director of the agency. This allowed me to understand what and how services were delivered to newly arrived refugees, as well as learn more how federal and state resettlement policies took shape on a local level. My time at the agency also allowed me to meet more Iraqi refugees, who later joined my study. I also had the opportunity for a few months to shadow the program officer of a nonprofit organization that served the Arab population of Philadelphia. There I was able to interview the staff about needs of the local Iraqi refugee community, as well as interview recently resettled refugees about their lives in the United States, which gave me a window into what life was like for refugees immediately after their arrival.

Positionality: A Familiar Outsider

As a Sudanese-Egyptian immigrant to this country, I held a complex insider-outsider position in relationship to my participants. I had never experienced, nor could I imagine, the horrors, loss, and pain of forced migration. I had never come face to face with the military devastation of my country and people at the hands of American neoliberal imperialism. I arrived in the United States as an adolescent with a firm command of the English language, a privilege that none of my participants had but yearned for daily. Being a fluent English speaker has allowed me to offer linguistic and navigational assistance to the Iraqi refugee families with whom I worked. As a Christian Arab American with no indications in my name of my Arab descent, I have not experienced the discrimination and stigma of being a Muslim in a post-9/11 context. Finally, unlike my participants, I am a U.S. citizen, while they were all permanent residents and several years away from becoming naturalized citizens. As a middle-aged unmarried woman, I was an anomaly among the adult female participants in my study since I did not share their identities as mothers and wives. In spite of these differences, I often felt as if I was among and "studying my own" (Shami 1988). Like my participants, I was born in the Middle East, and Arabic is my first language. Also, similar to my participants, I struggled to navigate the state institutions and everyday spaces in the United States when I first arrived, in spite of my ability to speak English fluently. And yet, it was undoubtedly easier for me to eventually become incorporated into my new context as an English speaker.

As a researcher who was privileged with linguistic, material, and navigational resources, I wrestled with the same deep sense of guilt other female ethnographers have encountered when they found themselves "caught inside webs of betrayal they themselves have spun; with stark clarity, when they realize that they are seeking out intimacy and friendship with subjects on whose backs, ultimately, the books will be written upon which their productivity as scholars in the academic marketplace will be assessed" (Behar 2003, 297). I was particularly uncomfortable with the image of building my career on the back of these women and their families, and giving nothing in return (Altorki 1988). As such, I made a concerted effort with assisting the families, including being available to the youth for tutoring and accompanying families when they needed linguistic and navigational assistance. In spite of these efforts, I realized that "no matter what help I could offer [my participants], I always felt that I was the one who came out ahead. I had no illusion of ever reaching a state of balanced reciprocity in the course of the fieldwork transaction" (Morsy 1998, 83). In sharing their lives with me, they have given me a gift I can never repay.

Notes

Introduction

1. Names of people and places have been changed to ensure anonymity.
2. In Iraq, parents are usually referred to as *Um,* "mother," or *Abu,* "father," of their eldest child. In this case, Fatima would be referred to as Um Jawad. However, to make the names of refugee parents more accessible to an English-speaking audience, I refer to them by a first name pseudonym.
3. A term of endearment in Arabic used among loved ones, meaning dear one or beloved.
4. I use the inclusive term *im/migrant* as a way to refer to all those who migrate, regardless of oftentimes strict and limited legal definitions attached to them.
5. This fact was corroborated by the United Nations Monitoring, Verification, and Inspections Commission, the U.S. State Department's Bureau of Intelligence and Research, the CIA, and the Defense Intelligence Agency—who all concluded that Iraq had no WMD. This did not thwart the Bush administration from the ultimate goal of regime change. The administration and its supporters established their own intelligence agency, the Office of Special Plans, that reported what the administration had claimed—Iraq had WMD.
6. These orders applied to all areas of the economy except oil, since it was acknowledged that any attempt to privatize the state oil company or to claim rights to untapped reserves before an Iraqi government was in office would be interpreted by Iraqis as an act of war.
7. De-Ba'athification was the process of removing the members and influence of the Ba'ath Party from public office in Iraq following the U.S.-led invasion of 2003.
8. These countries are ordered by the size of common borders that they share with Iraq: Iran, 905 miles; Saudi Arabia, 505 miles; Syria, 375 miles; Turkey, 218 miles; Kuwait, 149 miles; Jordan, 112 miles.
9. The division within the Muslim community emerged soon after the death of the Prophet Muhammad. The dispute was a political one about who should be selected as the Prophet's successor, also known as a caliph. While the Sunnis, who constitute the majority of Muslims in the world, accepted all of the caliphs who have held office, the Shi'a believed that only the fourth caliph Ali, who was both cousin and son-in-law to the Prophet, and his heirs are the rightful successors

(Marr and al-Marashi 2017). The Shi'a, who began as an underground political party, have since evolved into a distinct religious sect that adopted a different interpretation of Islamic law and have distinctive religious rituals and ceremonies. Every practicing Shi'a depends on a *mujtahid,* or a religious scholar. Arab Sunnis follow the *sunna,* or the customs of the Prophet, as well as the *shari'a,* or the body of Islamic law that is derived from the Quran and the *sunna.* Rather than giving leaders special authority, Sunnis look to the *ulama,* scholars and judges, to set and preserve community rules.

10. The exact origin of the Kurdish people is unknown, but Kurdish people claim that they descended from the ancient Medes, a group that resided in parts of modern-day Iran and Iraq from 500–600 BC. This claim cannot be substantiated since the Medes left no written record and no Kurdish literature existed before the twentieth century. Kurds have a distinct cultural and linguistic identity. The Kurdish language is an Indo-European language similar to Farsi, but many also speak Arabic. The current official languages of the Kurdish central government are Arabic and Kurdish.

11. Current estimates suggest that nearly 70 percent of Iraqi Muslims are Shi'a, and only 30 percent are Sunni.

12. The Turkmen are Turkish speakers who are a mostly Sunni Muslim, middle-class group. Turkmen, only 3 percent of the population, have been disproportionately represented in government.

13. Shi'a Farsi speakers were once nearly 2 percent of the population in 1980, but were mostly expelled from Iraq during its war with Iran.

14. While the Jewish community in Iraq once constituted 6 percent of the population, there are only a handful of Jews left in Iraq. The creation of Israel in 1948 made it impossible for them to continue residing in Iraq, and most left in 1951.

15. Christians have long lived in Iraq. The various sects in Iraq are Christian Assyrians, Armenians, Chaldeans, Greek Orthodox, Greek Catholics, and Latin Catholics and Syriacs, but they only constitute less than 3 percent of the population.

16. The Yazidis gained international attention as a result of their persecution and genocide at the hands of the Islamic State (IS). Ethnically and linguistically Kurdish, this group practices a monotheistic religion that draws from Zoroastrianism, Islam, and Christianity. Yazidis pray to Malak Taous, the Peacock Angel, the greatest of the seven spirits that emanate from the creator. Another name for Malak Taous is *shaytan,* the Arabic word for devil, which led some to believe that they are devil worshippers—the justification that the Islamic State used for the genocide of Yazidis in 2014.

17. The Mandeans follow a gnostic religion that originated two thousand years ago in Mesopotamia. Mandeans revere John the Baptist and believe in water's purifying force. A Mandean might be baptized thousands of times within their

lifetime. Before the American invasion of 2003, there were 60,000–80,000 Mandeans in the country, but most have relocated to neighboring countries.

18. The Arab Ba'ath Socialist Party was founded in Damascus in 1946 as a discussion group that grew into a small but robust political party. *Ba'ath* means "renaissance" or "resurrection" in Arabic. Ba'athist ideals—characterized by authoritarianism, mysticism, socialist-like values, and strong Pan-Arabist sentiments—were brought to Iraq by engineer Fouad Al-Rikabi, who first shared his ideas with Iraqi military officers and educated professionals.

19. Saddam Hussein was born in 1937 into a poor, rural family and was mostly raised by his uncle, who inculcated him with nationalist and anti-British ideals. After taking part in a failed assassination attempt on Qasim in 1959, Hussein was eventually imprisoned in 1963 along with other Ba'athists after news of a coup in the works reached Qasim. He spent three years in jail before he escaped and began working with the underground arm of the Ba'ath Party. These early experiences had an enormous impact on Hussein, shaping his personality and leadership style. "His secretiveness, suspiciousness, and his distrust of outsiders sprang from years of being hunted—and hunting others—and from his own considerable talents in organizing conspiracy" (Marr and al-Marashi 2017, 153).

20. Hussein mistrusted both the Shi'a population of Iraq, who he believed were loyal to Iran, and the Kurds, whose demands for independent governance continued. By the mid-1970s, Ba'athists drove thousands of Kurds across the border to Iran, who were followed by thousands more who fled the ruthlessness of the regime.

21. In spite of these achievements, opposition to Hussein came from inside the Ba'ath Party and other groups, including the Liberal Party, the Communists, as well as the Kurds who sought autonomy, and the Shi'a who resented Hussein's treatment of Iran, all of whom would eventually experience his wrath.

22. Beginning in 1983, reports emerged of Iraqi use of nerve gas and mustard gas. The worst of these attacks was the Anfal (meaning "spoils" in Arabic) military campaign against the Kurds in the north of Iraq, where an insurgency against him had erupted. This scorched-earth effort aimed at virtually wiping out Kurdistan by any means necessary, including the use of chemical weapons. Entire villages were cleared and thousands of villagers, including the elderly, women, and children, were transported to detention centers where they "disappeared." Those who resisted were killed on the spot. The Anfal campaign also resulted in the displacement of 1.5 million people and the utter destruction of rural Kurdish infrastructure and agricultural lands (Black 1993). While no accurate figures are available, it is estimated that over 100,000 Kurds were killed in the Anfal Genocide.

23. The sole exception to the draconian sanctions was the 1995 Oil for Food Program, which allowed Iraq to sell up to US$1 billion of oil every ninety days and use the proceeds for humanitarian supplies to the country (De Santisteban

2005). Even under this program, food scarcity persisted and malnutrition in Iraq continued to be a grave concern, particularly for children, the unemployed, and the poor. The UN finally lifted all ceilings on Iraq's oil production in 1999, but it wasn't until 2002 that the UN allowed the import of civilian goods.

24. In the 1980s, the Iraqi dinar was worth US$3 before the sanctions. By the late 1990s, 2,200 dinars traded for US$1.

25. Forty percent of the cluster bombs dropped by U.S. forces failed, and unexploded bombs all over the country continue to threaten lives of civilians, especially children who cannot recognize them, on an everyday basis.

26. On April 9, 2003, with the help of a corporal armed with a tank, a group of Iraqis toppled a statue of Saddam Hussein. This televised event became an international symbol of the fall of the regime.

27. While the army and police force of the Ba'ath Party had brought about tyrannical surveillance, oppression, and repression during its reign, it also provided a semblance of security and stability to its citizens due to the suppression of crimes and the banning of guns under Hussein's regime.

28. Looting became a form of survival as Iraqis became increasingly desperate. Perhaps the most devastating instance of looting was that of Baghdad's National Museum, which contained priceless historical artifacts and treasures. The cost of looting has been estimated at US$12 billion.

29. ISIS eventually changed its name to the Islamic State of Iraq and the Levant, and then simply the Islamic State (IS).

30. In 2014, the IS captured Sinjar, an area primarily inhabited by Yazidis, where they immediately killed thousands of men and boys, and abducted women and girls as sex slaves. Nearly 80,000 Yazidis fled to the mountains, where they struggled with access to clean water and food. Christians and other minorities in other areas, such as Mosul, were given a choice to convert or to flee—most chose to flee.

31. It was not until *after* the United States withdrew from Vietnam that it began resettling hundreds of thousands of Indochinese refugees, who were framed as those "voting with their feet" for democracy during the Cold War.

32. White supremacist and misogynist politics, and popular prejudices fed by media images of women of color abusing welfare such as the iconic "welfare queen" propagated by the Reagan administration, were central in restricting AFDC from the late 1960s to the 1990s.

33. Seeing this, toward the end of his presidency, Reagan softened his approach and even extended the program to include more recipients.

34. The term *American exceptionalism* is believed to be originally coined by Alexis de Tocqueville in 1831 and has referred to the historical perception of the uniqueness of the United States as compared to other developed nations, due to its distinctive origins, doctrine, and history, and its remarkable political and religious institutions (Shafer 1991).

3. Public Education

1. For a detailed account of the events that led Zeina's family to leave for Syria, and their initial experiences in the United States, see chapter 2.

4. Young Adult Education

1. Urban refugees reside in urban settings in host communities, among non-refugees, rather than living in camps.

2. See chapter 3 for Layla's family's migration history.

5. Healthcare

1. As outlined in chapter 4, Hussein dropped out of Liberty High after ninth grade to help earn enough money to support his family. His older brother Seif, who aged out of high school at twenty-one, struggled for a year in the Second Chances Program, attempted to earn a GED, and was then forced to leave his educational aspirations behind to work fulltime and help support his family.

Conclusion

1. *Outmigration* is a term used by refugee resettlement agents to indicate refugees moving away from the original city where they were resettled. This is a very common experience among refugees who move to other U.S. cities to join other friends or relatives from their native country once their state-funded health insurance has lapsed and/or after they have received their green card, which is sent to the first address that United States Citizen and Immigration Services has on file.

2. In my last meeting with Nadia, I had asked her, "What are your thoughts on citizenship, particularly since you are close to getting your green card and will eventually become an American citizen?"

3. The number of refugees to be admitted is a task that falls to the president, commonly referred to as the *presidential determination*.

4. The Trump administration also proposed the dismantling of the Bureau of Population, Refugees, and Migration's international assistance funding (PRM) to be subsumed under the United States Agency for International Development. This would have deleterious effects on PRM's ability to effectively assist refugees overseas. The Trump administration also issued the closure of all U.S. Citizenship and Immigration Services international field offices. These offices have been critical for refugee resettlement, and were particularly vital for processing applications that allow refugees to join family members in the United States. Office closures will inevitably increase family separation (Refugee Council USA 2019).

5. The first iteration of the "Muslim ban" included Iran, Iraq, Libya, Somalia, Sudan, Syria, and Yemen. In later iterations of executive orders that banned refugees, Iraq was removed from the list, but it was later expanded to include Egypt, Mali, North Korea, Palestine, and South Sudan, with the rationale that refugees from these countries required "enhanced vetting."

6. In 2017, the Trump administration fundamentally changed the admission categories from country of origin to four distinct categories: those who fled religious persecution, Iraqis who assisted U.S. missions abroad, refugees from the "northern triangle" (El Salvador, Guatemala, Honduras), and all other refugees. This had a devastating effect on the entry of Iraqi refugees.

7. The SIV program benefited those employed by or on behalf of the U.S. government in Iraq any time between March 2003 through September 2013, who "have experienced or are experiencing an ongoing serious threat as a consequence of that employment" (Refugee Council USA 2019). The Refugee Crisis in Iraq Act created a direct access program, known as Priority 2 (P2), to allow U.S.-affiliated Iraqis to apply directly to the United States for asylum, rather than go through the referral process via the UNHCR.

8. This amount ranges from $925 to $1,150 and is typically used to pay for the first few months of rent. In order to "stretch" refugees' resettlement fund, many resettlement agencies procure housing for refugees in the least costly neighborhoods, which translates to areas with the least resources, such as financially strapped and overcrowded schools.

9. The UNHCR gives priority to people who fall in the following categories: those who have legal or physical protection needs, survivors of violence and/or torture, children and adolescents at risk, those in need of family reunification, and those who lack foreseeable alternative durable solutions.

10. During the time that this study was conducted, 2011–2014, Pennsylvania was among the many states that did not expand Medicaid coverage to cover many low-income individuals—a measure that the ACA enacted in an effort to address the gaps in the healthcare system.

11. Recent estimates place the healthcare system as worth nearly $8.5 trillion, which mostly benefits health insurance companies, organized medicine, and pharmaceutical companies.

12. The current healthcare system is funded through a fragmented financing system that includes "employment-based health insurance, individual insurance, payroll taxes, income taxes, business taxes, state and local taxes, payments by patients, and the federal deficit" and is the principal factor behind the high cost of healthcare in the U.S. (Fuchs 2018, 15). A switch to universal healthcare would immediately save hundreds of billions of dollars, and save much more in the long term.

Bibliography

Abu El-Haj, T. R. 2010. "'The Beauty of America': Nationalism, Education, and the War on Terror." *Harvard Educational Review* 80 (2): 242–75.

Abu El-Haj, T. R. 2015. *Unsettled Belonging: Educating Palestinian American Youth after 9/11.* Chicago: University of Chicago Press.

Abu El-Haj, T. R., and S. W. Bonet. 2011. "Education, Citizenship, and the Politics of Belonging: Youth from Muslim Transnational Communities and the 'War on Terror.'" *Review of Research in Education* 35 (1): 29–59. https://www.bbc.com/news/world-asia-58283177.

Abu El-Haj, T. R., G. Kaloustian, S. W. Bonet, and S. Chatila. 2018. "Fifi the Punishing Cat and Other Civic Lessons from a Lebanese Public Kindergarten School." *Journal on Education in Emergencies* 4:13–44.

Abu El-Haj, T. R. A. Ríos-Rojas, and R. Jaffe-Walter. 2017. "Whose Race Problem? Tracking Patterns of Racial Denial in US and European Educational Discourses on Muslim Youth." *Curriculum Inquiry* 47 (3): 310–35.

Al-Hamzawi, A. O., A. J. Rosellini, M. Lindberg, M. Petukhova, R. C. Kessler, and R. Bruffaerts. 2014. "The Role of Common Mental and Physical Disorders in Days Out of Role in the Iraqi General Population: Results from the WHO World Mental Health Surveys." *Journal of Psychiatric Research* 53:23–29.

Ali, A. I. 2017. "Trumpal Fears, Anthropological Possibilities, and Muslim Futures." *Anthropology & Education Quarterly* 48 (4): 386–92.

Altorki, S. 1988. "At Home in the Field." In *Arab Women in the Field: Studying Your Own Society,* edited by S. Altorki and C. F. Al-Solh, 49-68. New York: Syracuse University Press.

Alvarez, P. 2019. "Resettlement Offices Close as Fewer Refugees Are Allowed into the US." *CNN,* September 20, 2019. https://www.cnn.com/2019/09/20/politics/refugee-resettlement/index.html.

Anderson, B. 2006. *Imagined Communities: Reflections on the Origin and Spread of Nationalism.* London: Verso.

Anyon, J. 1981. "Social Class and School Knowledge." *Curriculum Inquiry* 11 (1): 3–42.

Arendt, H. (1951) 1979. *The Origins of Totalitarianism.* New York: Harcourt Brace.

Arendt, H. (1943) 2009. *We Refugees: The Jewish Writings.* Edited by J. Kohn & R. H. Feldman. New York: Schocken.

Arnove, A. 2000. "Iraq under Siege: Ten Years on." *Monthly Review* 52 (December): 14–25.

Arnot, M., H. Pinson, and M. Candappa. 2009. "Compassion, Caring and Justice: Teachers' Strategies to Maintain Moral Integrity in the Face of National Hostility to the 'Non-citizen.'" *Educational Review* 61:249–64.

Baglieri, S., and J. H. Knopf. 2004. "Normalizing Difference in Inclusive Teaching." *Journal of Learning Disabilities* 37 (6): 525–29.

Banks, J. A., and C. A. M. Banks, eds. 2019. *Multicultural Education: Issues and Perspectives.* Hoboken, N.J.: John Wiley & Sons.

Bartlett, L., M. Mendenhall, and A. Ghaffar-Kucher. 2017. "Culture in Acculturation: Refugee Youth's Schooling Experiences in International Schools in New York City." *International Journal of Intercultural Relations* 60:109–19.

Bayoumi, M. 2008. *How Does It Feel to Be a Problem: Being Young and Arab in America.* New York: Penguin.

BBC News Visual Journalism Team. 2021. "Afghanistan: How Many Refugees Are There and Where Will They Go?" *BBC,* August 31, 2021. https://www.bbc.com/news/world-asia-58283177.

Bean, F. D., J. V. Van Hook, and J. E. Glick. 1997. "Country of Origin, Type of Public Assistance, and Patterns of Welfare Recipiency among US Immigrants and Natives." *Social Science Quarterly* 78, no. 2 (June): 432–51.

Behar, R. 2003. *Translated Woman: Crossing the Border with Esperanza's Story.* Boston: Beacon.

Benei, V. 2008. *Schooling Passions: Nation, History, and Language in Contemporary Western India.* Stanford, Calif.: Stanford University Press.

Berlant, L. 2007. "Slow Death (Sovereignty, Obesity, Lateral Agency)." *Critical Inquiry* 33 (4): 754–80.

Berlant, L. G. 2011. *Cruel Optimism.* Durham, N.C.: Duke University Press.

Berman, C. E. 2011. "Bordering on Conventional: The Politics of Iraqi Resettlement to the US and Europe, 2003–2011." *Refuge: Canada's Journal on Refugees* 28 (1): 123–36.

Besteman, C. 2016. *Making Refuge: Somali Bantu Refugees and Lewiston, Maine.* Durham, N.C.: Duke University Press.

Black, George. 1993. *Genocide in Iraq: The Anfal Campaign against the Kurds. A Middle East Watch Report.* New York: Human Rights Watch. https://www.hrw.org/reports/1993/iraqanfal/.

Blanchett, W. J. 2006. "Disproportionate Representation of African American Students in Special Education: Acknowledging the Role of White Privilege and Racism." *Educational Researcher,* 35 (6): 24–28.

Bonet, S. W. 2011. "Educating Muslim American Youth in a Post 9/11 Era: A Critical Review of Policy and Practice." *High School Journal* 95 (1): 46–55.

Bonet, S. W. 2018. "So Where Are the Promises of This America? Where Is the Democracy and Where Are the Human Rights?: Refugee Youth, Citizenship Education, and Exclusion from Public Schooling." *Curriculum Inquiry* 48 (1): 53–69.

Bonet, S. W., and A. Taylor. 2020. "I Have an Idea!": A Disabled Refugee's Curriculum of Navigation for Resettlement Policy and Practice. *Curriculum Inquiry* 50 (3): 242–61.

Bowles, S., and H. Gintis. 1976. *Schooling in Capitalist America: Educational Reform and the Contradictions of Economic Life.* Chicago: Haymarket.

Boyden, J., J. de Berry, T. Feeny, and J. Hart. 2002. "Children Affected by Conflict in South Asia: A Review of Trends and Issues Identified through Secondary Research." *Refugee Studies Centre,* RSC Working Paper No. 7, University of Oxford.

Burde, D. 2014. *Schools for Conflict or for Peace in Afghanistan.* New York: Columbia University Press.

Burnett, A., and M. Peel. 2001. "Asylum Seekers and Refugees in Britain: Health Needs of Asylum Seekers and Refugees." *BMJ: British Medical Journal* 322 (7285): 544.

Campeau, K. 2018. "Adaptive Frameworks of Chronic Pain: Daily Remakings of Pain and Care at a Somali Refugee Women's Health Centre." *Medical Humanities* 44 (2): 96–105.

Carnevale, A. P., N. Smith, and J. Strohl. 2010. *Help Wanted: Projections of Job and Education Requirements Through 2018.* Washington, D.C.: Georgetown University Center on Education and the Workforce.

Centers for Disease Control. 2014. "Iraqi Refugee Health Profile." https://www.cdc.gov/immigrantrefugeehealth/profiles/iraqi/index.html.

Christopher, A. S. 2016. "Single Payer Healthcare: Pluses, Minuses, and What It Means for You." Harvard Health Publishing: Harvard Medical School, June 27, 2016. https://www.health.harvard.edu/blog/single-payer-healthcare-pluses-minuses-means-201606279835#:~:text=What%20is%20a%20single%20payer,financing%20healthcare%20for%20all%20residents.

Coady, M. R., C. Harper, and E. J. De Jong. 2016. "Aiming for Equity: Preparing Mainstream Teachers for Inclusion or Inclusive Classrooms?" *Tesol Quarterly* 50 (2): 340–68.

Collins, K. M. 2013. *Ability Profiling and School Failure: One Child's Struggle to Be Seen as Competent.* Milton Park, UK: Routledge.

Connor, D. J. 2008. *Urban Narratives: Portraits in Progress, Life at the Intersections of Learning Disability, Race, & Social Class,* Vol. 5. New York: Peter Lang.

Cook, B., C. Dodds, and W. Mitchell. 2003. "Social Entrepreneurship—False Premises and Dangerous Forebodings." *Australian Journal of Social Issues* 38 (1): 57–72.

Crane, K. R. 2021. *Iraqi Refugees in the United States: The Enduring Effects of the War on Terror.* New York: NYU Press.

Crawford, N. C. 2013. *Civilian Death and Injury in the Iraq War, 2003–2013.*

Brown University, Watson Institute for International and Public Affairs. https://watson.brown.edu/costsofwar/papers/2013/civilian-death-and-injury-iraq-war-2003-2013.

Cummins, J., V. Bismilla, S. Cohen, F. Giampapa, and L. Leoni. 2005. "Rethinking Literacy Instruction in Multilingual Classrooms." *Orbit* 36 (1): 22–26.

D'Addario, S., D. Hiebert, and K. Sherrell. 2007. "Restricted Access: The Role of Social Capital in Mitigating Absolute Homelessness among Immigrants and Refugees in the GVRD." *Refuge: Canada's Journal on Refugees* 24 (1): 107–15.

Deeney, J. 2013. "Teacher Layoffs Are Bad; Aide Layoffs Might Be Worse." *The Atlantic,* June 13, 2013. https://www.theatlantic.com/national/archive/2013/06/teacher-layoffs-are-bad-aide-layoffs-might-be-worse/276977/.

DeLauro, R. L. 2015. "Why America Should Save SNAP." *Harvard Law School Journal on Legislation* 52 (2): 267–308.

Denvir, D. 2014. "Another Student Dies after Falling Sick at Philly School with No Nurse on Duty (PhillyLabor.com Editorial Follows Story)." *PhillyLabor.* http://phillylabor.com/another-student-dies-after-falling-sick-at-philly-school-with-no-nurse-on-duty-phillylabor-com-editorial-follows-story/.

Derous, E., H. H. Nguyen, and A. M. Ryan. 2009. "Hiring Discrimination against Arab Minorities: Interactions between Prejudice and Job Characteristics." *Human Performance* 22 (4): 297–320.

De Santisteban, A. V. 2005. "Sanctions, War, Occupation and the De-development of Education in Iraq." *International Review of Education* 51 (1): 59–71.

Dewachi, O. 2017. *Ungovernable Life: Mandatory Medicine and Statecraft in Iraq.* Stanford, Calif.: Stanford University Press.

Dryden-Peterson, S. 2015. *The Educational Experiences of Refugee Children in Countries of First Asylum.* Washington, D.C.: Migration Policy Institute.

Dryden-Peterson, S. 2016. "Refugee Education in Countries of First Asylum: Breaking Open the Black Box of Pre-resettlement Experiences." *Theory and Research in Education* 14 (2): 131–48.

Editors of *Black Issues in Higher Education,* J. Anderson, and D. N. Byrne. 2004. *The Unfinished Agenda of Brown v. Board of Education.* Hoboken, N.J.: John Wiley and Sons.

Eggebø, H. 2010. "The Problem of Dependency: Immigration, Gender, and the Welfare State." *Social Politics: International Studies in Gender, State & Society* 17 (3): 295–322.

Ferri, B. A., and D. J. Connor. 2006. "Challenging Normalcy: Dis/ability, Race, and the Normalized Classroom." In *Reading Resistance: Discourses of Exclusion in Desegregation & Inclusion Debates,* 127–41. New York: Peter Lang.

Fillmore, L. W., and C. E. Snow. 2000. "What Teachers Need to Know about Language." Opinion paper, Center for Applied Linguistics, August 23, 2000. https://files.eric.ed.gov/fulltext/ED444379.pdf.

Forgacs, D. 1988. *An Antonio Gramsci Reader: Selected Writings, 1916–1935.* London: Lawrence & Wishart.

Fraser, N. 1994. "Reinventing the Welfare State." *Boston Review* 19 (1): 1–7. https://bostonreview.net/archives/BR19.1/fraser.html.

Fraser, N., and W. K. Bedford. 2008. "Social Rights and Gender Justice in the Neoliberal Moment: A Conversation about Welfare and Transnational Politics." *Feminist Theory* 9 (2): 225–45.

Fuchs, V. R. 2018. "Is Single Payer the Answer for the US Health Care System?" *Journal of the American Medical Association* 319 (1): 15–16. https://europepmc.org/article/med/12915433.

Gabriel, T. 2013. "Budget Cuts Reach Bone for Philadelphia Schools." *New York Times,* June 16, 2013. http://www.nytimes.com/2013/06/17/education/budget-cuts-reach-bone-for-philadelphia-schools.html.

Galbraith, J. K. 2006. "Some Notes on Entrepreneurship and Welfare State." *Industrial and Corporate Change,* 15 (1), 203–7.

Gearan, A. 2020. "Thousands of Afghans and Iraqis Are under Threat for Helping Americans. Now They Hope Biden Will Help Them Resettle in the United States." *Washington Post,* December 30, 2020. https://www.washingtonpost.com/politics/biden-refugees-visas/2020/12/30/572c00fc-3e4f-11eb-9453-fc36ba0.

Geertz, C. 1973. "Thick Description: Toward an Interpretive Theory of Culture." In *The Interpretation of Cultures: Selected Essays.* New York: Basic Books.

Ghaffar-Kucher, A. 2009. "Citizenship and Belonging in an Age of Insecurity." In *Critical Approaches to Comparative Education,* edited by F. Vavrus and L. Bartlett, 163–78. New York: Palgrave Macmillan.

Golshan, T. 2017. "Trump's Travel Ban Is the Most Difficult for Refugees." *Vox,* June 29, 2017. https://www.vox.com/policy-and-politics/2017/6/26/15873690/supremecourt-travel-ban-refugees.

Gonzalez, J. 2003. "Slaughter Every Night: Democracy Now Interview." *Outlook India,* September 13, 2003. https://www.outlookindia.com/website/story/slaughter-every-night/221464.

González, N., L. C. Moll, and C. Amanti, eds. 2004. *Funds of Knowledge: Theorizing Practices in Households, Communities, and Classrooms.* New York: Routledge.

Gorst-Unsworth, C., and E. Goldenberg. 1998. "Psychological Sequelae of Torture and Organised Violence Suffered by Refugees from Iraq." *British Journal of Psychiatry* 172 (1): 90–94.

Graham, K. 2009. "Asian Students Describe Violence at South Philadelphia High." *Philadelphia Inquirer,* December 3.

Haines, D. W. 1988. "The Pursuit of English and Self-Sufficiency: Dilemmas in Assessing Refugee Programme Effects." *Journal of Refugee Studies* 1 (3–4): 195–213.

Haines, D. W. 2010. *Safe Haven: A History of Refugees in America.* Sterling, Va.: Kumarian.

Haines, D. 2022. "Prologue." In *Refugee Resettlement in the United States: Loss, Transition, and Resilience in a Post-9/11 World,* edited by M. K. Watson and P. Gopalan. New York: Routledge.

Halpern, P. 2008. *Refugee Economic Self-Sufficiency: An Exploratory Study of Approaches Used in Office of Refugee Resettlement Programs.* Office of the Assistant Secretary for Planning and Evaluation, US Department of Health and Human Services, November 2008. https://aspe.hhs.gov/reports/refugee -economic-self-sufficiency-exploratory-study-approaches-used-office-refugee -resettlement.

Hardt, M., and A. Negri. 2020. *Empire.* Cambridge, Mass.: Harvard University Press.

Harper, C., and E. De Jong. 2004. "Misconceptions about Teaching English-Language Learners." *Journal of Adolescent & Adult Literacy* 48 (2): 152–62.

Harper, C. A., and E. J. de Jong. 2009. "English Language Teacher Expertise: The Elephant in the Room." *Language and Education* 23 (2): 137–51.

Hartman, S. V. 1997. *Scenes of Subjection: Terror, Slavery, and Self-Making in Nineteenth-Century America.* New York: Oxford University Press.

Harvey, D. 2003. *The New Imperialism.* Oxford: Oxford University Press.

Harvey, D. 2007. *A Brief History of Neoliberalism.* New York: Oxford University Press.

Harvey, D. 2010. *Social Justice and the City.* Athens: University of Georgia Press.

Hedges, C., and L. Al-Arian. 2009. *Collateral Damage: America's War against Iraqi Civilians.* New York: Nation Books.

Hehir, T. 2002. "Eliminating Ableism in Education." *Harvard Educational Review* 72 (1): 1–33.

Hein, J. 1993. "Refugees, Immigrants, and the State." *Annual Review of Sociology* 19:43–59.

Henrekson, M. 2005. "Entrepreneurship: A Weak Link in the Welfare State?" *Industrial and Corporate Change* 14 (3): 437–67.

Hoffmann, D. E., and A. J. Tarzian. 2001. "The Girl Who Cried Pain: A Bias against Women in the Treatment of Pain." *Journal of Law, Medicine & Ethics* 29 (1): 13–27.

Human Rights First. 2019. "U.S. Refugee Resettlement Remains at Record Lows Halfway Into FY 2019." Fact Sheet: April 2019. https://www.humanrightsfirst .org/sites/default/files/Refugee_Admissions_April_2019.pdf.

Ignatieff, M. 2002. "Nation-Building Lite." *New York Times Magazine,* July 28, 2002. https://www.nytimes.com/2002/07/28/magazine/nation-building-lite .html.

Ignatieff, M. 2003. "The American Empire: The Burden." *New York Times Magazine,* January 5, 2003. https://www.nytimes.com/2003/01/05/magazine/the -american-empire-the-burden.html.

Ignatieff, M. 2011. "Human Rights as Politics and Idolatry." In *Human Rights as Politics and Idolatry.* Princeton, N.J.: Princeton University Press.

Inhorn, M. C. 2018. *America's Arab Refugees: Vulnerability and Health on the Margins.* Stanford, Calif.: Stanford University Press.

Ismael, S. T. 2008. "The Lost Generation of Iraq: Children Caught in the Crossfire." *International Journal of Contemporary Iraqi Studies* 2 (2): 151–63.

Iraqi Body Count. 2013. "Iraqi Deaths from Violence in 2012." https://www .iraqbodycount.org/analysis/numbers/2012/.

Iraqi Body Count. 2022. https://www.iraqbodycount.org/.

Jaffe-Walter, R. 2016. *Coercive Concern: Nationalism, Liberalism, and the Schooling of Muslim Youth.* Stanford, Calif.: Stanford University Press.

Jacobsen, K. 2006. "Refugees and Asylum Seekers in Urban Areas: A Livelihoods Perspective." *Journal of Refugee Studies* 19 (3): 273–86.

Jamil, H., M. Farrag, J. Hakim-Larson, T. Kafaji, H. Abdulkhaleq, and A. Hammad. 2007. "Mental Health Symptoms in Iraqi Refugees: Posttraumatic Stress Disorder, Anxiety, and Depression." *Journal of Cultural Diversity* 14 (1): 19–25.

Jamil, H., J. Hakim-Larson, M. Farrag, T. Kafaji, I. Duqum, and L. H. Jamil. 2002. "A Retrospective Study of Arab American Mental Health Clients: Trauma and the Iraqi Refugees." *American Journal of Orthopsychiatry* 72 (3): 355–61.

Jones, C., and J. Rutter. 1998. "Mapping the Field: Current Issues in Refugee Education." In *Refugee Education: Mapping the Field,* 1–11. Sterling, Va.: Stylus.

Katz, M. B. 2010. "Public Education as Welfare." *Dissent* 57 (3): 52–56.

Kempner, J. 2014. *Not Tonight: Migraine and the Politics of Gender and Health.* Chicago: University of Chicago Press.

Kibler, E., V. Salmivaara, P. Stenholm, and S. Terjesen. 2018. "The Evaluative Legitimacy of Social Entrepreneurship in Capitalist Welfare Systems." *Journal of World Business* 53 (6): 944–57.

Klein, N. 2007. *The Shock Doctrine: The Rise of Disaster Capitalism.* New York: Henry Holt.

Koh, H. H. 2002. "On American Exceptionalism." *Stanford Law Review* 55:1479–527.

Konish, L. 2019. "This Is the Real Reason Most Americans File for Bankruptcy." *CNBC,* February 11. https://www.cnbc.com/2019/02/11/this-is-the-real-reason -most-americans-file-for-bankruptcy.html.

Koyama, J. 2013. "Resettling Notions of Social Mobility: Locating Refugees as 'Educable' and 'Employable.'" *British Journal of Sociology of Education* 34 (5–6): 947–65.

Kozol, J. 1988. *Savage Inequalities*. New York: Crown.

Kozol, J. 2005. *The Shame of the Nation: The Restoration of Apartheid Schooling in America*. New York: Crown.

Krieg, G., W. Mullery, and T. Yellin. 2017. "Trump's Promises." *CNN Politics*, May 31. http://www.cnn.com/interactive/2017/politics/tracking-trumps-promises/.

Ladson-Billings, G. 2006. "From the Achievement Gap to the Education Debt: Understanding Achievement in US Schools." *Educational Researcher* 35 (7): 3–12.

Lee, T. 2014. "Another Philadelphia Student Dies at a Public School with No Nurse." *MSNBC*, May 22. https://www.msnbc.com/msnbc/another-student -dies-school-no-nurse-msna334541.

Linton, S. 1998. "Disability Studies/Not Disability Studies." *Disability & Society* 13 (4): 525–39.

Lipman, P. 2011. "Contesting the City: Neoliberal Urbanism and the Cultural Politics of Education Reform in Chicago." *Discourse: Studies in the Cultural Politics of Education* 32 (2): 217–34.

Lipman, P. 2013. *The New Political Economy of Urban Education: Neoliberalism, Race, and the Right to the City*. New York: Routledge.

Lipman, P., J. Smith, E. Gutstein, and L. Dallacqua. 2012. *Examining CPS' Plan to Close, Turn-Around, or Phase Out 17 Schools*. Data and Democracy Project: Investing in Neighborhoods, Research Paper Series, Paper 3. http:// voorheescenter.red.uic.edu/wp-content/uploads/sites/122/2017/10/2012 -Examining-CPS-plan-to-close-turn-around-or-phase-out-17-schools.pdf.

Lipset, S. M. 1997. *American Exceptionalism: A Double-Edged Sword*. New York: W. W. Norton.

Love, B. L. 2014. "'I See Trayvon Martin': What Teachers Can Learn from the Tragic Death of a Young Black Male." *Urban Review* 46 (2): 292–306.

Madsen, D. L. 1998. *American Exceptionalism*. Jackson: University Press of Mississippi.

Maira, S. M. 2009. *Missing: Youth, Citizenship, and Empire after 9/11*. Durham, N.C.: Duke University Press.

Majerol, M., V. Newkirk, and R. Garfield. 2015. *The Uninsured: A Primer. Key Facts about Health Insurance and the Uninsured in the Era of Health Reform*. Henry H. Kaiser Family Foundation, Commission on Medicaid and the Uninsured. https://files.kff.org/attachment/primer-the-uninsured-a-primer -key-facts-about-health-insurance-and-the-uninsured-in-the-era-of-health -reform.

Malos, S. 2010. "Post-9/11 Backlash in the Workplace: Employer Liability for Discrimination against Arab-and Muslim-Americans Based on Religion or National Origin." *Employee Responsibilities and Rights Journal* 22 (4): 297–310.

Marr, P. & I. al-Marashi. 2017. *The Modern History of Iraq.* Boulder, Colo.: Westview.

Masterson, D. 2010. "An American Dream: The Broken Iraqi Refugee Resettlement Program and How to Fix It." *Harvard Kennedy School Review* 10:4–7.

McCluskey, M. T. 2003. "Efficiency and Social Citizenship: Challenging the Neoliberal Attack on the Welfare State." *Indiana Law Journal* 78 (2): 783–876.

McLoyd, C. 2014. "Living Proof: Transnational Black Youth Theorizing Racism, Justice, and Education." Unpublished PhD dissertation, University of Pennsylvania Graduate School of Education, Philadelphia.

McNevin, A. 2006. "Political Belonging in a Neoliberal Era: The Struggle of the Sans Papiers." *Citizenship Studies* 10 (2): 135–51.

McWilliams, J. A. 2016. "Teaching amidst Precarity: Philadelphia's Teachers, Neighborhood Schools and the Public Education Crisis." *Workplace: A Journal for Academic Labor* 26:20–33.

McWilliams, J. A. 2019. *Compete or Close: Traditional Neighborhood Schools under Pressure.* Cambridge, Mass.: Harvard Education Press.

McWilliams, J. A., and S. W. Bonet. 2016. "Continuums of Precarity: Refugee Youth Transitions in American High Schools." *International Journal of Lifelong Education* 35 (2): 153–70.

Meekosha, H. 2011. "Decolonising Disability: Thinking and Acting Globally." *Disability & Society* 26 (6): 667–82.

Mehan, H. 2000. "Beneath the Skin and between the Ears: A Case Study in the Politics of Representation." In *Schooling the Symbolic Animal: Social and Cultural Dimensions of Education,* edited by B. A. U. Levinson, K. M. Borman, M. Eisenhart, M. Foster, A. E. Fox, and M. Sutton, 259–79. Lanham, Md.: Rowman & Littlefield.

Mehan, H., A. Hertweck, and J. L. Meihls. 1986. *Handicapping the Handicapped: Decision Making in Students' Educational Careers.* Stanford, Calif.: Stanford University Press.

Mendenhall, M., L. Bartlett, and A. Ghaffar-Kucher. 2017. "'If You Need Help, They Are Always There for Us': Education for Refugees in an International High School in NYC." *Urban Review* 49 (1): 1–25.

Menken, K. 2010. "NCLB and English Language Learners: Challenges and Consequences." *Theory Into Practice* 49 (2): 121–28.

Mink, G. 1998. *Welfare's End.* Ithaca, N.Y.: Cornell University Press.

Mirza, M. 2010. "Resettlement for Disabled Refugees." *Forced Migration Review* 35 (July): 30–31.

Moravcsik, A. 2005. "The Paradox of US Human Rights Policy." In *American Exceptionalism and Human Rights,* edited by M. Ignatieff, 147–50. Princeton, N.J.: Princeton University Press.

Morrice, L. 2007. "Lifelong Learning and the Social Integration of Refugees in the UK: The Significance of Social Capital." *International Journal of Lifelong Education* 26 (2): 155–72.

Morris, M. D., S. T. Popper, T. C. Rodwell, S. K. Brodine, and K. C. Brouwer. 2009. "Healthcare Barriers of Refugees Post-resettlement." *Journal of Community Health*, 34 (6): 529.

Morsy, S. 1988. "Fieldwork in My Egyptian Homeland: Toward the Demise of Anthropology's Distinctive-Other Hegemonic Tradition." In S. Altorki & C. F. Al-Solh, (Eds.), *Arab Women in the Field: Studying Your Own Society*, edited by S. Altorki and C. F. Al-Solh, 69-90. New York: Syracuse University Press.

Müllersdorf, M., V. Zander, and H. Eriksson. 2011. "The Magnitude of Reciprocity in Chronic Pain Management: Experiences of Dispersed Ethnic Populations of Muslim Women." *Scandinavian Journal of Caring Sciences* 25 (4): 637–45.

Nayeri, D. 2019. *The Ungrateful Refugee: What Immigrants Never Tell You.* New York: Catapult.

Nezer, M. 2013. *Resettlement at Risk: Meeting Emerging Challenges to Refugee Resettlement in Local Communities.* Washington, D.C.: Hebrew Immigrant Aid Society. https://www.hias.org/sites/default/files/resettlement_at_risk_1.pdf.

Nguyen, M. T. 2012. *The Gift of Freedom: War, Debt, and Other Refugee Passages.* Durham, N.C.: Duke University Press.

Olsen, L. 1997. *Made in America: Immigrant Students in Our Public Schools.* New York: New Press.

Ong, A. 1999. *Flexible Citizenship: The Cultural Logics of Transnationality.* Durham, N.C.: Duke University Press.

Ong, A. 2003. *Buddha Is Hiding: Refugees, Citizenship, the New America.* Berkeley: University of California Press.

Otterbein, H. 2015. "Philly Is the 4th Most Segregated Big City in the Country." *Philadelphia Magazine,* September 22, 2015.

Pappas, B. 2013. "How Budget Cuts Affect Special Education Programs." National Priorities Project, April 29, 2013. https://www.nationalpriorities.org/blog/2013/04/29/how-budget-cuts-affect-special-education-programs/.

Perna, L. W., and A. Jones. 2013. *The State of College Access and Completion: Improving College Success for Students from Underrepresented Groups.* New York: Routledge.

Polk, W. R. 2005. *Understanding Iraq: The Whole Sweep of Iraqi History, from Genghis Khan's Mongols to the Ottoman Turks to the British Mandate to the American Occupation.* New York: Harper Collins.

Popal, G. R. 2000. "Impact of Sanctions on the Population of Iraq." *EMHJ-Eastern Mediterranean Health Journal* 6 (4): 791–95, 2000.

Pryma, J. 2017. "'Even My Sister Says I'm Acting Like a Crazy to Get a Check':

Race, Gender, and Moral Boundary-Work in Women's Claims of Disabling Chronic Pain." *Social Science & Medicine* 181: 66–73.

Puar, J. K. 2017. *The Right to Maim: Debility, Capacity, Disability.* Durham, N.C.: Duke University Press.

Quillian, L., A. Heath, D. Pager, A. H. Midtbøen, F. Fleischmann, and O. Hexel. 2019. "Do Some Countries Discriminate More than Others? Evidence from 97 Field Experiments of Racial Discrimination in Hiring." *Sociological Science* 6: 467–96.

Ramsay, G. 2018. *Impossible Refuge: The Control and Constraint of Refugee Futures.* New York: Routledge.

Reddy, S. 2017. *British Empire and the Literature of Rebellion: Revolting Bodies, Laboring Subjects.* Cham, Switzerland: Palgrave McMillan.

Refugee Council USA. 2019. *Where Are the Refugees? Drastic Cuts to Resettlement Harming Refugees, Communities, and American Leadership.* https://rcusa.org/wp-content/uploads/2019/07/RCUSA-Report-1.pdf.

Research for Action 2018. *Patching the Leaky Pipeline: Recruiting and Retaining Teachers of Color in Pennsylvania.* https://www.researchforaction.org/publications/patching-the-leaky-pipeline/.

Rogers, K., and N. Fandos. 2019. "Trump Tells Congresswomen to 'Go Back' to the Countries They Came From." *New York Times,* July 14, 2019. https://www.nytimes.com/2019/07/14/us/politics/trump-twitter-squad-congress.html.

Rosenbloom, S. R., and N. Way. 2004. "Experiences of Discrimination among African American, Asian American, and Latino Adolescents in an Urban High School." *Youth & Society* 35 (4): 420–51.

Rubin, B. C. 2007. "'There's Still Not Justice': Youth Civic Identity Development amid Distinct School and Community Contexts." *Teachers College Record* 109 (2): 449–81.

Said, E. W. 1979. *Orientalism.* New York: Vintage.

Sainsbury, D. 2006. "Immigrants' Social Rights in Comparative Perspective: Welfare Regimes, Forms in Immigration and Immigration Policy Regimes." *Journal of European Social Policy* 16 (3): 229–44.

Saleh, Z. 2020. *The Human Cost of U.S. Interventions in Iraq: A History from the 1960s through the Post 9/11 Wars.* Watson Institute for International and Public Affairs, Brown University, October 13, 2020. https://watson.brown.edu/costsofwar/papers/2020/IraqHistory.

Salman, K. F., and L. K. Resick. 2015. "The Description of Health among Iraqi Refugee Women in the United States." *Journal of Immigrant and Minority Health* 17 (4): 1199–205.

Sarroub, L. K. 2013. *All American Yemeni Girls: Being Muslim in a Public School.* Philadelphia: University of Pennsylvania Press.

Savell, S., and 5W Infographics. 2019. "This Map Shows Where in the World the U.S. Military Is Combatting Terrorism." *Smithsonian Magazine,* January/February, 2019. https://www.smithsonianmag.com/history/map-shows-places-world-where-us-military-operates-180970997/.

Schäfer, G., K. M. Prkachin, K. A. Kaseweter, and A. C. de C Williams. 2016. "Health Care Providers' Judgments in Chronic Pain: The Influence of Gender and Trustworthiness." *Pain* 157 (8): 1618–25.

School District of Philadelphia. 2018. https://www.philasd.org/about/.

Scott, J. C. 1990. Domination and the Arts of Resistance: Hidden Transcripts. New Haven, Conn.: Yale University Press.

Shafer, B. E. 1991. *Is America Different?: A New Look at American Exceptionalism.* Oxford: Clarendon.

Shaklar, J. N. 1991. *American Citizenship: The Quest for Inclusion.* Cambridge, Mass.: Harvard University Press.

Shakya, Y. B., S. Guruge, M. Hynie, A. Akbari, M. Malik, S. Htoo, A. Khogali, S. A. Mona, R. Murtaza, and S. Alley. 2012. "Aspirations for Higher Education among Newcomer Refugee Youth in Toronto: Expectations, Challenges, and Strategies." *Refuge: Canada's Journal on Refugees* 27 (2): 65–78.

Shami, S. 1988. "Studying Your Own: The Complexities of a Shared Culture." In *Arab Women in the Field: Studying Your Own Society,* edited by S. Altorki and C. F. Al-Solh, 115–38. New York: Syracuse University Press.

Shalaby, C. 2017. *Troublemakers: Lessons in Freedom from Young Children at School.* New York: New Press.

Shapiro, J. P. 1994. *No Pity: People with Disabilities Forging a New Civil Rights Movement.* New York: Times Books.

Siegler, K. 2019. "Popular Refugee Resettlement Programs Closing under Trump Administration." NPR, September 12, 2019. https://www.npr.org/2019/09/12/759967768/popular-refugee-resettlement-programs-closing-under-trump-administration.

Smith, A. M. 2008. "Neoliberalism, Welfare Policy, and Feminist Theories of Social Justice: Feminist Theory Special Issue: Feminist Theory and Welfare." *Feminist Theory* 9 (2): 131–44.

Smith, J. C., and C. Medalia. 2015. *Health Insurance Coverage in the United States: 2014.* Current Population Reports, U.S. Census Bureau. https://www.census.gov/content/dam/Census/library/publications/2015/demo/p60-253.pdf.

Somers, M. 2008. *Genealogies of Citizenship: Markets, Statelessness, and the Right to Have Rights.* Cambridge: Cambridge University Press.

Soss, J., R. C. Fording, and S. F. Schram. 2011. *Disciplining the Poor: Neoliberal Paternalism and the Persistent Power of Race.* Chicago: University of Chicago Press.

Soylu, A., and T. A. Buchanan. 2013. "Ethnic and Racial Discrimination against Immigrants." *Journal of Business and Economics* 4 (9): 8548–81.

Spada, N., and P. M. Lightbown. 2009. "Interaction Research in Second/Foreign Language Classrooms." In *Multiple Perspectives on Interaction*, 163–81. New York: Routledge.

Statistical Atlas. 2019. "Overview of Philadelphia, Pennsylvania." https://statisticalatlas.com/place/Pennsylvania/Philadelphia/Overview.

Stermac, L., A. K. Clarke, and L. Brown. 2013. "Pathways to Resilience: The Role of Education in War-Zone Immigrant and Refugee Student Success." In *Handbook of Resilience in Children of War*, edited by C. Fernando and M. Ferrari, 211–20. New York: Springer.

Stevenson, J., and J. Willott. 2007. "The Aspiration and Access to Higher Education of Teenage Refugees in the UK." *Compare* 37 (5): 671–87.

Stiker, H. J. 2019. *A History of Disability*. Ann Arbor: University of Michigan Press.

Storey, K. 2007. "Combating Ableism in Schools." *Preventing School Failure: Alternative Education for Children and Youth* 52 (1): 56–58.

Takeda, J. 2000. "Psychological and Economic Adaptation of Iraqi Adult Male Refugees: Implications for Social Work Practice." *Journal of Social Service Research* 26 (3): 1–21.

Tang, E. 2015. *Unsettled: Cambodian Refugees in the New York City Hyperghetto*. Philadelphia: Temple University Press.

Tasha, S. 2021. "How Many Americans Are Uninsured." Policy Advice, February 23, 2021. https://policyadvice.net/insurance/insights/how-many-uninsured-americans/.

Taylor, A. 2012. "Addressing Ableism in Schooling and Society? The Capabilities Approach and Students with Disabilities." *Philosophy of Education Archive*, 113–21.

Taylor, A. 2020. "Embodied Refusals: Conceptualizing Civic Dissent with Students Labeled with Disabilities." *Educational Theory* 70 (3): 277–96.

Taylor, E. M., E. A. Yanni, C. Pezzi, M. Guterbock, E. Rothney, E. Harton, J. Montour, C. Elias, and H. Burke. 2014. "Physical and Mental Health Status of Iraqi Refugees Resettled in the United States." *Journal of Immigrant and Minority Health* 16 (6): 1130–37.

Taylor, S., and R. K. Sidhu. 2012. "Supporting Refugee Students in Schools: What Constitutes Inclusive Education?" *International Journal of Inclusive Education* 16 (1): 39–56.

Thomas, H. 2011. "No Refuge for Iraqi Refugees: How the United States Can Improve Its Refugee Resettlement Policies." *California Western International Law Journal* 42 (1): 189–220.

Thorpe, H. 2017. *The Newcomers: Finding Refuge, Friendship, and Hope in an American Classroom.* New York: Scribner.

Tinke, C. 2009. "Rights, Social Cohesion and Identity: Arguments for and against State-Funded Muslim Schools in Britain." *Race, Ethnicity and Education* 12 (3): 539–53.

Tolbert, J., K. Orgera, and A. Damico. 2020. "Key Facts about the Uninsured Population." Kaiser Family Foundation, November 6, 2020. https://www.kff .org/uninsured/issue-brief/key-facts-about-the-uninsured-population/ #:~:text=However%2C%20beginning%20in%202017%2C%20the,2016%20 to%2010.9%25%20in%202019.

Tyrrell, I. 1991. "American Exceptionalism in an Age of International History." *American Historical Review* 96 (4): 1031–55.

United States Citizenship and Immigration Services. 2020. "Refugee Processing and Security Screening." https://www.uscis.gov/humanitarian/ refugees-and-asylum/refugees/refugee-processing-and-security-screening.

United Nations High Commissioner for Refugees. 2018. *Working with Persons with Disabilities in Forced Displacement.* https://www.unhcr.org/4ec3c81c9 .pdf.

United Nations High Commissioner for Refugees. 2019. "Iraq Refugee Crisis." https://www.unrefugees.org/emergencies/iraq/.

United Nations High Commissioner for Refugees. 2021. "Figures at a Glance." https://www.unhcr.org/en-us/figures-at-a-glance.html.

United Nations Educational, Scientific and Cultural Organization. 2019. *Migration, Displacement, and Education.* Global Education Monitoring Report. https://en.unesco.org/gem-report/report/2019/migration.

United States Department of Health and Human Services. 2022. "Services for Survivors of Torture." Office of Refugee Resettlement. https://www.acf.hhs .gov/orr/programs/refugees/services-survivors-torture.

Ware, L. P. 2002. "A Moral Conversation on Disability: Risking the Personal in Educational Contexts." *Hypatia* 17 (3): 143–72.

Watson Institute of International and Public Affairs. 2020. "Costs of War: Iraqi Refugees." https://watson.brown.edu/costsofwar/costs/human/refugees/iraqi.

Werner, A., and K. Malterud. 2003. "It Is Hard Work Behaving as a Credible Patient: Encounters between Women with Chronic Pain and Their Doctors." *Social Science & Medicine* 57 (8): 1409–19.

Werner, A., L. W. Isaksen, and K. Malterud. 2004. "'I Am Not the Kind of Woman Who Complains of Everything': Illness Stories on Self and Shame in Women with Chronic Pain." *Social Science & Medicine* 59 (5): 1035–45.

Willis, P. 1997. *Learning to Labour: How Working Class Kids Get Working Class Jobs.* Aldershot, UK: Ashgate.

Wingfield, M. (2006). "Arab Americans: Into the Multicultural Mainstream." *Equity & Excellence in Education* 39 (3): 253–66.

Winthrop, R., and J. Kirk. 2008. "Learning for a Bright Future: Schooling, Armed Conflict, and Children's Well-Being." *Comparative Education Review* 52 (4): 639–61.

Woolhandler, S., D. U. Himmelstein, M. Angell, and Q. D. Young. 2003. "Proposal of the Physicians' Working Group for Single-Payer National Health Insurance." *Journal of the American Medical Association* 290 (6): 798–805.

Worabo, H. J., K. H. Hsueh, R. Yakimo, P. A. Burgess, and S. M. Farberman. 2016. "Understanding Refugees' Perceptions of Health Care in the United States." *Journal for Nurse Practitioners* 12 (7): 487–94.

World Health Organization. 2020. "Iraq Crisis." https://www.who.int/emergencies/crises/irq/en/.

Yemane, R. 2020. "Cumulative Disadvantage? The Role of Race Compared to Ethnicity, Religion, and Non-white Phenotype in Explaining Hiring Discrimination in the US Labour Market." *Research in Social Stratification and Mobility* 69: 100552.

Young, I. M. 1990. *Justice and the Politics of Difference.* Princeton, N.J.: Princeton University Press.

Zine, J. 2001. "Muslim Youth in Canadian Schools: Education and the Politics of Religious Identity." *Anthropology & Education Quarterly* 32 (4): 399–423.

Index

ableism: deficit-minded, 195; norms for disability, 88, 90, 192
Abu Ghraib prison scandal (2004), 137
Affordable Care Act (ACA, Obamacare): income-based, 159; Medicaid versus, 160–61; provisions of, 159–60; refugees' experience of, 159–62, 197; universal healthcare and, 198
Afghanistan, humanitarian crisis in, 22, 199
Afghanistan War, justification for, 11
Aid to Families with Dependent Children (AFDC, 1935–97), restrictions on, 214n32
al-Arian, L., 149
al-Askari mosque, al-Qaeda bombing of, 20, 37
al-Bakr, Ahmed Hasan: coup of, 14
Albright, Madeleine, 18
Ali, caliph: Shi'a followers of, 211n9
al-Qaeda, 11; al-Askari mosque bombing, 20, 37
Al-Rikabi, Fouad, 213n18
Al Sahir, Kathem, 36
Al-Zaidi, Muntadhar, 36
Americans with Disabilities Act (1990), Title II of, 89
Anfal campaign, against Kurds, 213n22
anthropology, educational: on social cohesion, 102
Anyon, J., 109
Arendt, H.: "We Refugees," 135–36

asylum, U.S.: effect of Covid-19 pandemic on, 183; for Iraqi refugees, 22, 179. *See also* refugee crisis, Iraqi

Ba'ath Party: crime suppression by, 214n27; ideals of, 213n18; opposition to Hussein, 213n21; persecution of Kurds, 213n20; physicians' affiliations with, 150; Shi'a revolt against, 15; wealth of, 18
Baghdad: American military violence in, 39–41; destruction of communications in, 11
Biden administration, refugee resettlement under, 183
bin Laden, Osama: Hussein and, 4, 10, 11
BIPOC peoples, reparations for, 180
British Mandate, Iraq under, 5, 13
Bureau of Population, Refugees, and Migration (PRM, U.S.): funding of resettlement, 45, 181; Trump administration on, 182, 215n4
Bush, George H. W.: Gulf War of, 6, 10, 17, 148–51
Bush, George W., 36; exceptionalism rhetoric of, 19
Bush administration (George W. Bush): American imperialism under, 18–19; establishment of Homeland Security, 137; refugee resettlement under, 21–22; regime change goals, 211n5; rhetoric of

earners' sacrifices in, 133; ways of
knowing, 194. *See also* parents, Iraqi
families, refugee: cash assistance for,
50, 60, 185, 187; cultural orientation
presentation for, 44; dispossession
of, 4, 53; effect of global neoliberalism on, 7; hidden savings of, 63–64;
poverty among, 52–53, 169; quality
of life for, 44
Federal Bureau of Investigation, resettlement programs under, 182
Ferri, B. A., 88
Fisk, Robert, 40
food stamps. *See* Supplementary
Nutrition Aid Program
Fording, R. C., 55, 56
Free Health Care Clinics, 162
Friedman, Milton, 9, 10

general education development
(GED), 175; with ESL component,
131; language needs for, 125–26, 131;
obstacles for, 131–32, 133, 215n1;
testing, 80, 131
Geneva Convention, 137
girls, Iraqi refugee: feminist liberal
assumptions concerning, 106; hijab
of, 105, 106. *See also* youth, Iraqi
refugee
Guantanamo Bay, detainees' rights at,
137
Gulf War (1990–91), 10, 178; DU use
in, 150–51; destruction of infrastructure, 148, 149; effect on infant
mortality, 149; effect on Iraqi
health, 148–49; food insecurity following, 149; sanctions following, 6;
targeting of civilians in, 148

Hartman, Saidiya, 28, 29, 53
Hashemite monarchy, overthrow of, 14

health, Iraqi refugees', 141–45; aftereffects of war on, 150; chronic
problems, 145–46, 153, 157–59, 168,
170–71, 175, 196; effect of American
imperialism on, 144, 170–71; effect
on employment, 146; factors affecting, 144–45; mobility problems, 142,
159, 176; pre-resettlement, 144
Health and Human Services, Department of: resettlement programs
under, 45
healthcare, Iraqi, 15; access to, 170;
devastation of, 5, 143, 148, 169, 171;
effect of Gulf War on, 149; effect of
U.S. occupation on, 149–50; flight
of physicians from, 150
healthcare, Iraqi refugees', 2; access
to, 6, 169–73, 196–99; access to
Medicaid, 160–62; across borders,
151–52; assumptions concerning,
158; barriers for, 6, 31, 173; barriers of language for, 54, 128–29,
133, 135, 143, 152–56, 160; changes
needed for, 196–99; communication with physicians, 152, 153–55;
cultural barriers for, 156; desperation for, 162–63; for disability,
142–43, 163–64; Free Health Care
Clinics, 162; gender bias in, 152–53;
as individual responsibility, 173;
in Kuwait, 142; mandated screenings in, 152; navigation of, 155–56,
160, 165–67; referral system in,
155–56, 163, 165, 197; Refugee
Medical Assistance program for,
142; resettlement programs on,
145, 160; return to Iraq for, 162–63,
176; right to, 170–71; in Syria, 143;
use of volunteers for, 154–55; in
U.S. welfare state, 25, 142; women's,
141–42; for youth, 31, 83. *See also*

Islamophobia: facing Iraqi refugees, 4; Iraqi youths' experience of, 30, 98–107, 110, 193–94; organizations combatting, 101–2; political rhetoric of, 193; in refugee policies, 31; Donald Trump's, 100

Israel, creation of, 212n14

Jaffe-Walter, R., 106

Jews, Iraqi, 14, 212n14

Jordan: cost of living in, 152; Iraqi refugees in, 91, 92, 134, 151–52

Justice, Department of: intervention in Islamophobia, 102

Kaiser Commission on Medicaid and the Uninsured, 161

Katz, Michael, 23

Khomeini, Ayatollah, 15

Klein, N., 10

Koyama, J., 52

Kozol, Jonathan, 24

Kurdi, Alan, 199

Kurds, Iraqi, 13; Anfal campaign against, 213n22; Ba'athist persecution of, 213n20; cultural/linguistic identity of, 212n10; ethnic identity of, 14; Hussein's attack on, 15; origin of, 212n10

Kuwait: Hussein's invasion of, 17; medical care in, 142

labor: citizenship through, 29, 53–55, 117, 139; conditions and terms of, 55; cutbacks in, 62; decommodification of, 23; incentivization of, 75; neoliberal market for, 189; "reserve army" of, 53; self-disciplined, 53–55. *See also* employment, Iraqi refugees'

labor, domestic: welfare support for, 23

labor, low-wage: as barrier to education, 123, 126, 131, 133; difficulty of advancing from, 54–55; disciplining effect of, 74; educational curriculum for, 109; funneling of refugee students into, 196; neoliberal pipeline into, 117; refugees', 46–49, 50–55; reproduction of workers for, 109; self-betterment through, 50–55; subsidies for employers, 55–56; systems enforcing, 56

LanguageLine (phone interpretation service), 50

language skills, refugees': assistance with, 208–9; barriers to healthcare, 54, 128–29, 135, 143, 152–56, 160; decreased support for, 192–93; difficulty of acquiring, 51, 54–56, 138, 184–85; effect on employability, 46, 50–53, 54, 128–29, 133; financial support for, 185; for general education development, 125–26; for mental health system, 165, 168; penalties for emphasizing, 51; prioritization of self-sufficiency over, 50–52, 138; reading and writing, 54; self-betterment through, 50–53; support needed for, 56. *See also* English as Second Language

Mandeans, Iraqi, 14; beliefs of, 212n17

market: citizenship in, 77; in civil society, 25; fundamentalism, 26; neoliberal, 27; social rights' protection from, 27

Medicaid: versus ACA, 160–62, 197; access to, 27, 197; expansion of, 161

Medicare-for-all, 198

mental health, Iraqi refugees': anxiety, 60, 69, 82, 88, 131, 144, 163–65, 168; changes needed for, 197; depression,

paternalism, neoliberal, 28, 75, 76, 77, 188
Pennsylvania: educational age limits in, 196; Medicaid in, 161, 197
Philadelphia: adult education classes in, 131, 195–96; Arabic-speaking immigrants, 2, 101–2; cost of living in, 185; educational segregation in, 103; Iraqi refugees in, 43–45, 98; minimum wage in, 129; nonprofits for refugees, 101–2, 208; outmigration from, 175; refugee mental healthcare in, 83–84, 88; refugee resettlement agencies, 167. *See also* School District of Philadelphia
political life, power relations and, 67–68
the poor: exclusion from civic participation, 28; market pressures on, 23; public education for, 24–25; resistance by, 69
posttraumatic stress disorder (PTSD), Iraqi refugees', 169
poverty, Iraqi refugees, 2, 29, 52–53, 61–63, 77, 116, 169, 177
power relations: political life and, 67–68; public/hidden transcripts of, 67–69
privatization, capitalist, 10
property rights, private, 9
Puar, Jasbir, 147–48, 149
public assistance programs, 23–24; correction of assumptions in, 188; human cost of, 59–60; need for expansion, 188; post-resettlement support under, 187; public notions of, 66; reduction of dependence on, 76; refugee/nonrefugee, 22, 75, 188; surveilling nature of, 65–66, 73, 77. *See also* welfare

public sphere, market mechanisms in, 26

Qasim, Abd al-Karem: coup of, 14; Hussein's assassination attempt on, 213n19

racism, disadvantaging of students by, 103
Ramsay, G., 178
Reagan administration: on Iraqi sanctions, 16; SNAP under, 24; on "welfare dependency," 184
Reception and Placement Grants, 22, 45
Refugee Act of 1980, 51, 185, 187
refugee crisis, Iraqi: U.S. response to, 21–23. *See also* asylum, U.S.
Refugee Medical Assistance, state-funded, 142
refugees: access to healthcare, 6, 160–62, 169–73; Afghani, 199; assimilation of, 25; Cambodian, 3–4; discouragement from seeking justice, 68–69; effect of income increases on, 63; English language classes for, 50–51, 54, 128; ethnographic studies of, 4–5, 205–9; experience of loss, 135; indebtedness for citizenship, 29, 53–55; institutional surveillance of, 63–66, 73, 77; Jewish, 135–36; as market actors, 75, 76; meaning for America, 135; optimism among, 135–36, 138–39; as other, 4, 106, 193; pre-migratory histories of, 7, 52, 75–76, 89, 113–14, 173; presidential determination of admittance, 215n3; relation with nation-state, 2, 133, 134; reports to welfare agencies, 63; "reproductive

exile" for, 6; resistance to welfare state, 60, 66–73, 77; responsibilities of, 60; rights of, 29, 59–60, 67, 73–77, 80–81, 177; sense of belonging for, 7; in service of capitalism, 5; silencing of, 69; social knowledge of, 188; South Sudanese, 172; stateless, 135–36; support for retraining, 56–57, 185, 186; Syrian, 182, 199; testing of institutional limits, 68; Ukrainian, 183; urban, 117, 215n1; U.S. benefits from, 134; of World War II, 48; worldwide number of, 180

refugees, Indochinese: following Vietnam War, 214n31; resettlement of, 49; retraining of, 49; under SIV program, 183

refugees, Iraqi: Affordable Care Act experiences, 159–62; airfare for, 45; arrival in America, 43–45; aspirations of, 34, 42–43, 55, 81, 107–11, 126–32, 169; assisting military missions, 183; broken promises for, 136; business ventures of, 64–66; caseworkers for, 22, 34, 43–45, 47; critique of America, 7, 76–77, 134–39; critique of citizenship, 2, 76–77, 135, 177; "cruel optimism" of, 178; debilitation of, 145–73; debts incurred by, 61; debt to resettlement country, 53; desire for belonging, 136; diminished expectations among, 129–34, 171–72; discourses of injustice, 74; discrimination against, 98, 101–8, 111; distrust of law enforcement, 102; double displacement of, 178, 184; earlier refugees and, 7; effect of American imperialism on, 30, 43, 74–75, 144, 170–72; effect of Covid-19 pandemic on, 183; expectations

placed on, 29, 178; expectations for support, 60; experiences of dissonance, 74; failures toward, 5, 29, 136; faith in United States, 132–33; financial responsibilities of, 33–34, 42; financial support for, 1, 22, 60, 127, 128, 185–86; food stamp access, 24, 61, 62–63, 67, 69; housing insecurity for, 45; human rights of, 126, 137; intergenerational tensions among, 7; internal displacement of, 20; interrogation of liberal ideals, 136; Islamophobia affecting, 4, 30, 98–107, 110, 193–94; in Jordan, 91, 92, 134, 151–52; as laboring subjects, 7, 30, 34, 50–55, 180; language barriers of, 46, 50–54, 128–29, 133, 143, 152–55, 160; liminality of, 6; navigational support for, 1, 185, 208; navigation of healthcare system, 155–56, 160, 165–67; under neoliberal state, 30, 43, 74–75, 138–39, 144, 170–72, 178; numbers of, 21, 180–83; outmigration from original resettlement, 215n1; penalties for deferring employment, 51; as percentage of Iraqi population, 179; post-resettlement funding cuts, 181; post-resettlement life of, 34, 43–55; poverty among, 2, 29, 52–53, 61–63, 77, 116, 169, 177; pre-resettlement health of, 144; pre-resettlement programs for, 181; professional class, 16, 20, 47, 49, 52, 186; on promise of America, 134–39; punitive welfare encounters of, 60–69, 73–74; Reception and Placement Grants for, 22, 45; reductions in wages, 62; relation to American nation-state, 2; repayment to America, 135; second-generation, 52–53; sense of

war, preemptive: UN ban on, 11
War on Terror, 4; effect on Iraqi refugees, 6; imperialism of, 8; refugees
from, 200
Way, N., 104
wealth, redistribution of, 180, 188
weapons of mass destruction (WMD):
claims of, 10–11, 19; UN Security
Council on, 17
welfare: consequences for democracy,
76; effect of income increases on,
63; effect of neoliberalism on, 22,
66, 74–77, 172, 178, 184, 187; entrepreneurship and, 66; hidden transcripts of, 68; increase in recipient
numbers, 187; paternalism in, 75,
76, 77; prioritizing of employment
in, 187; public-private distinctions
in, 189; "queens," 214n32; refugee
rights and, 73–77; service to white
citizens, 77; social partnerships for,
66; as social vice, 187. *See also* public assistance programs; resettlement, refugees'
welfare agencies: deception of, 69–73;
decreasing support from, 59, 60–61,
69; documents from, 60, 67; inflexibility of, 74; limiting of settled life,
59, 66, 74; punitive policies of, 30,
59, 60–69, 73–74; refugees' reports
to, 63; refugees' resentment of,
69–73; subsidies for employers,
55–56; surveillance by, 63–66, 73,
77; use of state power, 56
welfare state, U.S.: acknowledgement
of refugee challenges, 74; citizenship in, 25–26, 29; disciplinary
actions of, 30; dismantling of, 6–7;
domestic labor in, 23; fundamental changes for, 188; healthcare in,

25, 142; Iraqi refugees under, 2, 7,
206; male-headed households in,
23, 189; moral obligations of, 75;
neoliberal, 22, 66, 74–77, 172, 178,
184, 187; public education, 24–25;
resistance to, 60, 66–73, 77; social
insurance in, 25; "work first" agenda of, 56. *See also* public assistance
programs; resettlement programs,
U.S.; Supplementary Nutrition Aid
Program
welfare states, Western: social insurance programs of, 23
Willis, P., 108
women: head of households, 188–89;
unpaid labor of, 23
women, Iraqi refugee: communication
with physicians, 153; healthcare bias
against, 152–53; hijab of, 92, 99, 100,
106, 128, 141, 145
women of color, popular prejudices
against, 214n32
women's rights, in Iraq, 16
World War II, displaced persons of, 48

xenophobia: in refugee policies, 31;
Trump's, 4

Yazidis, Iraqi, 14; ISIS persecution of,
212n16, 214n30
Yemen: education in, 127, 129–30, 132;
Iraqi refugees in, 80, 98, 100, 127;
refugees' status in, 98, 129–30
young adults, Iraqi refugee: aging out
of education, 122–26, 130; aspirations of, 138–39; belief in exceptionalism, 139; delay of adulthood
for, 121; educational experiences
of, 30–31; as laboring citizens, 139;
pathways to higher education for,

SALLY WESLEY BONET is assistant professor of educational studies at Colgate University.